*f*P

THE

GREATEST GAME

*The Yankees, the Red Sox,
and the Playoff of '78*

RICHARD BRADLEY

FREE PRESS

New York   London   Toronto   Sydney

Free Press
A Division of Simon & Schuster, Inc.
1230 Avenue of the Americas
New York, NY 10020

First Free Press hardcover edition March 2008

FREE PRESS and colophon are trademarks of Simon & Schuster, Inc.

For information about special discounts for bulk purchases, please contact
Simon & Schuster Special Sales at 1-800-456-6798 or business@simonandschuster.com

Manufactured in the United States of America

1   3   5   7   9   10   8   6   4   2

Library of Congress Cataloging-in-Publication Data
Bradley, Richard.
The greatest game : the Yankees, the Red Sox, and the playoff of '78 / Richard Bradley.
p.   cm.
1. New York Yankees (Baseball team)—History.   2. Boston Red Sox
(Baseball team)—History.   I. Title.
GV875.N4B73 2008
796.357'640974—dc22
200745382

ISBN-13: 978-1-4165-3438-9
ISBN-10:   1-4165-3438-5

For Carter, Grey, Haley, Kenna,
and all the future fans

Contents

INTRODUCTION

It's going to be Yaz, Goose Gossage thought. *In the bottom of the ninth, it's going to be me against Yaz.*

The relief pitcher was back in his hotel room after drinking beers with his teammates at Daisy Buchanan's on Newbury Street. The Yankees hung out there when they came to Boston to play the Red Sox. Thurman Munson, Lou Piniella, Sparky Lyle, Reggie Jackson, Bucky Dent—it felt like the whole team was out drinking. The 1978 Yankees were a tough crew. They liked to party, razz one another, throw back a few—even if they were playing the biggest game of their lives the next afternoon, which they were. It was better than sitting around at your hotel. Thinking. Getting nervous. Getting tense. You didn't want that much time to think.

But Gossage couldn't shut out thoughts of the next day. After he and his teammates drifted off to their rooms for the night, he tried to sleep, and that's when the game bored into his head and started to buzz around inside his skull. The Yankees versus the Red Sox in a one-game playoff to determine the winner of the American League East Division. The two teams with the best records in either league, and those records happened to be the same—99 wins and 63 losses. After 162 games, the regular season had ended in a tie. Baseball hadn't seen such an outcome for thirty years, since 1948, when the Red Sox and the Cleveland Indians took part in the first such playoff. And for almost thirty years after 1978, the sport would not see it again.

A couple of weeks before the last day of the season, when the Red Sox trailed the Yankees in the standings by two games, officials from the two teams had flipped a coin to see, in the event that there were a one-game playoff, which team would be the host. The Red Sox won the toss but didn't expect anything to come of it. Since late July the Yankees had been winning nearly three of every four games they played,

ix

and even the Red Sox players doubted that they would catch them. They were wrong. The Sox won 11 of their last 12, including their last seven straight, to stay within one of the Yankees. Then, on October 1, both teams had a game against considerably weaker opponents—the Yankees against the mediocre Cleveland Indians, the Red Sox against the hapless Toronto Blue Jays. Much to the surprise of both the Red Sox and the Yankees, the Yankees lost. The Red Sox, however, did not.

As a result, baseball's two best teams would be facing each other in a 163rd game. The winner would take on the Kansas City Royals in the league championship series, the prelude to the World Series, but both teams were confident that whoever won this game was the best team in baseball. This game, they felt, was like an entire World Series compressed into one afternoon at Fenway Park. And that was why Richard Michael Gossage, best known as "Goose," had a feeling that, come the ninth inning, he would be on the mound. Closing out games was his specialty.

It's going to be Gator for as hard as he can go for as long as he can can go, Gossage thought. *And then . . .*

"Gator" was Ron Guidry, the team's soft-spoken, left-handed ace, who in his second full season had compiled an astonishing record of 24–3, the best in the majors and one of the best in baseball history. Game after game that 1978 season, Guidry had been almost unhittable. He threw a rising fastball in the mid-nineties, setting up a wicked slider that darted in on right-handed hitters. Guidry disguised the pitch somehow; batters couldn't see the spin on it. The slider looked like a straight-up fastball, but then, just as a batter started his swing . . . it made hitters look silly.

Guidry, however, had pitched just three days before, one day less than his usual rest between starts, and Gossage, the big, strong relief pitcher, suspected that Guidry wouldn't have his best stuff.

Gator for as long as he can go, and then it's going to be me. Against Yaz.

That night, Carl Yastrzemski, successor to the great Ted Williams and Red Sox star since 1961, lay in bed and thought about the game the next day. He tried to picture in his head the pitchers he would be facing—Guidry and Gossage. He'd faced them plenty of times before. What did they like to throw? What did they like to throw against him? What did they like to throw against him at Fenway? That was what Yastrzemski did before games. He was always thinking, always preparing, so deep inside his head that some of his teammates felt like they barely knew him.

Carl Yastrzemski had turned thirty-nine years old that season. He was well past his prime, eleven years older than he had been in the miracle season of 1967, when an unheralded Red Sox team came from nowhere to win the pennant. Yaz won the Triple Crown that year, leading the league in batting average, home runs, and runs driven in. No player in either league has done so since. But now, after seventeen seasons in the majors, Yaz's body was starting to break down. His back hurt him constantly; one of his vertebrae was digging into the surrounding tissue. Since August he had worn a steel back brace whenever he played. His wrists ached from an awkward check swing early in the season. Before each game, Yaz had them wrapped so heavily he looked like a burn victim. He couldn't run with his former daring, and more and more he played first base instead of his usual position in left field in the shadow of the thirty-seven-feet-high left-field wall, Fenway's famed Green Monster. First base was easier on the body—less running.

None of that, though, would matter in this game. As Gossage knew, Yastrzemski was the last man you'd want coming to the plate with the game on the line. He was unflappable, and he performed brilliantly under pressure. On that last day of the '67 season, when the Sox had to beat the Minnesota Twins to win the division, he went 3–4 with three runs batted in. Yaz was just tough. Midway through the season, the doctors wanted to hospitalize him so his back would heal. Yaz walked out on them. Blocks away from the hospital, he came across a construction site and picked up a shovel, the closest thing to a bat he'd seen in days. He picked it up and started to swing. If his back could handle the shovel . . .

When he was a kid, the son of a Long Island potato farmer, Yastrzemski had done much the same. In the summers, he'd toss hundred-pound bags of potatoes onto a tractor. On winter nights, bundled up against the cold, he'd trudge up a long hill to the family garage and swing a lead bat for hours, hundreds of times, peeling off the layers of coats and sweaters as he warmed up. Night after night, Yastrzemski went to that garage to practice his swing and build his strength. Twenty years later his swing was still powerful, just less frequent. Yaz had always been mainly a fastball hitter. Now, in the twilight years of his career, fastballs were about the only pitch he'd swing at. Breaking balls, curves, changeups—unless he guessed fastball, and guessed wrong, Yaz would stand and watch them go. And if Gossage and

Yastrzemski did face each other, the two men's individual strengths would make the confrontation particularly compelling: a fastball hitter against a fastball pitcher. For Gossage was even faster than Guidry—over short stretches, anyway—and maybe the fastest in the game. So against Gossage, Yaz would get his chances, and that was as it should be. You didn't want to come at a legend throwing junk. Gossage would match his strength against Yastrzemski's.

The two men tried to sleep, but couldn't, and lay in their beds wondering. What would the next day be like? Surely there would be two on, two out. Bottom of the ninth, the season on the line. Maybe the greatest chapter in the greatest rivalry in baseball and beyond. Was there a more intense, more passionate, more historic rivalry in all of sports? Going back to the turn of the twentieth century, the competition between the Red Sox and the Yankees wasn't just about two teams, but also about two cities, two regions, two cultures, two different ways of looking at the world. Whether you rooted for the Yankees or the Red Sox had something to do with your outlook on life, your reverence for tradition versus your tolerance for change—even, perhaps, how you saw the United States itself. There weren't many rivalries in sports you could say that about.

Fate, destiny, logic, whatever you wanted to call it—that was how the two teams had wound up here. The Sox and the Yankees had battled for six months now. Back in April, they'd started from two very different places. The Yankees had won the World Series in 1977, but even in spring training they seemed weary of the infighting that had plagued them the prior season, when manager Billy Martin and Reggie Jackson and Thurman Munson feuded and fought for months, and owner George Steinbrenner played the team like a puppeteer. Steinbrenner was "the kind of owner," right fielder Lou Piniella said in April 1978, "that likes a 163-game lead with 162 games left." Now, even the off-season was exhausting. "This club can't take it for another year," Piniella said.

The Red Sox, on the other hand, were optimistic, and with good reason. Defense? Player for player, theirs was better than the Yankees', and the Yankees themselves would probably have admitted that. Offense? In 1977, their third baseman, Butch Hobson, had 30 home runs and 112 runs batted in, and he was the *last* batter in the Red Sox lineup. Ahead of him came Yaz, of course, and catcher Carlton Fisk, former MVP Fred Lynn, the powerful George "Boomer" Scott, and the slugger Jim Rice, who would go on to have the finest offensive season in baseball in decades. The 1978 Red Sox might have had the strongest-hitting lineup in the team's storied history. They even had some speed, a Red Sox rarity, to go with the power. In the off-season, they had acquired second baseman Jerry Remy from the California Angels; Remy had stolen 41 bases for the Angels.

Pitching had been the club's weakness in 1977, when not a single Red Sox pitcher had won more than twelve games. But in the off-season the team had traded for the young and promising Dennis Eckersley and signed Mike Torrez, a right-hander who'd won 17 games for the Yankees the year before, with two more victories in the World Series against the Los Angeles Dodgers. Torrez had been with four teams before joining the Yankees, but from 1974 to 1977, even as he was traded from coast to coast, he'd won 68 games. After the advent of free agency in 1975, Torrez had taken charge of his own future. His father had been a Mexican immigrant who worked on the railroad for a living; Torrez wanted a better life. He played out his contract with the Yankees and signed a seven-year deal with their enemies in Boston for a million dollars more than the Yanks were willing to pay. New York fans called him a traitor. He told them to talk to George Steinbrenner.

Baseball was changing in the 1970s. With the recently obtained right to sell their services on the open market, players were acquiring new wealth and power; the days when even the greatest players were simply handed a contract every spring and told to sign it were gone forever. But this good fortune was also costing the game some of its former pleasures. The lure of seven-figure contracts separated players not just from their old teams, but from the writers who wrote about them, the fans who rooted for them, and even the teammates they played alongside. As wealth began to isolate the players, press coverage grew tougher and more invasive, while the fans, stunned and angry at the amounts of money these baseball players—baseball players!—were making, not to mention their sudden ability to pick up stakes and move to another city, were starting to look upon the athletes like racehorses—worse than that, even. Fans in the 1970s would hurl curses and objects at the players with whom they once felt kinship—beer, hot dogs, cherry bombs, bolts. Such vitriol reflected the fans' frustration over the uncomfortable ways in which baseball, the most tradition-conscious of American sports, was undergoing rapid and disconcerting change. It also showed how the violence and anger of the late 1960s and early 1970s was seeping into baseball stadiums, no matter how much those fortresses of constancy and tradition tried to filter out the cultural transformations, both good and bad, coursing through the country.

The game was changing, and even as the players tried to capitalize on that, they struggled to preserve the sense of joy so vital to the sport, that element of eternal boyhood so hard for most of them to articulate but so crucial to their love of the game. They welcomed the money that free agency brought. Who wouldn't? But money wasn't why this generation of athletes started playing baseball. When they were boys, no one went into baseball to get rich, because the vast majority of players never would. In backyards and on dusty playgrounds, in inner-city parks and on high school diamonds, they played baseball because when they were young they listened to the game on the radio and watched it on television, sometimes in color, but more often in grainy black and white. They saw Jackie Robinson steal home or Mickey Mantle race to make a catch in center field, or heard the crack of Ted Williams's bat sending another line drive into right field at Fenway Park, and that's what they wanted to do when they grew up: play baseball like their heroes. They never dreamed of making hundreds of thousands of dollars a year, much less millions, just for playing a game. They played baseball because they loved the sport, and for many of them it was the only thing they knew how to do.

Rich Gossage had been a free agent when he was signed by the Yankees after five years with the White Sox and one with the Pirates. When he came to the Bronx that spring of 1978, he learned how brutal the fans could be when you were being paid enormous sums of money but didn't perform brilliantly from day one. Gossage blew a few games early, on the road. Then, on opening day at the Stadium, when Gossage was announced with the rest of the Yankees, the fans had booed and booed, like nothing the twenty-six-year-old Gossage had ever heard. Playing for the White Sox, the fans had never been anywhere near as vocal—or hostile. He stood disbelieving in a line of Yankees, the jeers and catcalls cascading down upon him. Gossage was one of the game's most intimidating players. He stood six feet three inches tall and weighed 210 pounds, and pitched with his cap yanked down low so that opposing batters couldn't see his eyes. On his first day in his new stadium, Gossage stood on the field, alone in front of 50,000 people, and pulled his hat down to hide the fact that he was crying.

The 1978 season was like that for the Yankees and the Red Sox—gritty, emotional, fiercely competitive. It was also, as the writer Roger Angell said at the time, a *painful* season. All of those qualities contributed to the drama of the 1978 American League East pennant race. In the first months of the season, the Sox raced to a fourteen-game lead over the Yankees, who bickered and fought with one another as they had the year before. Then, in mid-July, Yankee manager Billy Martin simply imploded, the result of too much pressure and too many scotch-and-waters. One night he told two reporters that his most famous player was a liar and the team's owner was a crook, and the next day, as he unsuccessfully fought back tears, he announced his resignation in the lobby of a Minnesota hotel.

The Yankees hired a new manager, the quiet, self-assured Bob Lemon, who didn't say much, just wrote out the lineup card and let the players play. And even as the Red Sox started to lose, the Yankees started to win. A fourteen-game deficit became eight . . . then four . . . then none . . . and suddenly, in early September the Yankees had a three-game lead. No team in American League history had ever come back from fourteen games down. Red Sox fans, always the first to put the worst on the table—it hurt less that way—were calling their team's slide the greatest choke in baseball history.

And then the Red Sox surprised those fans by picking themselves up and fighting back.

The playoff started at two-thirty in the afternoon on October 2. Inside Fenway Park, 32,925 fans would watch as if the weight of a combined 324 games was riding on every pitch, because it was. For Red Sox fans, whose team had come tantalizingly close but fallen short for some sixty years, the weight of decades was riding on the outcome. This game was not just about who would go on to play the Kansas City Royals; both the Yankees and the Red Sox were sure they could beat the Royals. It was about everything that had come before it. You could trace a line from the men involved in this game back to the origins of the Red Sox–Yankee rivalry at the beginning of the century, and from there back to the very beginning of baseball in the United States, before the Civil War. Yet you could also look forward and see that, whoever won on this October day, when it was done everything was going to change—faster, probably, than baseball had ever changed before. That was one reason why players on both teams agreed it was the most important game of their careers. It felt not just like a singular moment, but also like a fragile one, a rare convergence of tradition and rivalry and timelessness that would not be easily, if ever, re-created.

Outside Fenway Park that afternoon, Red Sox fans lamenting their failure to acquire tickets would mill around Kenmore Square, carrying signs with obscene sentiments and harassing any Yankee fan reckless enough to flash his pinstripes. And beyond Fenway, north to Vermont, New Hampshire, and Maine, south to Rhode Island, Connecticut, New York, and New Jersey, and west across the entire country, fans would play hooky from work or school to park themselves in front of their televisions and watch a game that would burn itself into their memories, a game that reminded them of why they loved baseball, of how beautiful it felt to win and how much it hurt to lose, of the reassuring constancy of the expected and the inevitability of the unpredictable, of struggle and hope and redemption and disappointment and all the ways in which baseball was like life itself. Much of that feeling would be inspired by a light-hitting shortstop named Bucky Dent, whose uncharacteristic moment of greatness changed his life forever and would become one of the sport's iconic events. And much of the emotion would result from a showdown between a fiery but anxious relief pitcher and an intense, driven veteran near the end of his career, desperate to win it all for the very first time.

After 162 games, the New York Yankees would fly from New York to Boston and Goose Gossage would sit in his hotel room, thinking that the game between his team and the Red Sox would probably come down to a single confrontation between him and Carl Yastrzemski. Meanwhile, Yastrzemski lay in bed and wondered if he would get a chance to win the game for his team, bringing the Red Sox and himself one huge step closer to the goal that had so long escaped him: winning a World Series.

CHAPTER 1

THE YANKEE SPRING

The New York Yankees should have been a happy, rested group in the spring of 1978. They had just won a world championship and had no reason to believe that they couldn't do it again. The previous October, the Yankees had won their first World Series since 1962, beating the Los Angeles Dodgers in six games and ending a long and frustrating era of mediocrity. They had done so in dramatic fashion. The Yanks had won their division in a tight race against the Red Sox; though they took two of three from the Sox in early September, it was not until October 1, when the Orioles beat the Red Sox to knock Boston from contention, that the Yankees won the division. Then, for the second straight year, New York had eked out a playoff win by beating the Kansas City Royals in the bottom of the ninth inning in the fifth game. In the sixth game of the World Series against the Dodgers, played at Yankee Stadium, the Yankees watched as one of their teammates performed one of the most remarkable feats in baseball history. Beginning in the second inning, right fielder Reggie Jackson had stroked three decisive home runs in consecutive at-bats, and he had required just three swings to do it. Like everyone else at Yankee Stadium, the Dodgers were overwhelmed by Jackson's power. New York's Mike Torrez pitched well, and the Yankees won the game, 8–3, and the Series along with it.

But afterward, the Yankees sounded as if they had finished last instead of first. Outfielder Roy White and catcher Thurman Munson skipped the team's victory parade; White felt that he had been mistreated by manager Billy Martin, and Munson was exhausted and angry after a season filled with conflict. During the off-season, he would demand to be traded to Cleveland, saying that he wanted to play with a team closer to his wife and children, who lived in Canton, Ohio. Jackson had threatened to quit if Martin remained as manager.

1

"The hardest thing I ever went through in my whole life was last summer," he said. Their teammates were almost as frustrated. "It's been the toughest year mentally that I've ever had," Lou Piniella said. "If the season had dragged on two more weeks, I don't think I could have made it." Piniella wasn't usually one to complain, but his mood was so low that he considered quitting. "You don't have to be one big, happy family to concentrate on playing ball, but if everything isn't going to be tranquil, we might as well write off next year," he said.

The World Series victory, and the strangely inconsistent hard feelings, represented a culmination of developments set in motion in January 1973, when the Yankees were bought by a group of investors dominated by George Steinbrenner, an aggressive and impatient heir to a Cleveland shipbuilding company. Steinbrenner's father, Henry, had owned Kinsman Marine Transit, a five-boat fleet that transported goods across the Great Lakes. After graduating from Williams College in 1952, George Steinbrenner would eventually run Kinsman and lead a takeover of the American Shipbuilding Company, a much larger firm. But Steinbrenner wasn't interested in simply being a wealthy man in an unglamorous business. He'd always had an interest in sports. He ran track and played football at Williams, and coached football at Northwestern and Purdue before going to work at Kinsman. In November 1972, when Steinbrenner heard that CBS, which owned the Yankees, wanted to sell the team, he put together a group of partners that bought the team for a bargain sum of $10 million. Of that sum, Steinbrenner himself put in just $833,333.

The decade of CBS's ownership had been bleak. For fifty years preceding, the Yankees had been baseball's most successful and storied team, their history stocked with such names as Ruth, Gehrig, Heinrich, DiMaggio, Mantle, Ford, Rizzuto, Martin, Berra, and Maris. They won three championships in the 1920s, then another in 1932. From 1936 to 1939, the Yankees won four straight World Series. They won in 1941, 1943, and 1947. Then, a golden era: between 1949 and 1958, they won the World Series seven times, including a remarkable five straight from 1949 to 1953. From 1947 to 1964, the Yankees won fifteen pennants and ten World Series.

But when CBS purchased the team from owners Dan R. Topping and Del E. Webb for $11 million in 1964, the Yankees were growing old. Though the team had won the Series in 1961 and 1962, and appeared in the Series in 1963 and 1964, its stars were aging and there were few comparable replacements on the horizon. In a span of five years the Yankees lost second baseman Bobby Richardson, shortstop Tony Kubek, pitcher Whitey Ford, and center fielder Mickey Mantle to retirement. Partly because the team was slow to sign black and Hispanic players—the Yankees didn't bring up their first African-American, catcher Elston Howard, until 1955, and the pace didn't quicken much during the next decade—the team was decreasingly competitive. In 1965, the Yankees plunged to sixth; the next year, they finished last, for the first time since 1912. For the rest of the decade, the Yankees ranged from mediocre to crummy. Attendance sagged, partly because of the quality of play and partly because of the deteriorating neighborhood around Yankee Stadium, an area that over the course of the 1960s had become poorer, dirtier, and less safe. With the support of New York City mayor John Lindsay, Yankee Stadium was to be renovated and enlarged in 1974 and 1975, but that was still no guarantee that fans would come to a tough neighborhood to see a struggling team. In 1972, the Yankees finished fourth and attendance was under a million. CBS chairman William Paley decided it was time to sell, and dispatched team president Mike Burke to search for potential buyers. Eventually he found Steinbrenner, who had earlier tried to buy the Indians only to have the deal fall through.

The sale was announced on January 3, 1973. "I won't be active in the day-to-day operations of the club at all," Steinbrenner said. "I can't spread myself so thin. I've got enough headaches with my shipping company." That vow of separation was broken even before it was made. With the papers not yet signed, Steinbrenner clashed with Burke, who still aspired to run the team, over a six-figure contract Burke had negotiated with outfielder Bobby Murcer; Steinbrenner thought it was too much money and berated Burke mercilessly over the agreement. In late April, Burke resigned, telling friends, "I'll be fine when I get this knife out of my back." Steinbrenner's minority partners would remain virtually unknown, their level of visibility reflecting their lack of influence in the running of the team. At the end of the season, Yankees manager Ralph Houk, considered one of baseball's finest managers, also quit, telling his players that it would be impossible for any manager to enjoy autonomy with Steinbrenner in charge. Steinbrenner replaced him with Bill Virdon, a mild-mannered former center fielder who had managed the Pittsburgh Pirates for two years.

The Yankees were now entirely George Steinbrenner's franchise, and he set out to remake them. His partner in restoration was new president Gabe Paul, sixty-three, a longtime baseball executive with an eye for talent and a gift for making smart personnel moves. Paul, then the Indians' president, had introduced Steinbrenner to Burke, and Steinbrenner brought him to the Yankees. Some thought he joined them, in a sense, before the sale of the team had been completed: in November 1972, the Yankees had acquired a young third baseman from the Indians named Graig Nettles, a left-handed hitter with power whose fielding was good and getting better. Since Paul, who made the trade for the Indians, was himself negotiating to join the Yankees, many observers saw a conflict of interest, but Paul always denied any impropriety. In December 1973, the Yankees picked up right fielder Lou Piniella, whose best days were ahead of him, for relief pitcher Lindy McDaniel, whose best days were not. In April 1974, again from the Indians, Paul acquired first baseman Chris Chambliss, an excellent defensive player who had been American League rookie of the year in 1971, and the versatile relief pitcher Dick Tidrow. In October 1974 Paul would ship Bobby Murcer, one of the few Yankee bright lights of the late '60s and early '70s, to San Francisco for the speedy Bobby Bonds (who would in turn be dispatched to California one year later for pitcher Ed Figueroa and outfielder Mickey Rivers).

The Yankees also had some tough and talented veterans who were becoming the core of the team. Catcher Thurman Munson, who had come up from the minors in 1969 and was the 1970 American League rookie of the year, was one of the best at his position in either league. Sparky Lyle, a lefty relief pitcher with a vicious slider, had been acquired in a 1972 trade with Boston for first baseman Danny Cater, a deal that worked out considerably better for the Yankees than it did for the Red Sox. New York was improving. In 1974, the team finished second, two games behind the consistently strong Baltimore Orioles, with a record of 89–73. The Red Sox were another five games back.

In theory, many of Paul's personnel moves were made without the knowledge or participation of George Steinbrenner, who in November 1974 was suspended from baseball for two years. Three months earlier, Steinbrenner had pled guilty to two counts of campaign fraud; Steinbrenner was said to have violated campaign finance laws in 1972 by pressuring employees of his shipping firm to donate to Richard Nixon's Committee to Re-Elect the President. Steinbrenner gave $25,000 "bonuses" to eight of his employees, then instructed them to give that money to Nixon's reelection campaign, an illegal circumvention of limits on donations. He then tried to cover up the money trail.

The Yankee owner would claim that Richard Nixon's henchmen had pressured him into the scheme by threatening an antitrust investigation of American Shipping. But there was no evidence of such pressure, and in August 1974 Steinbrenner filed his guilty plea. Thanks in large part to the efforts of his brilliant trial lawyer, Edward Bennett Williams, he received only a $20,000 fine. The consequences in baseball were more severe: Commissioner Bowie Kuhn banned Steinbrenner from having any involvement with the team for two years. (Kuhn later reduced the term to fifteen months.) While the suspension was personally embarrassing and painful for Steinbrenner, it had little practical impact. It could stop him from showing up at Yankee Stadium, but it could not and did not stop him from using the telephone. And so it was, on Old-Timers' Day, August 2, 1975, that George Steinbrenner fired Bill Virdon, whom he found lackluster and boring, and hired Billy Martin to manage his team. The Yankees were an unimpressive 53–51 at the time, and Steinbrenner was in a hurry.

Alfred Manuel "Billy" Martin, Jr. was an unlikely Yankee, for he resembled none of the types that defined Yankee teams. He was not dignified and graceful, like DiMaggio, or an all-American farmboy, like Mantle, or stoic and gracious, like Gehrig. He was a lifelong underdog, a runt and a troublemaker, and the Yankees, with the exception of the CBS years, were never underdogs. Perhaps that was why the desire to be a Yankee had permeated Martin's life since he was a boy; Billy Martin wanted the peace of mind, the confidence and ease, the aura of comfortable success, that the New York Yankees promised.

Born on May 16, 1928, he was the grandson of Italian immigrants on his mother's side who came to the United States in 1879 and settled in West Berkeley, California, in the first decade of the twentieth century. He would be called "Billy" because his maternal grandmother used to pick him up and say "Bellissimo," and a shortened version stuck. His mother was Jenny Catherine Salvini and his father was a local musician named Alfred Manuel Martin. They had neither a good marriage nor a long one. Before Billy was even born, Jenny gave Alfred a watch, which he in turn gave to a fifteen-year-old girl he was courting. Jenny discovered the betrayal, found the girl, and physically beat her. Jenny then proceeded to throw Alfred Martin out of her house, hurling his clothes onto the lawn and smashing the windows of his car. She was pregnant at the time. Billy would be raised by Jenny and her second husband, a short-order cook named Jack Downey.

As a boy in a tough, working-class neighborhood, Martin did three things, all of them fiercely: he played baseball, he chased girls, and he fought. "I didn't like to fight, but I didn't have a choice," Martin would explain. "If you walked through the park, a couple of kids would come after you. When you were small, someone was always chasing you. I had to fight three kids because I joined the YMCA. They thought I was getting too ritzy for them." That was how Martin saw himself—as an outsider, a little guy, who was either being dragged back to his lowly roots or scorned by the "ritzy" people. He was a small boy, but wiry and physically fearless. His most distinctive features were unfortunate ones—a long, thin nose, floppy ears, and crooked teeth. He was often teased about them, and he usually responded violently. "From the time I was twelve, I awoke every morning knowing there was a good chance I was going to have to get into a fight with somebody," Martin said. More often than not, he was the instigator of those fights, sucker-punching his opponents, who sometimes did not even know that they had done something to offend Martin. And no matter how many people Billy hit, his mother assured him that he had done the right thing. The other boys only got what they deserved.

Martin carried that me-against-the-world attitude, a combustible mix of courage and insecurity, pride and fear, into his play on the baseball diamond. He'd take people out at second, but resented it if they did the same. To exact revenge, he'd slam the ball into a player's teeth, or swat a guy—hard—in the face with his glove. Such tactics supplemented his abilities. Martin was not a natural athlete but a hard worker with unrelenting intensity. That was why he always wanted to be an infielder. He lacked the patience to play outfield; he wanted to be in the thick of things. As a senior at Berkeley High School, in 1946, he was an all-star in his local league, but he couldn't play in the all-star game because of—of course—a fight. During an earlier game against a crosstown school, a fan had razzed Martin, calling him "Pinocchio." Martin didn't take it for long before he dropped his glove, jumped into the stands, and began punching the fan. Then he slugged the umpire who tried to break up the fight.

Growing up, Martin was a Yankee fan. The Yankees were the elite of baseball, and they also had Italian-American stars such as Phil Rizzuto, Tony Lazzeri, and, above all, Joe DiMaggio. In an era when most games weren't nationally broadcast, they were also the team that a California kid was most likely to hear about. But Martin could not simply go from high school in the Bay Area to the Yankees, although if his desire was the only prerequisite, Martin would have. So in the spring of 1946 Martin finagled a tryout with the local professional team, the Oakland Oaks of the Pacific Coast League, and its well-traveled manager, a former journeyman outfielder named Charles Dillon "Casey" Stengel. As Stengel watched, Martin fielded ground ball after ground ball, always confident, always aggressive, always asking to be hit another. Stengel signed him to a contract of two hundred dollars a month and said, "He's a hard-nosed, big-nosed player." Martin didn't mind such words when they came from Stengel, who would become like a father to him.

Martin played a year for an Oaks minor league team in Idaho Falls, Idaho, and then, in Phoenix in 1947, he had a remarkable season, driving in 173 runs. At the beginning of 1948, he was with the Oaks. The next year, Stengel left to manage the Yankees, and in October 1949 he convinced Yankee general manager George Weiss to buy Martin's contract from the Oaks. Martin, who by that point was making $9,000 a year, would start at $7,500 with the Yankees, a slight he would never forget. Such parsimony from Weiss was hardly unique to him, but Martin took everything personally. Still, the tough kid from the wrong side of the bay was playing for the New York Yankees. He had overcome considerable odds just to get there.

Martin's first spring with the Yankees was in 1950. He was just twenty-two years old, but he quickly ingratiated himself with some of the veteran players, especially Joe DiMaggio, who liked the rookie's brashness. In 1951 Mickey Mantle arrived on the team, and he and Martin grew close; from that year until 1957, they roomed together. Both were small-town kids who liked to go out at night, drink, and enjoy the company of beautiful women, even though, as of 1952, both were married. Yet their nighttime pursuits would go largely unreported, because sportswriters didn't mention such behavior in those days. Whether traveling on trains with the team or going out to dinner with players, reporters spent far more time with their subjects then than they do now. They couldn't afford to jeopardize that access, and they usually wouldn't think of it anyway. Baseball players chasing pretty women? That was hardly news.

But Martin still fought, and his fights couldn't always be kept out of the papers. After the 1950 season, Martin got in a car accident and beat up the other driver. The man sued, and Martin had to pay him $2,658, a lot of money on a four-figure salary. Before a game in May 1952, Martin grew furious at Red Sox rookie Jimmy Piersall, who was teasing Martin about his nose, calling him that hated "Pinocchio."

Somehow the two men convened under the stands behind home plate, and before other players could separate them, Martin punched Piersall twice in the face. In July, St. Louis Browns catcher Clint Courtney slid hard into Martin at second base, and Martin tagged him between the eyes with the ball for the third out. (Courtney wore glasses.) When Courtney followed Martin toward the Yankee dugout, Martin abruptly pivoted and slugged him in the jaw.

Fighting was something that Martin couldn't shake; it was part of his identity, part of the edge that helped him compete against more gifted athletes, and though he had reached the highest level of his sport he remained an insecure and angry man. There was, by this point, no objective reason for such feelings of inadequacy; the 1950s Yankees were perhaps the most consistently excellent squad in the history of the game. Led by Mantle, Rizzuto, catcher Yogi Berra, and pitchers such as Allie Reynolds and Ed Lopat, they won the pennant six times from 1950 to 1956, dominating baseball like no team before or since. Through it all, Martin was a mainstay, a player whose talent wasn't really measured by statistics but by less quantifiable contributions—the hard slide that broke up a double play, the unerring way he organized the infield defense, the insightful pointers he gave to his teammates, the opponents' signs he endeavored to steal. In the dugout he would sit next to Stengel, constantly asking questions, pestering the manager for information, and, as time passed, making suggestions himself. Martin was obsessed with winning, and he would try any trick to gain an advantage; one of his favorites was to take a quick step forward in the batter's box just as the pitcher was starting his motion, in hopes of breaking his concentration. At the same time he grew devoted to the ethos of those great Yankee teams, their spirit of professionalism and sacrifice. No matter how you comported yourself off the field, when you were playing the game you executed the fundamentals, you played with intensity and confidence, and you cared more about the betterment of the team than about your own statistics. And if you made a mistake, you didn't follow it with an excuse; you admitted your error.

Somehow, Martin was always playing better than he should have been able to. With the bases loaded in the seventh inning of the seventh game of the 1952 World Series against the Dodgers, Martin made a sprinting catch of a Jackie Robinson pop-up and saved the game for his team. The next year, when the Yankees won their fifth straight Series, Martin was the most valuable player; he had 12 hits against the Dodgers, batted .500, drove in 8 runs, and set World Series records for most hits and most total bases (23). The previous holder of that record was Babe Ruth. Martin would never equal that performance, but he consistently played brilliantly under pressure. His average over five World Series was .333, about .80 points higher than his career .257 mark. The only year that the Yankees did not win the pennant between 1951 and 1956, Martin's years on the team, was 1954. Martin spent that season in the military.

But Martin found it hard to enjoy success. Even when things were going well—perhaps especially then—he worried that he wasn't good enough, that he was on the verge of losing all that he had attained. In his years with the Yankees, he was treated for insomnia, hypertension, and "acute melancholia," according to a profile in the *Saturday Evening Post*. In 1953, he became addicted to sleeping pills, taking two a night throughout the season, along with his usual heavy doses of alcohol. While recovering from a knee injury in 1952, he admitted, he was so "frightened, I couldn't sleep, thinking about all the guys who washed out with bad legs. I couldn't eat. I vomited everything." Concerned teammates picked Martin up and put him on a scale. At about 160, he was normally thin. Now he weighed 132 pounds.

"Mothers and fathers of kids think you get ahead on ability and opportunity," Martin said. "They don't know about the outside pressure. The guys who are happy playing ball are those who can adjust to the nuthouse they have to live in. Some of us can. Some can't. I've never been able to get a too steady grip on myself in this racket." He wasn't the only person to feel that way. A 1954 poll of baseball writers named him both the "unhappiest" and the "most conceited" Yankee. Martin's arrogance was the flip side of his insecurity. "I don't have much saved, and I don't expect I'll be asked to manage a team," Martin said in 1956. "If I'd opened a little pizza-and-scallopini restaurant or a used car lot when I was eighteen, I'd have more than I have now."

Babe Ruth had such prodigious talent that he could abuse his body relentlessly and still dominate his sport; when he chased women and drank the night away, he reveled in the sheer fun of such decadence, like a little boy with the desires and resources of a grown man. With Martin, broads and booze didn't look like fun; his pursuit of them felt desperate and needy and, as the years passed, more and more pathetic. He was as addicted to both as he had been to painkillers. His lament prompted his profiler, Al Stump, to conclude that the price of success in pro ball wasn't always worth the psychological toll it exacted. "Parents of precocious young ballplayers might well take Martin's case to heart," Stump cautioned. "A boy may have all the physical attributes and be bursting with ambition. The question is: When he gets up there, can he cope with the rest of it?"

Casey Stengel never worried much about Martin's fighting, which he thought useful—it could inspire Martin's teammates—or about his team's partying. When pitcher Don Larsen, who was known for liking a drink, crashed his car at about four o'clock one morning, Stengel told reporters, "He must have been mailing a letter." While many teams now ban even beer from the postgame locker room, Stengel's most severe restriction was that when the Yankees were playing at night, they shouldn't drink *before* the game. Asked about players chasing girls, Stengel replied, "It ain't getting it that hurts them, it's staying up all night looking for it. They gotta learn that if you don't get it by midnight, you ain't gonna get it, and if you do, it ain't worth it."

Martin's concern about his status with the team was not wholly unfounded; Yankee general manager George Weiss had never liked him. In 1950, when Martin first arrived from Oakland, Weiss informed him that he was sending Martin to the minors, and a furious Martin had shouted back, "I'll make you pay for abusing me like this. I'll get even!" Weiss had never forgotten that act of disrespect. He also worried that Martin was a bad influence on Mickey Mantle, and that their late nights were hurting Mantle's play. Martin responded that if Mantle weren't partying with him, he'd be carousing with someone else. While perhaps true, it was not a winning argument, and in the spring of 1957 Martin's position grew precarious with the arrival of two gifted rookies, infielders Bobby Richardson and Tony Kubek. In May, Martin gave Weiss another reason to trade him. On the 14th, Martin and some of his teammates, including Mantle, Berra, Whitey Ford, and Hank Bauer, hit the town to celebrate Berra's and Martin's birthdays. (Berra was turning twenty-two, Martin twenty-nine.) The happy group eventually wound up at the Copacabana club, where Sammy Davis, Jr. was singing. Martin and Bauer exchanged words with an obnoxious drunk at the next table. The night ended with a man from that group unconscious, suffering from a broken nose and head contusions. The incident made headlines, and Weiss was livid; he couldn't prove that Martin was the puncher, but he may not have cared. It seemed that wherever Billy Martin went, trouble soon followed.

On June 15, Weiss traded Martin to the Kansas City Athletics for no one in particular. The trade devastated Martin. He had been ripped from the only team he'd ever wanted to play for and sent to a club on its way to a 61–92 record and a seventh-place finish. Martin fumed that he was hardly the only drinker on the Yankees, just the most expendable—the fall guy. Perhaps most painful, Martin felt betrayed by Stengel, who had failed to protect him. In fact Stengel, knowing that Weiss was determined to rid himself of Martin, hadn't even tried to save his protégé. The trade seemed to confirm Martin's deepest fears— that he didn't belong on a winner, he didn't deserve a father. No matter how far he had come, he could still fall right back to where he started.

In the next four and a half years, Martin would play for six teams— the A's, the Tigers, the Indians, the Reds, the Milwaukee Braves, and the Twins. The quality of his play would decline, but his penchant for aggressive behavior would not. On August 5, 1960, Martin was playing for the Reds in a game against the Chicago Cubs, and Cubs pitcher Jim Brewer threw a pitch headed for Martin's head. Martin threw up his arm and the ball hit him on the elbow, but to his amazement, the umpire ruled that the pitch had hit his bat for a strike. On the next pitch, Martin swung and released the bat in the direction of the pitcher's mound. As he walked onto the field to retrieve it, Martin leaned over to pick up the bat, then suddenly punched Brewer in the face, breaking his jaw. A melee ensued. Brewer later sued Martin and won a $22,000 judgment; the Reds sent Martin on his way. The Yankee hero had become an aging and embittered journeyman. In April 1962, the Minnesota Twins, his last team, released Martin.

After twelve years in the majors, Martin's playing days were over, but his prediction that he would never become a manager proved wrong. Even as he was haunted by old demons—insecurity, aggression, addiction, fear—Martin would become one of baseball's best managers. He started as a scout with the Twins, whose owner, Calvin Griffith, recognized that while Martin's physical skills had deteriorated, his knowledge of the game was immense. Martin served more as a managerial aide for the Twins, evaluating and working with players, than as a traditional scout in search of new talent. As Jack Tighe, his manager with the Tigers, said of Martin, "The big thing he's going to do for us is make those players realize how good they are. He can get a guy to play better baseball."

Martin gradually worked his way up the Twins organization. In 1968 he became manager of the Twins' Triple-A team, the Denver Bears, which went from a record of 8–22 to winning 57 of its next 85 games. That success earned Martin a promotion to the big leagues, and in 1969 he led the Twins to a division title. But the season was marred when Martin got into a brawl with Twins pitcher Dave Boswell at a bar, beating Boswell so badly the pitcher had to be taken to the hospital to receive twenty stitches. "I had to stop the country club atmosphere," Martin explained. After the Twins lost to the Orioles in the division championship, Calvin Griffith decided, as George Weiss had before him, that Billy Martin simply wasn't worth the trouble, and fired his new manager.

But some team was always willing to take a chance on a winner, no matter the baggage he carried, especially one who led his teams in an exciting, aggressive style of play that brought fans to the stadium; 1.3 million people paid to see the Twins play at home in 1969, a team record. In 1971, Martin signed a two-year contract to manage the Tigers. As always, he insisted that his players practice a nearly cult-like loyalty to him and be willing to do whatever it took to win. Before a game against California that season, Martin and his players were going over the Angels' lineup. Someone mentioned that former Red Sox Tony Conigliaro had trouble seeing fastballs because of a horrific beaning he'd received in 1967; Conigliaro's left cheekbone was crushed and his left retina severely damaged, and he had struggled to return to baseball. On hearing about Conigliaro's blind spot, Martin instructed his pitcher to knock him down on the first pitch. "We're not going to baby sit him," Martin said. "He may be lying."

In 1972, the Tigers won their division after Red Sox shortstop Luis Aparacio slipped and fell rounding third base, costing his team a decisive game. In September 1973, though, the Tigers fired Martin; the team's management had wearied of his drinking, his womanizing, and his penchant for picking fights with opponents, management, his own players, and the press. But Martin was like a drug-addicted rock star whom no one wants to cut off; as long as he could be pushed out onto the stage to perform, as long as he won, someone would give Martin a job. He was promptly hired by the Texas Rangers. Again he created his own problems, fighting with management over player moves and flaunting his philandering. Even as he banned his players from bringing wives on the team's charter planes, he brought his own girlfriends. (Martin apparently feared that the players' wives might disclose his wanderings to his own wife.) Martin began criticizing the Rangers' management and ownership in the press, especially when he'd been drinking. On July 21, 1975, the Rangers fired him.

The pattern was by now clear: Martin made every team he managed better, and he increased attendance. But sooner or later he demoralized and alienated crucial players, offended management, spoke indiscreetly to the press, acted unprofessionally, and generally sabotaged his own success. Billy Martin thought that he could, or should, get away with anything as long as he won, and there was quite a lot that he could get away with. But always he pushed too far, until his employers decided that winning was not, in the end, the only thing that mattered.

George Steinbrenner was in this way both the best and the worst possible owner for Martin. Like Martin, Steinbrenner did believe that winning was the only thing that mattered, which was why he was willing to bring Martin to New York. Given his own fixation with control, Steinbrenner would never cede Martin the level of autonomy the manager felt he needed and deserved, but in order to promote his team's chances of winning, the owner was willing to accept new levels of self-destructive behavior from his manager. Other owners tolerated Martin's behavior to a point; Steinbrenner was willing to put up with more than anyone else. To some degree, he even encouraged Martin's drama.

"In New York," Steinbrenner said, "athletics is more than a game. The game is important, but so is the showmanship involved with the game." The owner had once done business with theater producer James Nederlander, and he compared running the Yankees to producing a Broadway show. "I learned something from being in the theater business. You can take a show on Broadway . . . and win a Tony Award because you have Lauren Bacall. And you can take another show just as good . . . but not have a hit, because you don't have a Lauren Bacall. That always stuck in my bonnet. Billy Martin is something more than just a baseball manager." He was a personality, a star—even, to employ a term then starting to become widely used, a celebrity. Steinbrenner had fired Bill Virdon because he found the man boring; now he had hired an entertainer.

As for Martin, his return to New York meant nothing less than redemption from exile. Asked how it felt to take the job that once belonged to Casey Stengel, Martin was on the verge of tears. "This is the only job I ever wanted," he said.

He inherited a team on the upswing. The Yankees had come close to winning their division in 1974, but the Orioles won 25 of their last 31 games and finished two ahead of New York. Despite the heroic efforts of Catfish Hunter, who pitched an astonishing 30 complete games in his first year with the Yankees, the 1975 American League East Division title would go to the Red Sox, who then participated in one of the most exciting World Series in baseball history, a seven-game thriller they lost to the Reds. But in that off-season, the Yankees traded for center fielder Mickey Rivers and pitcher Ed Figueroa from California, and for a quiet young second baseman named Willie Randolph from Pittsburgh. With those newcomers and a core of veterans such as Munson, Piniella, Sparky Lyle, and Catfish Hunter, the Yankees were becoming formidable. As if to confirm their restoration, they returned to Yankee Stadium in 1976 after two years spent in the garish Shea Stadium, home of the Mets.

Martin quickly showed his habit of judging players in terms of their perceived manliness. Early in the season, he saw pitcher Larry Gura carrying a tennis racket through a hotel lobby. Gura would later hear Martin conspicuously whispering about what a "sissy sport" tennis was—a country club sport. In May, Gura was shipped to the Royals for backup catcher Fran Healy, and in subsequent years he would delight in beating the Yankees. In 1977, before the Royals played at Yankee Stadium in the league championship, Martin publicly suggested that Gura might get hurt on his way to the stadium, and offered to protect him. But Gura was a fine pitcher for Kansas City, going 16–4 in 1978; the Yankees released Healy in May of that season.

New York won 97 games in 1976, finishing 10½ ahead of the Orioles. After beating the Royals in the playoffs, the Yankees headed to the World Series for the first time since 1964. Their opponent was the Cincinnati Reds, the famous Big Red Machine. "They're a good club, but we're the better club," Martin said. They were not; the Reds swept the Series. Martin was so distraught that in the top of the ninth in Game Four, he threw a ball at home plate umpire Bill Deegan, who promptly ejected him. Martin vanished into the trainer's room, sat down under a table, and started to cry.

The loss only heightened Steinbrenner's desire to win a championship. On November 18, he signed free agent Don Gullett, a left-handed pitcher who'd helped the Reds win the Series the previous two years. Eleven days later, he announced an even bigger move: the signing of Reggie Jackson, a so-so outfielder but a tremendous power hitter, for $2.5 million over five years.

With Martin as manager and Steinbrenner as owner, the Yankees were already a volatile mix. Jackson's arrival introduced that volatility to the ranks of the players. Certainly Jackson was one of baseball's great hitters. In ten years in the majors, he had hit 281 home runs, helping the A's win championships from 1972 to 1974. He was a thoughtful, introspective, and articulate man. He was also, in some ways, very much like his two new bosses. He liked attention from the media, he had a high opinion of his own abilities, and he enjoyed hearing himself speak. Before he even joined the Yankees, he'd been on the cover of *Time, Sport,* and *Sports Illustrated* magazines—no fewer than five times for *Sports Illustrated* alone.

But he was in important ways very different from his new manager. Martin had learned baseball in an earlier era, and he did not welcome change. He resisted Steinbrenner's suggestions that he pay more attention to statistical analysis, saying, "The computer never played baseball, and neither did the guy who uses it." He resented the fact that a manager's control over players was diminished by their free agent riches. If you fined a millionaire five hundred dollars, what difference did that make? Instead, Martin favored players whose work ethic and attitudes toward the game reminded him of his Yankee teams and, more specifically, of himself.

Reggie Jackson was not such a player. On the field, his skills—primarily the ability to hit a ball very hard and very far—all seemed to revolve around the promotion of individual glory. He could not bunt. He struck out more than any other player in the history of the game. His defense was poor, and he didn't work much at improving it. Martin, however, had toiled constantly to make himself a good player; for him a commitment to the sport meant valuing its small, subtle acts and knowing how to perform them. Jackson was a devotee of the grand gesture, the home run. He had little interest in making himself a well-rounded player; you would never hear stories of Jackson practicing his defense hour after hour. In one memorable Oakland A's game against Baltimore, an Oriole hit a double over the first base bag. A's first baseman Danny Cater (the same Danny Cater whom the Yankees would later ship to the Red Sox for Sparky Lyle) promptly turned and started arguing with the umpire, shouting that the ball was foul. Jackson, meanwhile, had picked up the ball and thrown it into the infield without looking. His throw struck Cater in the back of the head, prompting Catfish Hunter to say that that was the only time Reggie ever hit the cutoff man.

Jackson was, in fact, the ideal designated hitter, a new American League position created in 1973, a player who would bat but not play in the field. And that made him the antithesis of everything that Martin valued in a baseball player—yet he was hugely rewarded despite, or perhaps even because of, what Martin considered his disrespect for the game. Jackson was modern, and bound to clash with his tradition-obsessed manager. He wasn't just a baseball player, as Martin had been, so immersed in the sport that he could not imagine a life outside it, so desperate about his status within it that the thought of failure kept him staring at the ceiling when he tried to sleep. Martin never quite believed in his excellence; Jackson never doubted his. Such confidence liberated Jackson, giving him more perspective on baseball, a greater critical distance. As a free agent, he was one of the first players able to choose which team he would play for, and he selected the Yankees not just on the basis of how good they were, or how much Steinbrenner would pay him—other teams had offered more money—but how much media attention he could generate in New York and how valuable that attention would be in terms of endorsements, advertisements, and his own ego.

Martin played the game because he could do nothing else and never much wanted to. For Jackson, baseball was merely the foundation of the Reggie Jackson brand, a platform from which to launch other ventures. He was a sports commentator, a businessman, a real estate investor, and a millionaire (at a time when that was rare among baseball players) even before he joined the Yankees. While Martin worried that he'd never made much money in baseball, Jackson flaunted his wealth; he owned a collection of classic cars that included five Rolls-Royces. And money was not all he flaunted. Like Martin, Jackson loved the company of beautiful women, but his were usually more beautiful than those with whom Martin consorted and, because he was divorced, he did not have to hide their existence. A 1974 *Time* profile of Jackson said that "his typical evening will end with some dancing at the Playboy Club in San Francisco, where several Bunnies appreciate his company after work. For more substantial relationships, Jackson dates several white girls. . . ."

Of course Jackson was modern in a way that was, for baseball, still a relatively new phenomenon: he was black, or at least partially so. His father, Martinez Jackson, was the son of a black father and a Spanish mother; his mother, Clara, was black. Reginald Martinez Jackson was born May 18, 1946, and grew up in Wyncote, Pennsylvania, a prosperous suburb of Philadelphia. Race, Jackson always said, was not a prominent factor in his childhood; unlike Martin, Jackson never felt that he grew up on the wrong side of the tracks, whether physical, social, racial or ethnic. "My father didn't and still doesn't know what color is," he said. "I grew up with white kids, played ball with them, went home with them and more than one time beat up some punk trying to hurt them. I didn't know what prejudice was until I got to college and the football coach told me to stop dating white girls."

After two years playing baseball and football at Arizona State, Jackson was signed by the Kansas City Athletics in 1966 for an $85,000 bonus. The New York Mets actually had the first pick that year. But their general manager, George Weiss, who a decade earlier had been loath to integrate the Yankees, avoided Jackson because of his predilection for dating white women. Two years later, when the A's moved to Oakland, Jackson was their starting right fielder. That season he led the American League in home runs, with 29, but also strikeouts, with 171, and errors, with 12. The following year Jackson erupted, hitting 37 home runs before the All-Star break, looking like he would break Roger Maris's record of 61 home runs in a season, until he tailed off in the second half and finished with a still remarkable 47.

The A's dominated baseball in the early 1970s, winning the World Series in 1972, 1973, and 1974. With such pitchers as Catfish Hunter, Rollie Fingers, and Vida Blue and hitters such as Joe Rudi, Ray Fosse, and Sal Bando, they were a rambunctious, tough group who had learned to live with Jackson's ego and insatiable need for media attention. Jackson sought press, reveled in it, and rewarded those who gave it to him with the kind of quotes that sounded more like something Andy Warhol would say than a baseball player. "I'd rather hit than have sex," Jackson told *Time*. "To hit is to show strength. It's two against one at the plate, the pitcher and the catcher versus you . . . God, I do love to hit that little round sum-bitch out of the park and make 'em say, 'Wow!' " The magazine wrote of Jackson, "Though once a sloppy defenseman, rightfielder Jackson now makes a habit of circus catches and bullet throws to infield and home." Jackson did indeed have a powerful throwing arm. But the "circus catches" line might have been a nice way of saying that Jackson could make even routine fly balls look exciting.

For all the ink he attracted in Oakland, Jackson was restless; he knew he could get more attention and more money elsewhere, and at the beginning of the 1976 season he made no secret of his desire to become a free agent. The A's notoriously stingy owner, Charles Finley, promptly traded Jackson to Baltimore, on the theory that it was better to get something for him while that was still possible than simply to lose him to free agency. (One of the players Finley received in return was Mike Torrez, who had just won 20 games with the Orioles.) But Jackson wouldn't sign with Baltimore, to the frustration of local fans who pelted Jackson with hot dogs. At the end of the season, the courtship began. The Yankees wanted Jackson, as did the Padres and the Expos, among others. Could Reggie Jackson really play in Montreal or San Diego?

From the beginning, then—even before he arrived in spring training for 1977 in one of his Rolls-Royces—Reggie Jackson created tension. Thurman Munson fumed that Steinbrenner was paying Jackson more than Munson, though Steinbrenner had promised Munson that he would be the highest-paid Yankee. Then, in late May, the publication of a profile of Jackson in *Sport* magazine irritated Munson further. Robert Ward's article, "Reggie Jackson in No-Man's Land," quoted Jackson saying, "You know, this team, it all flows from me. I've got to keep it all going. I'm the straw that stirs the drink. It all comes back to me. Maybe I should say me and Munson. But he really doesn't enter into it. He's so damned insecure about the whole thing. . . . Munson thinks he can be the straw that stirs the drink, but he can only stir it bad." Those provocative quotations would create season-long tension not just between Jackson and Munson, but between Jackson and almost all the other Yankees. Thurman Munson was the team captain, but more than that, he was the team leader; insulting him was a terrible mistake.

Martin, of course, hadn't wanted Jackson on the team; he preferred Oakland outfielder Joe Rudi, who was quieter, less flamboyant, and played better defense. He disliked Jackson for numerous reasons, but prime among them was that he considered Jackson one of "George's boys," his derogatory term for players whom, he felt, the owner had foisted upon him. Relations between the two started bad and got worse, most notably in a June 18 game against the Red Sox at Fenway. In the sixth inning, Jim Rice lined a short fly ball toward Jackson in right. Jackson couldn't have caught the ball, but he certainly didn't run very hard to get it. An alert Rice noted Jackson's lackadaisical effort and quickly turned a single into a double. Martin—the man who'd made a sprinting grab of a pop-up to save the 1952 World Series—was livid, and instantly sent reserve outfielder Paul Blair out to replace Jackson. The Yankee right fielder was stunned; the game was being nationally broadcast on NBC's *Game of the Week*, and Martin was taking him out in the middle of the inning, humiliating him in front of millions of viewers. As soon as Jackson arrived at the dugout, he and Martin began screaming at each other, and would have come to blows if coaches Yogi Berra and Elston Howard hadn't physically inserted themselves between them.

Martin almost lost his job because of the incident—even for Steinbrenner, tolerating a manager who threatened to beat the daylights out of his star free agent was asking a lot—but it marked the peak of the Yankees' discontent, and after the incident the team pulled back from the edge of implosion. Though the bad feelings lingered, the Yankees began to win. Munson and Jackson hit well, Ron Guidry started to come into his own, Sparky Lyle was having a Cy Young Award–winning season, and the Yankees won 100 games. They then won 7 more in the postseason, culminating in Jackson's memorable Game Six performance. Three swings, three homers.

In the off-season, Steinbrenner did not sit still. To the amazement of Sparky Lyle, he signed right-handed relief pitcher Rich Gossage to a contract totaling $2,748,000. Lyle was making about $130,000 a year, and though he won that Cy Young Award for his pitching during the '77 season—a rarity for a reliever—suddenly he felt replaced with the arrival of a competitor who happened to be younger and making far more money than he was.

The pitching staff had gone through other changes. Mike Torrez had headed up to Boston, but the Yankees had also signed reliever Rawly Eastwick from the Reds and Andy Messersmith from the Braves. Between Eastwick, who was to pitch middle innings, and Dick Tidrow, Sparky Lyle, and Rich Gossage, the Yankees surely had the best bullpen in baseball. The starters were shakier. Leading the staff now was Guidry, who had gone 10–2 after the All-Star break. Both Hunter and Gullett, however, had struggled with sore arms in 1977, and that spring Hunter was diagnosed with diabetes. The Yankees were counting on Ed Figueroa, winner of 51 games in the previous three years. And they hoped that they could cobble together a fifth starter with either Ken Holtzman, acquired in a trade with the Orioles in 1976, or rookies Ken Clay and Jim Beattie.

The rest of the starting lineup stayed the same. Thurman Munson, coming off his third consecutive season hitting over .300 with 100 or more RBIs, would be behind the plate. Quiet, consistent Chris Chambliss was at first. Willie Randolph, a gifted young player already looking like an anchor of the team, was at second. Former White Sox shortstop Bucky Dent would be starting his second year with the team. Graig Nettles, whose fielding ability rivaled that of the legendary Brooks Robinson, handled third. In the outfield, the veteran Roy White, modest but capable, played left. Mickey Rivers roamed in center, and Reggie Jackson and Lou Piniella split responsibilities in right field and at designated hitter. The outfielders were a strong offensive group, but defensively they possessed liabilities. Both White and Rivers had weak arms. In 1976, *Sports Illustrated* had said of White that he had "a glove that goes clank in the night and an arm like Venus DeMilo's," and Rivers's hardest throws arced into the infield as if they were taking a Sunday constitutional. Jackson frequently looked tentative and awkward in the field. Piniella was solid, but no one would ever confuse him with Willie Mays.

As Martin started his third full year as manager, the most pressing question about the team was whether the Yankees could play another season without tearing themselves apart. Winning had cooled the antagonisms between Steinbrenner, Martin, Jackson, Munson, and the others. But how much and for how long?

At the end of spring training, the Yankees were 10–13, which didn't bother Martin, who didn't think that a team's record before the season started meant much. Steinbrenner, however, was already unhappy. In early April he warned Martin that the manager "better start pulling this team together." Martin vowed that he and Steinbrenner would get along. "George is a moody guy," he said. "He's going to have his moods. I understand that, because I'm moody too—when I'm losing ball games."

But it wasn't just when losing that Steinbrenner, Martin, Munson, and Jackson grew moody. The four men clashed because they were caught in the tensions of a game in transition. Steinbrenner brought a self-aggrandizing, media-hungry, free-spending style of ownership to a team whose ownership had typically been studied, efficient, and corporate. At the same time that Steinbrenner professed devotion to Yankee tradition, he was effecting radical changes to that tradition, participating in the new free agency scramble with almost reckless abandon. Martin, meanwhile, was a manager steeped in baseball's golden era and obsessed with control who could not accept that he could control neither everything about his team nor the larger course of the game—the new and massive sums of money, the greater media scrutiny, the changing balance of power between managers and players. Like Martin, Thurman Munson felt he should be rewarded for his traditional values—his work ethic, his willingness to play when injured, his leadership, his devotion to the subtle elements of the game. Instead, he worried that the rewards were going to a newcomer, Jackson, who manifested none of those traits but combined a singular hitting skill with a gift and a hunger for modern celebrity.

They were four very different personalities on a team that was trying to integrate all the changes shaking up baseball in the 1970s, even as they hoped to win their second World Series in two years. No matter that the spring had been relatively quiet—it seemed unlikely that such calm could persist.

CHAPTER 2

TOP OF THE FIRST

The crowd at Fenway was on its feet and cheering for Mike Torrez as he walked from the bullpen in right field to the dugout. They cheered as a minute or so later the Red Sox players trotted onto the field to take their positions, and they continued to cheer as Torrez stood on the mound throwing warm-up pitches. Some Yankee fans had managed to infiltrate Fenway Park, but most of the 32,925 fans on hand were passionate supporters of the home team. A coin flip had given the Red Sox that advantage. Whatever their allegiance, even before the first pitch, everyone understood that this improbable playoff between two old rivals was a special game. "If there is anything else going on in this world today, I don't know what it is," said Red Sox announcer Ned Martin. "If you don't believe baseball is our national pastime, you should be here at Fenway Park this afternoon," Yankee announcer Frank Messer said. "I have seen nothing like it. I have seen playoff games, I have seen World Series, and this has got to top anything I have seen in my baseball career."

It was a perfect day to play. The afternoon of October 2 was sunny and warm, with a light breeze and temperatures in the mid-sixties. Such days are cherished in Boston, for they are fleeting in October, when the days grow shorter, and the leaves turn yellow and crimson and orange; it would be only weeks until the frigid bite of winter clamped down on the Hub until at least April and the beginning of the next baseball season. So the warmth of this day felt like a gift, all the more appreciated because it would quickly pass. Labor Day had come and gone, the wet, gusty gray of November was imminent, but a brilliant autumn afternoon was still somehow timeless. New England never seems quite so perfect as on a sunny day in October, and the place to be in New England that day was inside Fenway Park.

October 2 was a Monday, so the fans in Fenway and the millions of people watching on television or listening on the radio were dodging their responsibilities. Those unable to escape from work or study turned on their televisions and radios in their stores and garages and offices. The weekday 2:30 P.M. starting time lent the game an even more vintage quality. Thanks to night baseball, there weren't many games of such import played during the day anymore. The very next evening, the winner of this game would face the Kansas City Royals, the American League West champions, in a night game at Kansas City.

If the day was a perfect backdrop, Fenway Park was the perfect site for such a game. Fenway is as idiosyncratic as the city in which it is located, sometimes gruff and cold, equally charming and eccentric. It is cozy. In 1978 you could cram only about 36,000 people into Fenway Park, and only then if three of four thousand of them were standing in the aisles. The seats were a tight squeeze, and many had views obstructed by support beams that do not exist in modern stadiums. By comparison, the cavernous Yankee Stadium, refurbished and reopened in 1976, seated about 55,000. The stands in Fenway came close to the field, and players spoke—sometimes with reverence, sometimes with dismay—of the intimacy of the place: when fans yelled to them, good or bad, the players heard their words. Other forces in baseball were working to create greater distances between fans and players, but here at Fenway, the two could still interact. For those who appreciated history, that was the charm of the park. Walking into Fenway in 1978 didn't feel all that different from walking into Fenway in 1958, or 1938.

Red Sox owner Charles Henry Taylor built Fenway Park between 1910 and 1912. He named the stadium for its location in the Fens, an area of tidal swamp that landscape architect Frederick Law Olmsted had helped transform into a freshwater lagoon and park. The Fens are now an attractive urban glade, but at the turn of the twentieth century they were less than scenic—an "unsightly and ill-smelling area of mud flats made more palatable by Frederick Law Olmsted's manipulations of the landscape," according to one Red Sox historian. But Taylor had his reasons for building where he did; he was an investor in the Fenway Realty Company, which owned large chunks of land in the neighborhood, and the new ballpark would substantially increase the value of Fenway Realty's holdings. Fenway was built to accommodate the entirety of a plot that Taylor had purchased, so its dimensions were larger than was then necessary, because the loosely wrapped baseballs used in 1912 didn't travel nearly as far as modern balls do. Right field was 302 feet down the line, but 380 feet at its deepest, while the deepest point in center field was 420 feet from home.

Perhaps Fenway's most distinctive feature was in left field: a twenty-five-foot-high wall intended to discourage fans from watching the games without a ticket. The wall was officially listed as 315 feet from home plate, but architectural blueprints suggest that it was more like 308 feet, and amateur geographers have put the distance at 304 feet. Even so, the left field wall was thought to be beyond batters' capabilities, and so a ten-foot-high mound sloping down from the wall was built to host standing-room crowds. Soon enough, batters found its distance. Red Sox left fielder Duffy Lewis would become so adept at running up and down the little hill that it became known as "Duffy's Cliff."

On April 20, 1912, the Red Sox played the first professional game in Fenway Park, against the New York Highlanders, winning 7–6 in eleven innings. The next season, the Highlanders would officially change their name to "Yankees."

In February 1933 the Red Sox were bought by a thirty-year-old millionaire named Thomas Austin Yawkey. The adopted son of William Yawkey, onetime owner of the Detroit Tigers, Yawkey was heir to a mining and lumber fortune estimated at $8 million to $20 million. The young millionaire had little interest in any business other than his new ball club and quickly commenced two projects: improving the Red Sox by paying top dollar for ballplayers, and renovating a stadium that, after twenty years of use, was starting to show signs of age. Painted a color known as "Dartmouth green," Yawkey's "New Fenway Park," completed in 1934, contained about eleven thousand seats more than the old Fenway. The left field wall was enlarged to its current height of thirty-seven feet and included an electric scoreboard, the first to use green and red lights as markers for balls and strikes. Unlike the rest of the stadium, though, it was covered in billboards. (The ads would be removed in 1947, when the wall was painted Dartmouth green, after which it acquired its famous nickname, the Green Monster.) Though there would be tweaks from time to time—the 1940 introduction of bullpens in right field, for example, which shortened the fences for the pull-hitting Ted Williams—this was essentially the stadium in which the Yankees and the Red Sox were playing.

Michael Augustine Torrez was a little nervous. He had tried to adhere to his regular game day routine, starting with some pancakes for breakfast, visualizing the Yankee lineup, mentally going over how he would pitch to each batter—what their weaknesses were, how he would set the hitters up so that he could exploit those weakness, and what his "out pitch" for each batter would be. The year before, he had been a member of the Yankees, and he sat and watched them hit. "I knew they all had weaknesses," he would recall. Still, this was hardly a typical game, and Torrez was an emotional man.

Torrez, thirty-one years old, wanted to beat the Yankees very badly on this day, not just because of the importance of the game but also for personal reasons. As a member of the 1977 Yankees, Torrez had felt that his contributions were insufficiently appreciated by the Yankee management, particularly owner George Steinbrenner. Beating them on this day would show them the error of their ways.

His career record against the Yankees, however, was not encouraging. In a little over two seasons in the American League, Torrez had compiled a 1–5 record against the New Yorkers, with a mediocre earned run average of 4.58 per nine innings. During the 1978 season, he was 1–3 against the Yankees, with a horrific ERA of 6.16. As a team, the Yankees were hitting .307 against him. But Torrez did have some momentum coming into the game: in his last start, against the Toronto Blue Jays four days before, Torrez had thrown a 1–0 shutout, and his season record of 16–12 with an ERA of 3.92 was certainly better than his record against his former team.

He was a right-handed pitcher with a good fastball, a slider that broke in on left-handed hitters, and a hard curveball. Torrez was six feet five and weighed about 220 pounds. "A big strong son of a bitch," said his teammate, the pitcher Dennis Eckersley, meaning it as a compliment. "He'd throw a lot of pitches, and he wasn't afraid to go 3–2 on a batter. He didn't make it look easy. But he was the type of guy who pitched good enough to win, whether it went 4–3 or 1–0." Torrez was not an elite pitcher, but he could be a very good one, and no one doubted his competitive fire. As Yankee broadcaster Phil Rizzuto put it that day, Torrez was "an excitable Latin type."

He was born in Topeka, Kansas, in 1946. His parents were Mexican-American, and his father worked as a carpenter on Santa Fe Railroad coaches. One of eight children in the family, Torrez threw the baseball hard from an early age. His father had only one good eye, and when Mike was ten, the boy was already hurling the ball with such velocity that his father decided that someone else—someone with two good eyes—should catch his son's throws. As a teenager, Torrez played

American Legion baseball, supporting himself by pumping gas from 11 P.M. to 7 A.M., sleeping for a few hours, then pitching in the afternoon or evening. In 1964, after a season in which Torrez went 13–1 with an ERA of 0.60, the Cardinals signed the eighteen-year-old to a $20,000 contract. He found out later that they were willing to pay twice that, but he wasn't in a position to negotiate; his family needed the money. When Torrez was a kid, he and his oldest brother would hunt for food—rabbits, quail, pheasants, deer. Once they arrived home toting 103 pheasants. "The Torrez family ate a lot of pheasant for the next month or so," he remembered. "There were many, many times that the game we shot and brought home supplied the food for our table."

After three years in the minor leagues, Torrez joined the Cardinals in 1967, a cocky rookie eager to make his mark. "I wanted to be like Don Drysdale and Bob Gibson," he said. "I wanted to learn how to pitch inside and be intimidating." That spring, Torrez was out for dinner with Cardinals center fielder Curt Flood when "Drysdale happened to walk in and Curt introduced me," Torrez said. "I said, 'Don, can I ask you—what would make a pitcher successful?' He says, 'Kid, I've seen you pitch. *Learn* to pitch. Learn to pitch *in*. Hitters don't like it when you pitch in. Learn to do that and you'll be successful in the big leagues.'

"And that's what I did," Torrez said. "I started learning how to pitch in."

He got help from Gibson, the Cardinals' famed right-hander, perhaps the most dominant pitcher in baseball—and certainly the most intimidating—during the late 1960s. Torrez had speed, but not craft. He didn't know how to throw a slider, a pitch that is like a combination of a fastball and a curveball—faster than the curveball, more of a break to one side or the other than the fastball. So Torrez pestered Gibson to teach him the secrets of throwing the pitch. "How do you throw that?" he'd ask. "Will you teach me?" Gibson would mutter his response: "Damn kiss-ass. Goddamn rookie." Finally, he gave in. Gibson showed Torrez how to grip the ball, how you snapped the wrist to give the pitch its telltale motion. As a good slider approaches the plate, a batter watching the ball should see a little round dot, like a zero, an optical illusion caused by the spinning laces. "Gibson taught me how to hold the ball and stay on top, like a football, then bring it down, boom, so you started seeing the spot," Torrez said. They were just throwing the ball back and forth, maybe thirty feet apart. But as he got the grip and the motion down, Torrez started backing up, throwing the pitch longer distances, approaching the sixty feet, six inches that is the distance between home plate and the pitching rubber. It took him a few weeks, but soon he was ready to throw the pitch in a game. That was when Torrez really started to become a pitcher.

Even so, Torrez never realized his potential with the Cardinals. In more than four years with the team, he would not win more than ten games in a season. Some thought that Torrez's fondness for going out at night, along with the demise of his first marriage, had something to do with that; one sportswriter dubbed him "the Knight of the Neon." In 1971 the Cards shipped Torrez to the Montreal Expos, a move that upset the young pitcher—the Cardinals were a top-notch organization, the Expos were not. In Montreal, he got married again, to a successful Canadian model named Danielle Gagnon, who, it was reported, earned at least forty dollars an hour in photo shoots (for lingerie ads, two hundred dollars an hour). On the field, Torrez was less successful. Expos manager Gene Mauch thought him inconsistent, immature, and sometimes overweight, and in December 1974 the Expos dispatched Torrez to the Baltimore Orioles. Torrez had a great year with the O's, going 20–9 with a 3.06 ERA, but in April 1976 Baltimore sent him to the Oakland A's in a multiplayer deal that landed the Orioles home run hitter Reggie Jackson. A year later, when A's owner Charlie Finley realized that Torrez intended to play out his option and become a free agent, Oakland traded Torrez to New York.

Amid all the coast-to-coast traveling, Torrez had become a much-improved pitcher. He credited Baltimore pitching coach George Bamberger, who helped tutor the great Orioles pitching staffs of that era. "He taught me how to pitch, how to think," Torrez said at the time. "You figure that in the course of a season you're going to have 35 or 40 starts. But you're only going to have your really good fastball about ten times. A pitcher learns to win when he doesn't have the good stuff. I probably threw a lot harder in St. Louis than I do now, but I didn't know how to get by. There are times now when I just have to mix things up for six, seven, eight innings, and then maybe I'll finally really get loose and let go those last couple of innings."

In 1977, Torrez went 14–12 with the Yankees, but he pitched best in the second half of the season, and then, in the Yankees' World Series victory against the Dodgers, he won the third and sixth games. Torrez became a hero in New York, but the real value of his postseason heroics was financial. After bouncing around the majors for a decade, Torrez wanted to take control of his career. Boosted by his World Series success, he filed for free agency.

It was just the second year in which players had that freedom. Before 1975, baseball teams had bound players through contractual language known as the reserve clause. Dating to the late 1880s, the reserve clause was intended to suppress financial competition between owners by stipulating that, at the end of a player's contract, "the club shall have the right . . . to renew this contract for a period of one year." In practical terms, the reserve clause meant that a player could never sign with another team unless he were traded, which kept the owners from bidding against one another. Even after retirement, a player was bound to the team for which he had once played.

Thus deprived of bargaining power, players had little choice but to accept the contracts they were offered at whatever salary the owner was willing to pay. (Adding insult to injury, the reserve clause also stipulated that each new contract need only be 80 percent of the preceding one.) Every so often, a player would feel so shortchanged that he refused to sign and play unless offered more money, but that tactic was only available to the handful of players whose skills were truly irreplaceable. It was also a surefire way to lose popular support: from Joe DiMaggio to Sandy Koufax, fans turned on players who held out for more money. They looked greedy. After all, they were being paid for playing a game. What did they have to complain about?

Over the decades, only the principled, the stubborn, and the desperate challenged the reserve clause. In the 1920s, a Baltimore team sued the National League over monopolistic practices that included the reserve clause. Arguing that the National League's anticompetitive behavior violated the Sherman Anti-Trust Act, the team took its case, *Federal Baseball Club of Baltimore, Inc.* v. *National League of Professional Baseball Clubs et al.*, all the way to the Supreme Court, only to lose when, in 1922, Chief Justice Oliver Wendell Holmes wrote that baseball was not a business but a sport, and therefore could not violate the laws of interstate commerce. That romantic but naïve legal distinction, which said so much about the way Americans wished to see baseball, would last for more than fifty years.

In 1947 a player named Danny Gardella, blacklisted by major league owners because he had joined the Mexican League rather than accept a lackluster contract from the New York Giants, sued baseball. After a barrage of negative press fueled by the owners—the Dodgers'

Branch Rickey charged that Gardella's labor activism was a sign of a "communistic tendency"—Gardella accepted an out-of-court settlement that allowed him to return to the major leagues. But Gardella would come to regret not pursuing his case; he later said that the settlement made him "feel like a Judas who had received his thirty pieces of silver."

In 1953, a Yankee minor leaguer named George Toolson filed another lawsuit. Because of the reserve clause, the Yankees had been able to keep him in the minor leagues indefinitely, he charged. They would not bring him up to the majors, but they didn't want another team to have him, either. As a result, Toolson was stuck in the minors and hampered in his ability to make a living. But in *Toolson* v. *New York Yankees, Inc.*, the Supreme Court affirmed the 1922 ruling.

The next challenge to the reserve clause, the most serious yet, came from Mike Torrez's former teammate Curt Flood. In October 1969, the Cardinals traded Flood to Philadelphia, a move he was first informed of by a sportswriter. Once considered perhaps the game's best center fielder, Flood was insulted by the manner in which he learned of the trade and less than enthused about playing in Philadelphia, a city with a reputation for hostility toward African-American players. Plus, the Phillies were an organization reputed to treat all its players badly, whether they were black or white. Sacrificing a $90,000 salary, Flood refused to go to Philadelphia, and instead moved to Europe for a year. With the help of Marvin Miller, the executive director of the Major League Baseball Players Association, Flood sued baseball commissioner Bowie Kuhn and Major League Baseball for $4.1 million, charging violation of antitrust laws.

In 1972 the Supreme Court heard the case of *Flood* v. *Kuhn*, and by a vote of 5–3 the court again reaffirmed the 1922 decision. (Justice Lewis Powell recused himself because he was a shareholder in Anheuser-Busch, which owned the Cardinals.) "The justices' reasoning seemed tortured and sentimental," wrote *New York Times* sportswriter George Vecsey, "as often happens when learned and powerful Americans confront sport, somehow assuming they should like it and endorse it, straining to seem like regular fellows." Flood, meanwhile, had attempted a comeback with the Washington Senators, to whom the Phillies had traded him when Flood would not play for them. After just 13 games, in which he hit .200, a dispirited Flood quit and returned to Europe, where he would live in self-imposed exile for the rest of the decade. In 1997, Flood, a longtime drinker and smoker, died of cancer at age fifty-nine.

Still, the tensions of arguing that a multimillion-dollar business with franchises all across the country was, in fact, not a business at all were increasingly evident. The year 1974 saw a watershed in the century-long struggle between players and owners: Oakland A's pitcher Jim "Catfish" Hunter became a free agent. Hunter was a right-hander with pinpoint control who anchored the A's staff through World Series victories in 1972, 1973, and 1974. In that third season he won 25 games, the fourth of an astonishing five consecutive 20-game-winning seasons. But when Charlie Finley failed to make a stipulated payment on Hunter's contract, Hunter and his lawyer notified the league that they considered the contract void. In December 1974, arbitrator Peter Seitz—empowered to consider such disputes by the bargaining agreement between the owners and the players—ruled in Hunter's favor. Seitz's decision made Hunter the first baseball player in the history of the major leagues with the legal right to leave one team and sign with any team he wanted.

The manic bidding that followed astounded Hunter—and gave baseball players a sense of just what the marketplace might hold for them were they allowed to test it. While Hunter enjoyed the off-season at his farm in Hertford, North Carolina, representatives from interested teams made pilgrimages to his lawyers' offices in nearby Ahoskie. Charlie Finley was paying Hunter $100,000 a year, which was slightly less than elite players around the league received. (Finley was notoriously cheap.) The Mets offered Hunter $2 million for a multiyear deal; the Indians, $2.4 million; Kansas City, $3.3 million. The Pirates suggested $2 million in cash and a limited partnership in five new Wal-Mart stores. The Red Sox proposed $3 million over five years, only to be topped by the Dodgers, who offered Hunter $3 million over two years—fifteen times what Hunter had been making. The San Diego Padres came in with the highest monetary offer, $4.5 million for five years.

In the end, Hunter signed with the Yankees for about $3.5 million—$100,000 a year for five years, plus various deferred payments such as college tuition for his children. There were other factors involved besides money: Hunter was close with Yankee scout Clyde Kluttz, and he wanted to stay in the American League. He also wanted to pitch for a team that played on grass, rather than artificial turf, which pitchers disliked because a ground ball was more likely to scoot through an artificial turf infield than a grass one.

Hunter was, of course, one of the greatest pitchers of the decade, a future Hall of Famer. Most players could not command anywhere near such sums on the free market. And, of course, Seitz ruled for Hunter on a technical issue—Finley's missed payment—rather than on the question of the legitimacy of the reserve clause. Still, Hunter's experience showed baseball players that they were worth more to the owners than the owners were paying them—far more. So, in 1975, Dave McNally of the Expos and Andy Messersmith of the Dodgers agreed to conduct a provocative experiment: Believing that the reserve clause allowed owners to renew their contracts for one year, but *only* one year, the two decided they would play the 1975 season without signing contracts. At the end of the season, they would declare themselves free agents. Backed by union head Marvin Miller, their plan worked: that December, arbitrator Seitz ruled that the reserve clause *was* only binding for one year (an act of logic for which the baseball owners quickly fired him). McNally had by this point retired, but in short order Messersmith signed a three-year contract with the Atlanta Braves for about $600,000 a year. The owners would again take the matter to court, but this time, and for the first time, they would lose.

The floodgates were open; baseball was about to undergo its most profound transformation since Jackie Robinson joined the Brooklyn Dodgers in 1947. The first, and most obvious, indicator of the changes brought on by free agency was an exponential rise in players' salaries. In 1967, the average baseball salary was $19,600; in 1975, $44,000. By 1977 that figure jumped about 75 percent, to $76,349. By 1985, the number was $371,000. Players were now making more money in a year than most of their predecessors had made during their entire careers.

Free agency would change far more than just the average salary; it shifted the fundamental balance of power in baseball from owners to players—and to a new entity, the sports agent. (Now that contracts could be negotiated, the players needed someone to do the negotiating.) It would diminish the power of the managers, who found their authority over players greatly weakened. What did it mean to fine a player $1,000 if he was making $500,000? And how could you bench an underperforming or obnoxious player when an owner had just announced to great fanfare that he had signed that athlete for several million dollars? Free agency would also change the relationships between players on the team, corroding the very concept of a team. When only a few thousand dollars separated one player's salary from another's, the differentials were not particularly divisive. But when the gap was tens of thousands, hundreds of thousands of dollars a year, friction between teammates invariably arose. Players would start "playing for their option year"—trying to pump up their individual statistics, sometimes at the expense of the team, when they knew they were on the verge of becoming free agents.

And, of course, free agency would change the nature of a team from a fan's perspective. Before free agency, fans would get to know the players on the teams they rooted for over a period of years. They lived with these players from season to season, grew attached to them, saw them as young rookies, athletes in their prime, wily veterans, and aging heroes. Fans not only knew the players as individuals, they also knew the culture, the attributes of the teams these individuals collectively composed. Before free agency, rooting for a baseball team was like immersing oneself in a Dickens serial. You knew the characters, and you knew that there would be many more chapters to come.

But after free agency, the relationship between fan and team changed. How could you root for a team with all your heart and soul when from year to year its players could up and leave for another city, another team? Or when from year to year your team would bring in unfamiliar faces, hired arms and rented bats with whom local fans had no emotional connection? The more you cared about your team, the more it broke your heart when your favorite player announced that he had just signed with another organization for more money than you could imagine an athlete being paid. Teams would adapt by signing players to long-term contacts; fans would adapt by taking a more intellectual and less emotional approach to the game, becoming ever more immersed in statistics and strategy. Or by simply becoming obsessed with winning. If you could not cheer for a team because you knew that team, had rooted for pretty much the same bunch of guys who were playing when you kissed a girl for the first time, drank too much in college, survived basic training, and married the girl next door—if you could no longer root for a team because they felt like a part of your extended family, then you might as well just cheer for them to win at any cost.

Following the 1977 World Series, Mike Torrez found himself in the perfect position to sign a lucrative contract: He'd just come off a season in which he'd won 17 regular season games and 2 more in the postseason. But Yankee general manager Gabe Paul did not consider Torrez an elite pitcher, merely a good one. The Yankees offered Torrez $1.5 million over five years, a relatively modest offer by the emerging standards of the new era. The Red Sox, in dire need of pitching, countered with $2.5 million over seven years. Torrez appreciated not just the money, but the longevity. "The big reason I signed with the Red Sox was for the security I received," he would say. "After all the times I had traveled to so many different teams, I just felt that the next stop I wanted to be my last one." And having played for the Yankees for just one season, the move to the archrival Red Sox didn't bother him. "I wanted to go to a team that had a shot" at the World Series, Torrez said, "and I thought, after facing the Red Sox in '77, that they were going to be one of the tougher teams in baseball in '78."

Torrez felt so sure of that, in fact, that shortly after he signed with the Red Sox he expressed his opinion that the Sox were better than his old team. "I know Boston has a better ballclub than the Yankees, offensively and defensively," he said in November 1977. He later told the *Boston Globe* that the Yanks would suffer from the same kind of turmoil they'd endured the previous year. "Graig Nettles hates Jackson," he told the *Globe*. "Thurman Munson hates Jackson. Jackson is not well-liked by many members of his team."

By October 1978, Mike Torrez was not particularly well liked by members of the Yankees, either. "He's been bad-mouthing us all year," Yankee third baseman Graig Nettles said. "We didn't appreciate that. If it wasn't for us, he wouldn't have been in the position to sign a $2.5 million contract."

The Yankees' Mickey Rivers, a speedy, mischief-making center fielder, would lead off the game for the Yankees on October 2. Batting second was the catcher, Thurman Munson, and third was right fielder Lou Piniella. The powerful Reggie Jackson was batting cleanup. Graig Nettles, another home run hitter, would hit fifth, followed by the solid-hitting first baseman Chris Chambliss. Left fielder Roy White, second baseman Brian Doyle, and shortstop Bucky Dent, a significant drop-off in power and average from the top six Yankee batters, constituted the bottom third of the order.

When Rivers was not in the field or on base, he shuffled from place to place as if exhausted, or conserving his energy, in a way that looked more reminiscent of an old man than a twenty-nine-year-old athlete. A left-handed hitter, Rivers stepped into the batter's box and waggled his bat, almost pushing it forward with his left forearm as he took his practice swings. Rivers was five feet ten inches tall and weighed maybe 165 pounds, and he was in some ways an ideal leadoff hitter. Bent from the middle almost at a right angle, he offered a small strike zone for Torrez. He didn't strike out much, and when on base, he was a constant irritant. With the California Angels in 1975, he had stolen 70 bases. But whether stealing or not, Rivers was a distraction and a threat. In 1976, the Yankees had acquired Rivers, along with pitcher Ed Figueroa, for center fielder Bobby Bonds, who like Rivers could steal bases and unlike Rivers could hit for power, but who also struck out about three times as frequently as Rivers. His first two seasons with the Yankees, Rivers had hit .326, but this season his numbers had dropped to .264, with 11 home runs and 48 runs batted in.

Rivers was an unconventional leadoff hitter in one way: in 555 at-bats that season, he had walked just 27 times. He did not like to work the count and try to catch a glimpse of every weapon in a pitcher's arsenal, but instead loved to swing at first-pitch fastballs. In the first game of a late September series the year before against the Red Sox, Rivers had lined three hits on first pitches. The next night, Red Sox pitcher Reggie Cleveland had begun the bottom of the first by nailing Rivers in the ribs. The game was in the Bronx, and as Yankee fans began hurling beer and other unpleasantries in Cleveland's direction, Carlton Fisk had trotted to the mound to ensure that his pitcher wasn't rattled. "Let's see the little bastard hit *that* first pitch," Cleveland had told Fisk.

As third baseman Jack Brohamer moved two steps in on the infield grass in case Rivers should bunt, Torrez started with a breaking pitch, thinking that Rivers would guess fastball and swing over the pitch. But Rivers took it low, for a ball. Torrez followed that with a high fastball. Ball two. Ball three was a slider, inside. Ball four was another high fastball, and Rivers dropped his bat and loped to first base.

None of Torrez's pitches had been even close to the strike zone, and now the Yankee that Torrez most wanted to keep off the bases was leading off first, hands in front of him, knees bent, rocking back and forth.

Torrez was annoyed with himself: he'd walked someone who hated not to swing. First baseman George Scott strolled to the mound. He told Torrez to settle down, try to get a double-play ball out of Munson. Torrez just nodded. That wouldn't be easy. Scott would have to hold

Rivers at first, leaving a larger-than-usual gap between first and second, and the right-handed-hitting Munson was gifted at punching the ball to the opposite field. Moreover, if Munson hit a soft ground ball to any defender, Rivers wasn't an easy out at second.

The five-feet-eleven, 190-pound Munson was not normally the Yankees' number two hitter, a batter who is expected, should the leadoff man get on base, to tailor his hitting to the advantage of the man on first—hit to right field to advance the runner, swing to make contact in a hit-and-run, swing if the runner breaks for second, so as to attempt to disrupt the catcher's throw. But the regular number two hitter, second baseman Willie Randolph, had pulled a hamstring muscle in the last week of the season, and his replacement, rookie Brian Doyle, was a poor hitter. Munson was one of the finest hitters in the sport. From 1975 through 1977, he had posted three consecutive seasons with a .300 average and at least 100 runs batted in. Now thirty-one, his body wearing down from the cumulative physical abuse of a decade behind the plate with the Yankees, Munson had tailed off this season, hitting .297 with just 6 home runs and 70 RBIs. Still, he was a threat. He struck out only about once every ten at-bats, and he had surprising speed for a catcher.

Munson was not picturesque at the plate. He had scraggly brown hair and a ragged mustache. His face was jowly and his eyes small. He was strong, with massive forearms and powerful legs, but his body looked lumpy, like one sack of potatoes stacked on top of another. In an era when players had more colorful nicknames than they generally do now—Rivers, for example, was "Mick the Quick"—Munson's nicknames were "Tugboat" and "Squatty Body." Few people actually called him those names, which hardly rolled off the tongue.

Approaching the plate, Munson spat. Standing outside the batter's box, he adjusted his batting gloves, meticulously undoing the Velcro strap on each, then pulling them tighter. Stepping into the box, he swung his bat in a downward arc, like a minute hand running counterclockwise, then clockwise in an upward arc, and finally horizontally across the plate. He tugged at his jersey, then placed his left hand on his helmet and settled it on his head. With his right foot, he dug a small trough in the dirt of the batter's box, for leverage during his swing. Holding the bat in his right hand, he tapped the outside edge of the plate with its head, then flipped it over so that he held the fat part of the bat, tapped the far edge of the plate with its knob, then rolled the bat into his left palm and touched the outside of the plate again with its head. Finally, he brought the bat up toward his right shoulder. Knees slightly bent, feet parallel, he awaited Torrez's pitch.

Standing on the mound, Torrez considered the batter. The two had not always gotten along. In a June 1975 game, when Torrez was an Oriole, Torrez first hit Munson in the elbow. In Munson's next at-bat, Torrez threw a pitch that hit Munson's bat and his shoulder. The third time Munson was up, Torrez uncorked a pitch that zoomed behind his head. The fourth time Munson came to the plate, he told Orioles catcher Ellie Hendricks that he was going out to the mound if Torrez threw at him again. After Munson grounded out, the two men shouted at each other, and Munson suddenly charged at Torrez. Munson tried to punch Torrez but missed, and as his teammates arrived, the fight quickly deteriorated into shouting and shoving. "He yelled at me when he came up," Torrez said, "and I yelled back at him. Then he said something again when he ran down to first base, and I threw him a kiss. Who did he think he is, God, that I can't pitch him inside?" The catcher and pitcher had made up when Torrez joined the Yankees, but they would never be best friends.

Munson liked to hit in Fenway; he liked thumping fastballs off the Green Monster. But Torrez knew that Munson had trouble with his slider. The pitch broke down and away from a right-handed batter, out of his power zone. If Torrez got ahead of Munson on the count, he'd make sure not to throw him anything in the middle of the plate, or up and away, because Munson could drive those balls to right field. If Torrez fell behind Munson, he wouldn't give in and throw inside, where Munson could pull the ball. The trick was to get two strikes on Munson and set him up for his out pitch, the slider.

As Torrez lifted his left leg to start his motion—a high kick—Rivers took off for second. It wasn't a called play; Yankee manager Bob Lemon let Rivers pick his moments. The pitch was a fastball high, and Munson declined to swing. Catcher Carlton Fisk caught the ball, leaping from his crouch, and hurled to second. It wasn't even close; Rivers had stolen the base during that high leg kick.

Torrez had now thrown five straight balls. In the Red Sox bullpen, reliever Bob Stanley started to warm up. With Rivers on second and none out, the Yankees were already threatening to take the lead.

On the next pitch, Torrez caught a break. His slider broke just outside the plate, but umpire Don Denkinger called it a strike to even the count. Munson complained to Denkinger that the pitch was a ball. Torrez's next pitch hit the exact same spot, and Denkinger gave it to

Munson. Two balls, one strike. Then a curveball inside; Munson swung over it. Two and two. A fastball in the dirt got by Fisk and rolled to the side of the plate, but not far enough for Rivers to advance. Three and two.

Torrez whirled around and threw the ball to shortstop Rick Burleson, who had tried to sneak behind Rivers at second. Rivers scrambled back in time to beat Burleson's tag. Still, the play showed how his presence could keep the pitcher from focusing on the batter.

With his slider so far more accurate than his fastball, Torrez went to it on the 3–2 count, and just as he had predicted, Munson was fooled by the pitch, swinging awkwardly and missing badly. The first out, a crucial out. A man on second with one away was very different, than, say, first and second with none out, or Munson rounding first and Rivers scampering home.

Right-handed Lou Piniella came to the plate. A platoon player, Piniella was hitting .314, with 6 home runs and 69 runs batted in in 130 games. Along with Munson, he was a contact hitter who didn't hit many home runs but rarely struck out. Piniella was a respectable outfielder, but he was really known for his hitting—and for his obsession with hitting. Just as Ted Williams would stand in the outfield swinging an imaginary bat, so would Piniella. "He'd be standing in right field, working on his swing," former Orioles pitcher Jim Palmer remembered. When he was at home with his wife, or in a hotel room on the road, he'd do the same. "I just envisioned pitches in certain areas," Piniella said. "If you can handle 'em in front of a mirror, you can handle 'em in front of a game."

Louis Victor Piniella was born August 28, 1943, in Tampa, Florida. Originally signed by the Indians in 1962, he was then drafted by the Washington Senators, then traded to the Orioles, then traded to the Indians, then selected by the Seattle Pilots, an expansion team, in 1968, and then, in 1969, traded to the Royals. Under the guidance of a patient manager named Bob Lemon, Piniella finally got a chance to play in Kansas City. He responded by hitting .282 with 11 home runs in 135 games and was, at age twenty-six, voted rookie of the year. If there was a rap against Piniella, it was that he wanted to hit so badly, he lacked discipline at the plate. "He's so anxious to hit the ball, he swings at everything," said George Strickland, a coach for the Royals, in 1968. "Good pitches, bad pitches, inside, outside, high or low. He doesn't let anything go by. Every time he's on base, he has earned his way with the bat. He never walks." And Piniella, who stood six feet two and weighed about two hundred pounds when he was in good shape, was not nimble. "He's no speed merchant," Strickland said.

Relentlessly self-critical, Piniella admitted that Strickland had a point. Ted Williams once told Piniella that "the best way to be a good hitter is to wait for his pitch." But, Piniella confessed early in his career, "I'm just not like that. I'm just a swinger." That was overly harsh: no player worked on his hitting more, or with more intensity, than Piniella. In one notorious incident, Piniella was practicing his swings behind a batting cage. After several imaginary pitches and corresponding swings, Piniella suddenly turned, hurled his bat, and shouted, "Dammit! I can't hit that stuff!"

When he wasn't throwing his bat, he was throwing his helmet. After a strikeout, Piniella would return to the dugout furious with himself, smashing water coolers and lightbulbs, once even throwing himself into a rain barrel. "Lou was a red-ass," Palmer said, using the baseball term for a fiery player. In 1964, the two men played minor league ball together in Aberdeen, South Dakota. Piniella was coming out of a stint in the military, Palmer recalled. "He hadn't played in about a year, and a ball goes through his legs. A fan yelled, 'Piniella, we're going to send you back to the bush leagues.' And Piniella looked at him and said, 'Where in the fuck do you think I am?' " Another time, Piniella lined out with the bases loaded. "Lou comes in, throws his helmet down, beats the shit out of it," Palmer said. "Steam coming out of his ears." A teammate named Bobby Litchfield looked at Piniella, and said, "Lou . . ."

"What the fuck do you want?" Piniella said.

"Even if you hit .300, Lou," Litchfield answered, "you're still going to break seven out of ten helmets."

Piniella just started laughing.

The Royals traded Piniella to the Yankees in 1973 for right-handed pitcher Lindy McDaniel, and the well-traveled player quickly became one of the most popular players on the team. Sometimes he played right field, sometimes he served as the designated hitter, after the American League created that hitting-only position in 1973. And sometimes he didn't play at all. For Piniella, that wasn't the worst thing. "If I had the attitude that I had to play everyday to be happy, I wouldn't be here right now," he said early in 1978. "I would have been in the free agent market last year and been making a hell of a lot more money elsewhere. I'd rather be a swing man on a championship team than a regular on another team."

Torrez thought the key to pitching to Piniella was to throw high and inside. Piniella like the ball over the plate or away and high, Torrez knew. He didn't like to be jammed. So Torrez would try to establish the fastball inside, then work the slider away, and perhaps mix in some curveballs to throw off the timing of Piniella's swing.

One fastball was enough. Piniella smashed a bouncing ball to third baseman Brohamer, who easily threw Piniella out at first. Torrez was one out away from getting out of the inning without any damage done—but not an easy out. Reggie Jackson, the designated hitter and fourth man in the Yankee batting order, was up next.

For Torrez, it was a dangerous situation. Jackson, a left-handed hitter, hit better against right-handers such as Torrez than against left-handed pitchers. Making the situation even more delicate, Jackson was usually a pull hitter, and the right-field foul pole was just 302 feet away. But even if Jackson didn't pull the ball straight down the line, there was still lots of room in Fenway's expansive right field in which to place the ball. "I don't know any other park that has a bigger field than right field in Fenway," said Dwight Evans, who from 1972 to 1990 probably defended that field better than any other Red Sox player has done. From the foul pole out to center field, the wall curves and angles until it has made virtually a ninety-degree turn. "It is very difficult to play," Evans said. "Everyone thinks the fences are low, but they come right to your armpit. And if you put your arm out to catch a ball, that's cement" underneath the padding. It was easy to get the wind knocked out of you, or crash into the wall and dislodge the ball.

And then there was the wind in Fenway, which is frequently strong and often changes direction, particularly in the early and late months of the season. At the moment, it was blowing from left field to right, but in October, the Fenway wind could be fickle and unpredictable.

Jackson was hitting .274, with 26 home runs and 90 runs batted in. Those are not awesome numbers by current standards, when a decrease in pitching quality, rule changes designed to promote offense, and steroid use have inflated offensive statistics. By the standards of the late 1970s, however, Jackson had had a very good year, particularly given the distractions that had occurred earlier in the season. Still, Torrez liked pitching to him; Jackson, he thought, had a vulnerable area high and away. If he could put a pitch there, he could minimize Jackson's formidable strength and bat speed. He might also be able to exploit the fact that Jackson loved to swing for home runs, and as a result struck out well over 100 times a season. Of course, Torrez still had to pitch

Jackson inside once in a while, to set him up for the outside pitch. And yes, Jackson was strong enough so that he could still hurt you hitting the ball to left field. It's just that he was *more* likely to inflict damage when he hit the ball anywhere else.

Torrez's first pitch was a fastball right over the plate. Jackson swung hard and missed it completely. Torrez was pleased. He thought the pitch was around 96 or 97 miles an hour, speeds he did not often reach. So he followed that with a breaking ball on the inside corner, and Jackson swung—and missed—with such force that he almost toppled over. Then came that fastball high and outside. But with a flick of his bat, Jackson connected. Rising high and toward the Green Monster, the ball looked like it might carry over the wall and give the Yankees a 2–0 lead. But in left field, Carl Yastrzemski reassured the fans; running toward the left field corner, he gave every indication that he would catch it. And when that left-to-right breeze pushed the ball down, Yaz did, just a few feet from the left-field corner, smoothly gloving the ball and then turning and running toward the Red Sox dugout. A difficult play; Yastrzemski made it look easy.

After an initial scare, Torrez had settled down and looked strong. Those nerves had passed. He felt confident. And the Red Sox were coming to the plate.

CHAPTER 3

The Boston Spring

In contrast to the Yankees, the Red Sox began their spring full of optimism and camaraderie. They had come close in 1977, finishing just 2½ games behind New York, tying with the Orioles for second place in the American League East. They had been, as usual, a powerful hitting team, but their pitching had disappointed: of the team's six starters, only one, Luis Tiant, had won as many as 12 games, and even Tiant had an ERA of 4.53.

So in the off-season, general manager Haywood Sullivan had engaged in a flurry of trades and free agent signings that improved the team, particularly its pitching staff, considerably. He signed Torrez for $2.5 million, and in March acquired twenty-three-year-old right-hander Dennis Eckersley from the Cleveland Indians. Eckersley had pitched well for the mediocre Indians, winning 40 games in three seasons, and he seemed poised to develop into one of the game's premier pitchers. And Sullivan signed free agent relievers Dick Drago and Tom Burgmeier to bolster a bullpen that had been often relied upon in 1977. His retooling did not stop with the pitching. He gave the California Angels a rookie pitcher, Don Aase, and cash for second baseman Jerry Remy, a local boy from Somerset, Massachusetts, who couldn't wait to get back to Boston. The Red Sox were never a fast team, and Remy would help to remedy that; he had stolen 41 bases in 1977. And Sullivan signed free agent Jack Brohamer, a veteran infielder, for three years at about $110,000 a year—an amount that just a couple of years before would have suggested that Brohamer was one of the league's elite players, but was now something of a modest free agent contract.

All this change made some baseball observers uncomfortable. Leigh Montville, one of the *Boston Globe*'s baseball writers, noted that "under the old rules, teams had to be built, teams had to be developed.

There were certain assets that could never be bought, that could only be found, throwing corncobs at barn doors and hitting three-sewer moonshots through plate-glass windows. Under the old rules, there were premiums on initiative and research and knowledge. The new world, the free agent world, puts the premium on only one factor and that factor is money." As a result, Montville declared, the Red Sox and the Yankees were the overwhelming favorites to win the World Series. "Nobody else matters in this baseball season. . . . The Red Sox and the Yankees are the entire story."

As they did every spring, Red Sox fans tried to hope. A World Series championship for their team was a distant memory—not many Sox fans were old enough actually to remember it—while disappointment and heartbreak were a much more recent and common occurrence. The last championship had come in 1918, when World War I was still being fought and a flu epidemic would kill more than 650,000 Americans. Perhaps more relevant, 1918 was two years before Red Sox owner Harry Frazee sold Babe Ruth to the Yankees for $125,000 cash and a $300,000 loan, on which the collateral was Fenway Park itself. In 1920 Ruth would hit .376, with 54 home runs and 137 runs batted in; in 1921, he would hit .378, with 59 homers and 171 RBIs. He would play for the Yankees until 1934. When Ruth left, he took the championships with him. Since the Series began in 1903, in which the Boston "Americans," as they were then known, beat the Pittsburgh Pirates, Boston had won five of the first sixteen championships. (There was no Series in 1904 due to squabbling between the two leagues.) After Ruth's departure, the Red Sox did not win another pennant until 1946, when a team stocked with stars such as Ted Williams, Johnny Pesky, Dom DiMaggio, and Bobby Doerr was beaten by the Cardinals in a seven-game World Series.

In the following years, they came close. In 1948, the Sox finished the regular season tied with the Cleveland Indians; both teams had a record of 96–58. The Sox had fallen a daunting twelve games out of first in July, then fought back to reach first place. On the last day of the season, they were a game behind Cleveland. At Fenway Park, they beat the Yankees, 10–5, while Cleveland lost to Detroit. Afterward, the Indians took an all-night train from Cleveland to play at Fenway. Cleveland was expected to start one of two veterans: the great Bob Feller or young Bob Lemon, a right-hander who'd already won 20 games. Instead, player-manager Lou Boudreau chose Gene Bearden, a 19-game-winning rookie who'd beaten the Red Sox twice. Red Sox manager Joe McCarthy chose Denny Galehouse, a thirty-six-year-old right-hander who'd never won more than 12 games in the majors. It was an unexpected choice; Galehouse would later claim that no other Sox pitcher wanted to pitch. Galehouse had a record of 8–7 with a 3.82 ERA, but he hadn't started a game in three weeks. It showed. The Sox were losing before the first inning was over. The final score was 8–3. Galehouse would never start another game in the major leagues.

Nineteen forty-nine brought more heartbreak. The Sox played tepidly the first half of the season and were twelve games behind the Yankees on July 4. But in the second half, the team pulled together and the Yankees slumped, and with two games to go, Boston led New York by a game. The team went to New York to play two games, needing to win only one to clinch the pennant. The Yankees won the first game, 5–4. In the second game, the Red Sox were down, 5–3, in the top of the ninth, with a man on base and two outs when catcher Birdie Tebbetts came to the plate. On the first pitch, Tebbetts popped to Tommy Henrich at first. The Red Sox had lost the pennant.

With the Yankees enjoying supremacy across both leagues, it would be eighteen years before the Red Sox finished higher than third. Through the 1950s and for most of the 1960s, Boston fans had little to cheer for: the team was undercut by bad management and Tom Yawkey's refusal to sign black and Latino players. Not until 1959 would Elijah "Pumpsie" Green integrate the Red Sox, making them the last team in the majors to field a black player. Green was too little, too late. As the Red Sox racked up losing seasons year after year, attendance plummeted, falling well below a million fans a season. The low point was 1965, when the team lost 100 games; for the final home game of that season, only 487 fans showed up at Fenway. The following year was slightly better, as power-hitting young players such as first baseman George Scott and outfielder Tony Conigliaro started to give the team new energy. They finished ninth, but they had shown signs of life.

Even so, what happened in 1967 was an almost inexplicable surprise: under the firm leadership of an intense new manager named Dick Williams, the youngest team in baseball somehow managed to win the pennant. Carl Yastrzemski, at twenty-seven the second-oldest Red Sox player, put together one of the greatest seasons in baseball history, winning the Triple Crown with a .326 batting average, 44 home runs, and 121 runs batted in. Tony C., as Conigliaro was known, had 20 home runs before August 18, when he was hit in the face by a pitch from

Angels pitcher Jack Hamilton and his season—his career, really—was ended. Pitcher Jim Lonborg went 22–9, and the Sox benefited from the late-season signing of Ken "Hawk" Harrelson. The Kansas City A's outfielder had made the mistake of declaring owner Charlie Finley "a menace to baseball," and Finley simply released Harrelson, who promptly found himself the subject of a bidding war. He'd been making $12,000 a year with the A's; the Red Sox signed him for $150,000. Yastrzemski, meanwhile, was astonishing. As the Sox scrambled for the pennant in the last twelve games of the season, caught in a down-to-the-wire race with the Tigers and the Twins, Yaz hit .523 with 16 runs batted in. On the last two days of the season, with the Sox having to beat the Twins to win the pennant, Yazstremski went 7–8 with 6 runs batted in. The Red Sox were finally back.

They would not win the Series against the Cardinals, thanks to the brilliant pitching of Bob Gibson, who won three of the seven games played. But there was no shame in losing to Gibson, one of the game's greatest pitchers. The Sox had already far surpassed expectations, and 1967 was a joyous season for the team and its fans. For the first time in a long time, fans and players could say "there's always next year" and actually think it meant something. After almost twenty years of bad baseball, the Impossible Dream team had restored vitality to the Red Sox tradition. Its unlikely success had made old fans care again while inspiring new ones.

The fans' hopes, however, that the team would follow that success with even greater good fortune would not pan out—at least, not the next year. For six years after '67, injuries, subpar seasons, and bad trades, such as sending Sparky Lyle to the Yankees for Danny Cater, would keep the Red Sox from returning to the World Series. The Baltimore Orioles and the Oakland A's didn't help as they ran roughshod over the rest of the American League in the early '70s. Not until 1975 did the pieces come together again for the Red Sox, and by that time they were an almost entirely different team than the upstarts of 1967. Yastrzemski was still there, of course, but he was surrounded by fresh faces. The pitching staff included Luis Tiant, a Cuban refugee of indeterminate age who baffled hitters with a smorgasbord of different pitches and motions, and Warren Zevon devotee Bill Lee, who baffled everyone with his penchant for bizarre behavior but also won 17 games. Behind the plate, a New Hampshire native named Carlton Fisk, the first truly great catcher in Red Sox history, had taken charge. Though second base was unsettled, Rick Burleson and Rico Petrocelli at short and third anchored the infield. And three new players, Jim Rice, Fred Lynn, and Dwight Evans patrolled the outfield from left to right. In right field, Evans was a defensive stalwart with a .274 batting average and 13 home runs. But Rice and Lynn overshadowed him. Both were rookies that year, and no two rookies on the same team ever had finer seasons. With a batting average of .331, 21 homers, and 105 RBIs, Lynn was not only the rookie of the year, but also the league MVP, the first time in baseball history a rookie had won that honor. Jim Rice had compiled virtually the same numbers—.309, 22, 102—when he was hit by a pitch and suffered a broken wrist on September 21.

The Sox won 95 games, finishing 4½ ahead of Baltimore and 12 games ahead of the Yankees. In the playoffs, the Sox swept the fading A's—free agency clearly did not bode well for a team united by its rabid dislike of Charlie Finley—and would face the powerful Cincinnati Reds in the World Series. Few expected the Red Sox to win. The Reds were a team without weaknesses. They had the best catcher in baseball, Johnny Bench, powerful outfielders such as George Foster and Ken Griffey, and an infield of legends-in-the-making that included Pete Rose and Joe Morgan. Though their pitching staff was slightly less daunting, it did include the young fastballer Don Gullett, who'd gone 15–4 with an ERA of 2.42. As in 1967, the Red Sox were the underdogs.

They almost pulled it off. The Sox forced the Reds to seven games, five of which were decided by one run and two of which went into extra innings. With the Sox down three games to two, Game Six would instantly become a classic when, in the bottom of the twelfth, Carlton Fisk pulled a line drive toward the left-field foul pole and hopped, skipped, and prayed his way toward first, practically commanding the ball to stay fair. Fantastically, it did—a game-winning home run. To no one's surprise, Game Seven was another drama and went into the ninth tied 3–3. The Reds pushed across a run in the top of the inning. In the bottom half, the Red Sox made two quick outs before Carl Yastrzemski, who had been clutch so often before, came to the plate. But Yaz could not re-create the miracle of the previous night, nor his own miracle of 1967. He lined a gentle fly ball to Cesar Geronimo in center field for the final out.

Heartbreak, again. To come so close . . . closer, even, than in 1967 . . . only to fall barely short, just as the Sox had done in 1948, 1949, and '67. Heartbreak was becoming the dominant emotion Red

Sox fans associated with their team. Others included frustration, disappointment, and a stubborn, head-shaking sort of love that endured the New England winters and burst forth anew each spring.

There was a bright side: the Sox were exciting again, and their unexpected grit had helped create a legendary World Series. If in 1967 the team had won back their own fans, now they and the Reds helped win back baseball's fans. At a time when the sport was losing its singular grip over American fandom to football, and many teams around both leagues were struggling with flat or declining attendance, the '75 Series captivated the country by reminding people of the glories of the game, the individual dramas set within the context of team culture and competition. The seventh game alone was watched by 75 million Americans.

That was the positive. The harder fact remained: the Red Sox still had not won a World Series in almost sixty years. For Yastrzemski, the loss was devastating; he knew that he could not count on many more chances to reach the Series. After 1967, he'd been confident that the Sox would be back soon, but things happened that no one could control and suddenly seven years had passed. He was thirty-six now, and couldn't wait another seven years. Neither could owner Tom Yawkey, who was gravely ill with leukemia. Even as Yaz's fly ball settled into Geronimo's glove, Yawkey knew that 1975 would be his last chance to enjoy the championship he had so long sought. It was the close of a sad chapter, one that his own attitudes toward management and race had helped to write: no one else in the history of baseball had ever owned a team for so long without winning at least one World Series.

Boston fans thought that, after such a gutsy showing, their team would be right back in the Series. As announcer Curt Gowdy predicted after the last out of Game Seven, "I think the Red Sox's future is ahead of them." Instead, 1976 was a grueling season in Boston. At the beginning of the season, Fisk, Burleson, and Lynn refused to sign new contracts, holding out for more money. In the history of the Red Sox, no player had ever done that; Yawkey's generosity was legendary. But even a wealthy man's largesse could not compete with the riches of an open market. All three players were represented by a tough, aggressive agent named Jerry Kapstein who saw how the economics of the game were quickly changing. The players' decision was wildly unpopular. Sox fans responded to the holdouts by jeering and cursing them when they came to the plate, and the conversation on Boston's talk radio, an increasingly powerful force in the city's sports culture, was not warm and friendly. Perhaps the players shouldn't have been surprised—fans had never responded well when players demanded more money—but they were taken aback by the hostility. The Red Sox were on the verge of a championship, and these three guys were getting greedy?

"I get hate mail a lot," Fred Lynn said at the time. "A lot of it is from fans who insist I should sign right away for the sake of the game. They say I should be the same kind of player that they knew about years ago."

Lynn, the laid-back Californian who played the game with such easy grace that writers sometimes accused him of not trying, occasionally gave fans the finger (perhaps in the spirit of Ted Williams, who more than once spat at Boston fans). "For the first time in my life, baseball isn't fun," he explained. Burleson would swear at the fans when he returned to the dugout. Fisk kept his feelings to himself, even though, as a local kid from New Hampshire, he probably felt the venom the most deeply. After the July 12 agreement that established the guidelines of free agency, the Sox quickly signed all three players, with Lynn getting a total of $1.65 million, Fisk receiving $900,000, and Burleson $600,000.

Waiting would have cost the organization more, as the Sox had seen just a few weeks before when the A's Finley had decided to hold a fire sale. Rather than see free agency decimate his team, he decided to sell his players before they could sell themselves. On June 15, the Yankees picked up pitcher Vida Blue for $1.5 million; the Sox bought outfielder Joe Rudi and relief pitcher Rollie Fingers from the A's for $2 million. But the deals didn't last long. The very next day, Commissioner Kuhn put them on hold and subsequently voided them, saying the agreements were not "in the best interests of baseball." The argument made little sense, since the players could become free agents and sell themselves to the highest bidder anyway, and after all, back in 1920 the Red Sox had sold perhaps the greatest player in the history of the game. But even without actually being consummated, the stunning deal only heightened the awareness that the business of baseball was becoming an increasingly prominent and intrusive aspect of the game.

Tom Yawkey died on July 9, 1976, a wrenching event for an organization that could barely remember another owner. Still, his tenure had been a mixed blessing for the Red Sox. He left ownership of the team to a trust controlled by his wife, Jean. It was an awkward arrangement that would complicate management of the Red Sox for years. For four decades, Yawkey had been the most generous of baseball owners, and his players were devoted to him because he paid them the game's highest salaries and genuinely cared about them. "He loved his players," Dwight Evans recalled. Evans had two sons with a genetic disorder, and Yawkey always asked after their well-being. "He'd come in and say hello to everyone before the game, go to each chair and talk to each person. He wouldn't talk baseball, just, 'How are your boys doing?' He was special."

Yawkey's death was particularly painful for Carl Yastrzemski. Yawkey was not close to many people and neither was Yastrzemski, but since Yaz joined the team in 1961, the two men had forged a relationship more like father and son than owner and player. In 1965, when Yastrzemski was in the hospital for a week with broken ribs from an encounter with a second baseman's knee, Yawkey came to visit every day. The two would sit and talk baseball for hours. "All I want is one pennant," he told Yaz.

Later Yawkey would change his mind and long to win a World Series. But the remark was revealing. As his critics suggested, Yawkey sometimes seemed more interested in bonding with his players than in winning championships. Some said that he coddled his players, especially Yastrzemski, and that his generosity made the players complacent. Certainly Yawkey's philosophy was vastly different from that of, say, George Steinbrenner, who believed that it was better to keep players on edge than leave them fully satisfied. The more a player worried about his status, Steinbrenner believed, the harder he was likely to play.

"Playing for Mr. Yawkey, you didn't have a grasp of what was going on with other teams," Yastrzemski recalled. "Playing with the Red Sox was like being a free agent when you had Tom Yawkey as an owner." If a player was short on cash, Yastzemski said, "Mr. Yawkey would ask, 'How much do you need?' Boom. He'd hand down a check for the guy, and never deduct it from his contract. That's the way Tom Yawkey was. We were more spoiled than other teams."

In 1967, Yastrzemski bought a piece of land in Boca Raton, Florida, and built a house on it. Not long after the home was completed, he was playing golf with his friend Sam Snead when the legendary golfer announced that he was selling his home. "I went and looked at it just to keep him quiet," Yastrzemski said. The house, closer to the water than his own, caught his fancy. "Sam told me what he wanted for it, and I said, 'I'll buy it, don't worry.' So now I got money tied up in one house, I need a loan real quick. I called Mr. Yawkey and said I needed a $200,000 loan. He said, 'You just built a house, why do you need another one?' I said, 'It's on the ocean . . . I'll pay you back when I sell my house.' And next thing, there's a check in the mail.

"Well, I sold my house a few months later, and I went upstairs [in Fenway Park] to give him a check. He tore it up and said, 'Thanks for the memories.' "

Particularly during the last years of Yawkey's life, many of the Red Sox had similar stories (though probably not of the same magnitude). Whether such generosity made the Red Sox play harder or less hard was debatable. What was certain was that Yawkey's refusal to sign African-American athletes until after every other team in the sport had done so was not only shameful, but hurt his team. The Red Sox, after all, had passed on the chance to sign Jackie Robinson. Instead of making history by signing Robinson and other minority players, the Red Sox would make history by going long decades without a championship.

Incredibly, the team's 1976 season of turmoil did not end with Yawkey's death. On July 21, general manager Dick O'Connell fired manager Darrell Johnson, architect of the 1975 season, on the grounds that "it is easier to change a manager than the whole club." His replacement was forty-three-year-old third base coach Don Zimmer, a repository of baseball lore and tradition who would become one of the most scorned figures in Red Sox history despite being one of the team's winningest managers.

Donald William Zimmer liked to joke that he had never received a paycheck outside of baseball, and the amazing thing about the line was that it was actually true: Zimmer had lived a life of baseball and little else. He was born in Cincinnati on January 17, 1931, the son of a fruit and vegetable wholesaler. Drafted out of high school by the Brooklyn Dodgers in 1949, Zimmer had all the makings of a great shortstop: He fielded brilliantly and was a strong hitter. From 1949 through 1952, he hit over .300 for Dodger minor league teams in Hornell, New York, Mobile, Alabama, and St. Paul, Minnesota. But his path to the big leagues was blocked by the presence of Pee Wee Reese, the great Dodger shortstop, and because of the reserve clause, there was nothing that Zimmer could do about it. In July 1953, he was leading the American Association in home runs and RBIs when he was hit around the left eye by a curveball. The pitch started out looking like it would hit Zimmer. He dived toward the ground. The curve dove with him.

Zimmer was rushed to the hospital, where doctors drilled holes on each side of his head to relieve the pressure from swelling of his brain. Later, they would plug the holes with "buttons" made of a rare metal called tantalum. Zimmer was in a coma for thirteen days. But he was tough and stubborn, and he was back with his team before the end of the season. In 1954, the Dodgers finally called him up, and he hustled to break into the starting lineup. Then, on June 23, 1956, he was hit again, this time by a fastball that fractured his cheekbone. Doctors were concerned that the retina on Zimmer's left eye was in danger of detaching, and so he was not allowed to play for the rest of the season. For six weeks he wore a blindfold; for six weeks after that the blindfold was replaced by pinhole glasses with shields on both sides. And still Zimmer came back. Baseball was all he knew, all he wanted to know. But Zimmer was damaged; the once-promising shortstop would never be more than a utility infielder.

The beanings changed the course of Zimmer's playing career, but they did have a positive consequence for baseball generally: They galvanized support for the universal use of batting helmets, then worn by only a handful of players. Brooklyn Dodgers president Walter O'Malley responded to Zimmer's second beaning by pushing plans to punish pitchers who threw at hitters. He proposed a rule under which, if an umpire thought that a pitcher was throwing wildly—or even if he was about to throw wildly—the umpire could wave the batter out of the box and force the pitcher to throw several practice pitches. If that weren't reassuring enough, the umpire could eject the pitcher from the game. "Most of the [beaning] incidents follow something that has upset the defensive club," O'Malley explained. "Sometimes the pitcher does it on his own, sometimes under orders. My plan would give a break in the routine, and so tempers would have a chance to cool and players get control of themselves again."

Supporters of O'Malley's idea argued that the growing prevalence of night baseball, first started in 1935 and used in every park but Wrigley Field by 1948, made such a rule even more important, since batters claimed that it was harder to see the ball at night than during the day. But critics, including Yankee pitcher Allie Reynolds, said the rule would never work. Pitching was hard enough, Reynolds argued, what with livelier balls, outfield fences, and stands that were increasingly close to the field, all of which encouraged hitters to dig in and swing away. Pitchers needed the brushback pitch to compete against hitters.

"I believe every hitter should wear a plastic helmet," Reynolds suggested instead. Sooner or later, all of them did. And though the helmets could not prevent all injuries, as Tony Conigliaro would learn, they made baseball a vastly safer sport.

The change came too late for Zimmer, though. He had problems seeing the ball and would never again be a threat at the plate. Instead he bounced around the majors, playing for the Dodgers, the Cubs, the Mets, the Reds, the Washington Senators, even going to Japan for a year. What else could he do? Baseball was his life. In 1951, he'd even gotten married on his minor league baseball field. His teammates formed an arch with their bats for the bride and groom to walk through. "He was baseball," third baseman Butch Hobson would recall. "That's what Don was. I remember when my first wife was having our second baby. I went to Don and said, 'Skip, we're getting ready to go on this road trip to Kansas City and my wife is going to induce.' He looked me in the eye and said, 'Let me tell you something, Hobs. I got two children, and do you know where I was when they were born? I was on the field.' "

In the late 1960s, Zimmer started managing minor league teams, and in 1972 the Padres hired him as their manager. Disgusted with what he considered a lack of commitment from the club's management, he quit the team a year later. In 1974, the Red Sox hired Zimmer to coach third.

Don Zimmer was not his sport's most articulate representative, or its deepest thinker, but he knew baseball. Like Billy Martin, he had been a player who could never coast on talent alone; he'd had to work harder than many just to stay in the game, and so he had studied its tactics and strategies. As was also the case with Martin, there was a type of player that Zimmer liked—hardworking, took instruction well, veteran—and a type of player he didn't. Martin didn't mind players who partied, as long as they performed. Zimmer, however, had a particular dislike for a group of players known for their carousing, a band of Red Sox rebels known as the Buffalo Head Gang. They included pitchers Bill Lee, Jim Willoughby, and Ferguson Jenkins, and outfielders Bernie Carbo and Reggie Cleveland. They called themselves that because of their shared opposition to Don Zimmer, whom they called "Buffalo Head," which was not intended as a compliment—buffalos, according to Jenkins, were "the ugliest animal alive." Zimmer had small eyes, a pudgy face, and big ears; he was not a clas-

sically handsome man. The Buffalo Heads' other nickname for him was
Gerbil, which Lee later changed to Hamster, because he said that was
more accurate—hamsters had fatter cheeks.

The members of the Buffalo Head Gang were free spirits straight out
of the 1960s. Lee had been labeled Spaceman by a teammate who got
fed up when Lee insisted on talking to the press about NASA. "We got
our own fuckin' Spaceman right here," he said. Of course, part of the
reason Lee and the other Buffalo Heads were spacey was because they
were, from time to time, stoned. "We did run the streets hard," Carbo
said. "We chased the women, we played hard, we drank hard, we did
drugs, and played hard."

"The '70s . . ." Dennis Eckersley, one of Lee's friends in 1978,
recalled. "I don't want to get into it, but it was just, anything goes. It
was a great time to be a player, it really was."

"I hung out with Bill Lee a few times," Eckersley said. "It was like,
'Oh my God, he *tries* to be crazy. He was very heady, almost poetic . . .
in a crazy way."

For at least some members, the Buffalo Heads' indulgences extended
beyond pot to the soundtrack drug of the disco era, cocaine. "They
would lay out lines of coke and they would have relay races," said Lee's
biographer, Richard Lally. "They would sniff, and then they'd pass the
folded dollar to the next guy and go all the way."

How much of this Zimmer knew is unclear. What was obvious was
that he hated the counterculture qualities of the Buffalo Heads. They
differed from the apolitical hard-drinking players of the '40s and '50s;
infused in their behavior was a left-wing critique of American society
and the management of baseball itself. Like Reggie Jackson, they were
talented enough to play the game and simultaneously critique it, something Zimmer was not. Mickey Mantle may have liked to drink—loved
to drink—but he was still an all-American hero, unlikely to say or do
anything political. Bill Lee, on the other hand, came from Southern
California, listened to rock music, quoted French deconstructionist
philosophers, and spoke in favor of busing in Boston, an emotional
issue that was tearing the city apart. The Buffalo Heads' politics made
Zimmer uncomfortable. He thought that their irreverent attitude hurt
the team, and he couldn't help but take their criticisms personally. If
they were the hippies, he was the square, the man in the gray flannel
suit, and what was old-fashioned was inevitably an easy target. Lee
could be extremely funny, and like Jackson, he sucked up media attention that relieved the other players from scrutiny they didn't want. But

he could also be cruel. "X-rays of Zimmer's head show nothing," Lee once said, a mean remark absent of context, especially callous given Zimmer's history of injury.

Zimmer's relationship with the Buffalo Head Gang would grow more tense in 1977 and 1978. In the meantime, there was still the rest of the 1976 season to play. Despite the upheaval from the contract holdouts, the overturned deal with the A's, Tom Yawkey's death, and Darrell Johnson's firing, the Red Sox finished the season by making the race at least a little closer. Although they finished 15½ games behind the Yankees, they did win 15 of their last 18 in September to eke out a third-place finish. And when the season was over, the Sox improved themselves by signing free agent relief pitcher Bill Campbell for $1 million over five years. "No one's worth that," said Campbell, who had previously been making all of $22,000 a year with the Twins. "But if they want to pay me, I'm certainly not going to turn it down." The Sox also got George Scott, a star of the '67 team, back from the Brewers, along with Bernie Carbo, a hero of 1975 who'd since been traded to Milwaukee.

The 1977 Red Sox were an extremely good team, finishing the season with a record of 97–64, even without a single pitcher winning more than 12 games. In almost any other year, that would have been enough. But with a record of 100–62, the Yankees were even better. And so the Sox went and picked up Mike Torrez, Jerry Remy, Jack Brohamer, Dennis Eckersley, Dick Drago, and Tom Burgmeier. They were already the best-hitting team in baseball. Now they'd improved their speed, their starting pitching, and their relief pitching. "I never dreamed that we'd be sitting here with the pitching staff we have," Zimmer said in spring training in 1978. "No one can say, 'There's no way they can beat the Yankees with that pitching.'"

At the end of that spring training, the Red Sox had a record of 15–11. "It was a camp to remember," the *Boston Globe*'s Peter Gammons wrote, "one of the most remarkable spring trainings in recent years." There were, however, some small worrisome signs. Butch Hobson, who had been bothered by a bad elbow in 1977, reinjured it diving for a ball; the team trainer hastened to say that the elbow was not as bad as it had been the previous year. Meanwhile, Gammons, the Sox's primary scribe that season, was already writing that if the Sox so much as started slowly, Zimmer would be in trouble. And in early April, Buffalo Head Jim Willoughby was sold to the White Sox—not a huge loss in terms of pitching, for Willoughby would go 1–6 with

Chicago, but it was a sign of Zimmer's desire to purge his team of the Buffalo Heads, and in response, Bill Lee lit a memorial candle to burn on Zimmer's desk. Unlike Willoughby, Lee was a pitcher whose talents justified managerial patience.

But these quibbles would barely have been heard amid the hubbub in the Yankee camp, and the Red Sox headed north from Florida struggling to contain their optimism. Boston hearts had been broken before, but this team looked like the real thing. Some said they were the finest squad in franchise history. Tiant, Torrez, Lee, and Eckersley gave the Red Sox their best starting pitching in a decade, if not longer. Fisk, Scott, Remy, Burleson, Hobson, Yaz, Lynn, Evans, and Rice— there wasn't a weak bat in the bunch, not even close. And defensively, they certainly had an advantage over the Yankees in the outfield. No one would say that Roy White, Mickey Rivers, Lou Piniella, and Reggie Jackson constituted a group of stalwart defenders.

A Red Sox championship, just out of reach for so many years, seemed finally at hand.

CHAPTER 4

THE BOTTOM OF THE FIRST

Warming up in the bullpen, Ron Guidry felt good, which came as a relief to the twenty-eight-year-old pitcher. For just the second time in the season, he was pitching with three days rest instead of his usual four; on September 29, he had beaten the Blue Jays, 3–1. Guidry never knew exactly what his stuff was going to be like until he started warming up, and that was even more true when he deviated from routine. But Guidry's control didn't seem hurt by the short rest, and that was crucial, because control was one of the qualities that made Guidry so effective. Not only could he throw fast, but he could put the ball where he wanted it with uncommon accuracy. In 266 innings pitched that season, Guidry had allowed just 72 walks. Only once in twenty-seven games had he walked as many as five batters.

Guidry was not sure, however, that he had his usual strength; he couldn't really determine that until he had pitched a few innings and felt how his body was holding up. He expected to have to compensate for his abbreviated rest. Instead of throwing 50 or 60 pitches at 95 miles an hour over nine innings, he'd throw maybe only 30. "I knew that I might not have the ability to throw 92-plus throughout the game," Guidry would recall. "I'm not going to try to throw a ball 95 miles an hour if I can get 'em out at 91."

With a record of 24–3 and an ERA of 1.72, Ronald Ames Guidry was nearing the end of one of the most remarkable seasons of pitching in baseball history. He had the highest winning percentage (.889) of any pitcher ever, and if not for a 2–1 loss to the Orioles in August, it would have been even better. His earned run average was the lowest for any left-hander since 1933, when the New York Giants' Carl Hubbell had an ERA of 1.66. Guidry had won the first 13 games he pitched that season, and he had thrown a total of 9 shutouts—the most by a left-hander in the American League since 1916, when a young Boston pitcher named Babe Ruth had done the same. Perhaps most important, fourteen times that year Guidry had won the day after the Yankees had lost, making it virtually impossible for the Yankees to go on a losing streak of any duration. His achievements were particularly remarkable given that 1978 was only his second full season with the Yankees, and that in 1976 he had come very close to quitting baseball altogether.

His mother had not even wanted him to play baseball. A boy in Guidry's hometown of Lafayette, Louisiana, had been killed by a ball that hit him in the chest and stopped his heart. "I don't want you doing this, Ronnie," his mother had said. "You'll get hurt." But one day when Guidry was seven, he was walking by a game in progress when a ball got away from an outfielder and rolled to him. Guidry picked it up and threw it past the catcher, a distance of about 250 feet. Soon after, his father bought him a fifteen-dollar glove.

Lafayette was a small, rural Cajun community whose working-class inhabitants were proud, tight-knit, and self-reliant. Guidry's youth was filled with sports and hunting—rabbit, geese, quail, ducks, frogs, and alligators. All that hunting was one reason why Guidry grew up quiet and patient, a man of few words; these were necessary attributes for tracking alligators in a swamp. His athleticism, however, came naturally. In addition to his powerful arm, Guidry was fast on the base paths—so fast that, later, when he was on the Yankees, he would occasionally be pressed into service as a pinch runner. And Guidry was strong—pound per pound, probably the strongest player on the team. He was not, however, a big man. Guidry was so lean, he looked like he still needed to hunt for food. The Yankees would list him at five-eleven and 160 pounds, but that wasn't true. "I weighed about 152 pounds," Guidry said, "but they always listed me at 160 because they said it didn't look good to have a pitcher at 150."

He was the star pitcher of his high school team and again at the University of Southwestern Louisiana, and in 1971 the Yankees signed him for $10,000 plus incentive bonuses of $7,500. For the next five years, Guidry bounced around the minors. Johnson City, Tennessee . . . Fort Lauderdale . . . Kinston, North Carolina . . . West Haven, Connecticut . . . Syracuse, New York. In late July 1975, Yankee manager Bill Virdon called Guidry up from Syracuse, and on the afternoon he arrived at Shea Stadium—the remodeled Yankee Stadium was not yet finished—Virdon sent Guidry to the mound in the seventh inning of a game against the Red Sox. Thurman Munson greeted him there. "Don't get nervous," Munson said. "Just throw strikes." Munson, who had never met Guidry, asked him what pitches he threw. A slider and a fastball, Guidry answered. "Okay," Munson said, "one's a fastball and two's a slider." But Guidry's slider wasn't particularly good, and his fastball was; for three innings, Guidry saw only one finger from Munson. That day, he shut out the Red Sox.

Subsequent efforts didn't go as well, and Guidry pitched infrequently for the rest of the year, especially after Billy Martin replaced Virdon on Old-Timers' Day. The incoming manager wasn't fond of unproven rookies. "A guy like Billy Martin, until he gets respect for you, it's going to be tough," Guidry said. "He never used me because I didn't have his trust."

The next spring, Martin sent Guidry back to the minors—the bullpen was full, Martin said. Guidry would not be back until May, again against the Red Sox. This time, they shelled him. For the next six weeks, Guidry rode the bench, until team president Gabe Paul informed him that he was once a headed back to Syracuse. "Let's go back to Louisiana and forget about this," the demoralized pitcher told his wife, Bonnie. He was twenty-six years old. Perhaps it was time to accept that baseball wasn't going to work out. But before taking that step, Guidry decided, he would call George Steinbrenner, and try to talk with the boss about his future. Once a day for three days, Guidry called, which was a feat for him because he didn't easily reach out. Steinbrenner never called back. So Ron and Bonnie packed their car, and instead of heading north to Syracuse, they drove west out of Manhattan on Interstate 80. Guidry didn't really know where he was going, just that that if he drove west long enough, eventually he'd find a road that would take him south to Louisiana.

After an hour had passed in silence, Bonnie turned to her husband and said, "Where are we going?" Back home, Guidry answered. To Lafayette. "What are you going to do when we get there?" his wife said. Guidry thought about that, pulled the car over, and decided to give baseball one more chance.

In his first game back at Syracuse, he started the eighth inning and struck out the side on ten pitches. A month later, he was with the Yankees again. For the most part, he pitched well this time, although Martin would only use him in meaningless mop-up situations. Then, in a late-season game against the Angels, he allowed a couple of runs—bloop hits, slow-roller singles, that kind of thing. After the game, George Steinbrenner summoned Guidry to his office. "When are you going to start pitching?" Steinbrenner said. Guidry was dumbfounded.

"All I know is, you better start striking people out or I'm going to ship you right back to Syracuse . . ." Steinbrenner continued. "Guidry, you will never be able to pitch in this league." Then Steinbrenner walked out of his own office.

The problem wasn't the fastball; Guidry could throw consistently in the mid-90s, and it wasn't just the speed of his pitch that made it tough to hit. Guidry's fastball moved. It rose; it darted away from right-handed hitters. "If it started out below the belt, by the time Thurman caught it, it would be above the belt," said Cliff Johnson, the Yankees' backup catcher. And the fastball seemed to pick up speed, to *jump*, just before it reached the plate. (The same thing had been said of Babe Ruth's fastball six decades earlier.) "Gator threw a hopping, hopping fastball," Johnson said. "People would ask me, 'Where did he get his velocity from?' Well, he didn't have anything tying him up. He was a slightly built guy. He didn't have a lot of muscles and things tying him up."

Certainly Guidry had a smooth, relaxed motion that allowed him to channel his strength. On the mound, he didn't glower or fidget or bury his face in his glove or tug at his cap. Instead, he pitched quickly and efficiently, looking as comfortable and casual as if he were throwing batting practice. "My mechanics were good enough that it didn't take a lot from me to throw a ball hard," Guidry said. "I had guys tell me that when they saw me on the mound, their first impression was, 'He's not going to throw that hard.' They said it was an *easy* hard—the look was deceiving."

But few pitchers can succeed on a single pitch, no matter how good it is. So Guidry found help from his teammates in the bullpen. Right-handed reliever Dick Tidrow taught Guidry how to be a pitcher, not just a thrower—how to mix speeds and locations, throwing a batter strikes low to get him thinking low, then coming back with a pitch chest-high—rather than simply rearing back and hurling one fastball after another. And one night, lefty Sparky Lyle, who was known for having a brutal slider, told Guidry that he needed another pitch. The fastball alone wasn't enough. "You throw hard," Lyle said, "harder than anybody else that we have, but you need to come up with another pitch to complement your fastball."

Guidry said that he'd never been able to throw a curve; he couldn't bend his arm the way a curve required.

"You and I throw a lot alike," Lyle told him. "You could learn to throw the same slider that I throw, but yours is gonna be harder because you throw harder."

The two pitchers began working together in the bullpen; every day Guidry would practice the pitch. Lyle told him not to worry about the speed of it, just throw it slow, work on the wrist motion, the snap at the end of the delivery, and the grip, the fingers over the ball but off to one side. That gave the ball a downward spinning motion, a challenge for batters, who find it easier to pick up a side-to-side spin than an up-or-down spin.

As Mike Torrez had with Bob Gibson, Guidry worked on throwing the ball with that little pop of the wrist at the end of the motion. But there was a crucial difference. Torrez's slider had the side-to-side spin that created the telltale red dot, the optical illusion created by the spinning seams. When hitters saw that dot, they recognized the pitch as a breaking ball. But Guidry's downward-spinning slider didn't create the appearance of the dot, and so it gave batters the impression that the pitch was a fastball. Then, just as it reached the plate, Guidry's slider would break hard, down and in on a right-handed batter.

After about a month of practice, one night in the bullpen Lyle turned to Guidry and said, "Tonight is a good time to throw it hard. Do the same thing we've been working with, but when you throw tonight, you throw that pitch as hard as you can."

Guidry threw a few fastballs to Dominic Scala, the bullpen catcher, to loosen up. Then, for the first time, he came with the slider as hard as he threw his fastballs. As Scala positioned his glove to catch the pitch, the ball suddenly twisted and plunged. "It hit the catcher in the knee," Guidry said. "I looked at Sparky, Sparky looked at me. He started clapping his hands and said, 'I think we got something.' "

As American League batters would come to learn, Guidry's slider was almost impossible to hit. "Guidry was a skinny little guy that threw gas," Dennis Eckersley recalled, "and he would throw that slider, and guys would swing and miss. That thing *disappeared*. I'd say, 'Why are you up swinging at that thing?' And they'd say, 'You're not up there. You don't know what it's like.' "

Guidry started the 1977 season with the Yankees, but not on a promising note. He pulled a muscle in his chest and couldn't get much speed on the ball. As a result, batters were teeing off against him, and one day Martin came up to Guidry and said, "If there's anybody in this league you can get out, let me know and I'll let you pitch to him."

Steinbrenner had wanted to trade Guidry in the off-season—other teams were certainly interested—and that spring he almost succeeded in sending him to the White Sox for a young, dependable shortstop named Bucky Dent. The deal fell through, partly because Gabe Paul, who was responsible for most of the Yankees' savviest personnel moves, opposed trading Guidry. Still, Guidry finished spring training with an ERA of 10.24. He wouldn't get to pitch in a regular season game until April 29, and even then it was only because the Yankees were suffering from a shortage of arms.

But then Guidry earned a save in a game, and after that, he got a start against Seattle; the Yankees had traded for an Oakland pitcher, a big right-hander named Mike Torrez, and Torrez hadn't yet arrived. Martin needed a starter. For eight innings, Guidry threw a shutout. It was the beginning of Guidry's arrival as a pitcher; the combination of that fastball and slider was kicking in. When Jim Palmer of the Orioles saw him, he thought, "This is unbelievable. It looks like he's throwing a javelin. He's a smaller version of Koufax, but instead of a curveball he has a slider."

"He threw everything on the same plane," said Red Sox right fielder Dwight Evans, a right-handed hitter. "It came in at the same height, and it either exploded away or it was a hard slider down and in. You couldn't really pick up the spin on his slider, so it'd look like a fastball, and then all of a sudden it would dart down."

"Right-handed hitters couldn't keep that slider fair," said Gene Michael, the Yankee shortstop turned coach. "You'd hit it off your ankle, off your foot."

As the 1977 season progressed, Guidry felt increasingly confident, and the results reflected his comfort level. "One day I woke up and I *knew* what pitching was all about," Guidry recalled. "I had quit throwing and had started pitching, and the slider was getting better every game and so was my control. . . . I started winning consistently, and for the first time it was fun to be playing baseball in the majors." Before the All-Star break, he was 6–5. After, he went 10–2. Perhaps the most satisfying win came against the Red Sox in September, the first game of a three-game series that would ensure the pennant for the Yankees. Guidry threw 140 pitches and beat the Sox, 4–2. Even so, not all the Red Sox were convinced. "He's got speed and nothing else," Jim Rice insisted. "He showed me nothing." Rice blamed the Red Sox's defeat on the dimensions of Yankee Stadium, which are considerably larger than those of Fenway Park, especially in left field. "We lost because of the ballpark," he insisted. "We're supposed to be playing in a ballpark, not the Grand Canyon." Guidry would remember those words.

The Yankees would go on to win the league championship series against Kansas City, and then beat the Dodgers in the Series. Guidry finished the season with a record of 16–7 and an ERA of 2.82, along with one playoff win and a World Series victory. He would not forget the hard things that he had lived through—the dismissive words Billy Martin and George Steinbrenner had said to him, the number of times he had been sent to the minors, the angry, helpless feeling he'd had driving west, headed vaguely toward Louisiana and home. Guidry was a proud man; he couldn't forget those things had he wanted to. But he had proved his skeptics wrong. In the space of a season, he had gone from being a player the Yankees wished to trade to being the indispensable man on the team's pitching staff, a fiercely competitive ace.

Nineteen seventy-eight would be his masterpiece.

He would face, in the bottom of the first inning, the Red Sox shortstop Rick Burleson, a right-handed hitter, and then the speedy second baseman Jerry Remy, a lefty, and finally Jim Rice, the Red Sox's most feared batter. He was, as usual, confident. Guidry had done well against the Red Sox in his career; his record against them was 3–1, and in 1978 the Red Sox team average against Guidry was a paltry .207.

And though you'd never know it to look at him, Guidry was excited. This was surely the biggest game of his career to date. He knew that, and he suspected that it would be the most important game of his entire career. Moreover, he loved to pitch in Fenway, surrounded by the mystique and the history of the ballpark. Pitching in Fenway felt special; the stands were always packed, the fans vocal, the stadium a crucible of baseball's past. Nor did he fear its cozy dimensions. Though Guidry was a left-handed pitcher, he didn't worry about right-handed hitters driving his fastballs over the Green Monster, just three hundred or so feet away. If batters connected against him—though they hardly ever did, home runs off Guidry were exceedingly rare—the energy of his pitches would be quickly converted into long drives. "If they're going to hit a ball off me over that wall," Guidry said, "it's gonna go out of any ballpark."

He hadn't talked much with Munson before the game. There wasn't a lot for the two to say; they'd played these Red Sox many times, and knew them. The Sox hitters wouldn't change. What might be different was Guidry's pitching, because of the short rest. But Munson would know what Guidry had well before the first inning was over—how much life he had in his fastball, how his slider was moving, if he was hitting his spots. In turn, Guidry trusted Munson to call pitches. Nobody, he thought, was better than Munson at calling a game.

Burleson came to the plate to start the Red Sox half of the inning. The red-headed shortstop was his team's sparkplug—fiery, emotional, intense. A red-ass, like Piniella. Don Zimmer, then a coach, had given him the nickname "Rooster" when he watched Burleson fielding ground balls in practice, his hair sticking up, staking out his position like a bantam rooster claiming his turf. He'd come to the Sox from their Pawtucket, Rhode Island, farm team in 1974 and almost immediately become the anchor of the team's defense, as well as one of the team's emotional leaders. During the 1977 season, Burleson had publicly announced that he "hated" everybody in pinstripes. "He was always kind of a miserable personality," his teammate, Jerry Remy, said fondly. "He was feisty. That was his baseball persona." In 1978, he had hit .248, with 5 home runs and 49 runs batted in. Those were low numbers for Burleson, who in each of the previous two years had batted about 45 points higher. But much of the drop was due to a torn ligament he'd suffered in July, and Burleson was since healed. Like all the Red Sox, he'd come to Fenway that day with his suitcase packed. If they won the game, they'd go straight to the airport, and Kansas City. Also, he wasn't happy about the way the Boston media had treated his team—how, on sports radio, in the *Boston Globe* and the *Herald American,* the armchair observers kept saying that the Red Sox had choked. It got under his skin.

Guidry started Burleson with a fastball; Burleson fouled it off. Burleson was aggressive, and in truth, neither team was stocked with patient hitters who liked to take pitchers and work the count. If Burleson got a pitch from Guidry he thought he could handle, he had to swing at it. The odds of getting another were low.

Pitching with his usual quick pace, Guidry came back with his slider, but missed high. Burleson next took a second slider for a strike. Hoping that Burleson would look for another slider on the 1–2 count—Guidry loved to throw that slider when he had two strikes on a batter—Guidry instead threw a fastball on the outside corner. The pitch was close, and umpire Don Denkinger called it a ball. Munson hesitated for a second, then threw the ball back to Guidry and said a few words to Denkinger. The catcher wanted to try to establish a wide strike zone early in the game, as well as plant the thought in the umpire's mind: Denkinger owed him one. A small complaint, at this point. If Munson had wanted to make a larger one, he would have held the ball while complaining to Denkinger, drawing attention to his displeasure with the call by interrupting the game. That tactic, however, could backfire by irritating Denkinger, and there was no reason to risk that just four pitches into the bottom of the first.

Using that nice, smooth delivery, Guidry came back with a fastball that was farther outside than the one before it, and Burleson watched it into Munson's glove. Denkinger raised his thumb to signal strike three. Burleson looked stunned and shook his head in amazement. From the dugout, Zimmer let Denkinger know that he'd missed the call. "I know where it was," Denkinger shouted back at him. In fact, he had missed the call, and he knew that, too. But he wasn't about to admit it to Zimmer.

Jerry Remy, the five-nine, 165-pound, left-handed-hitting second baseman, came up next. As he walked into the batter's box, Munson started talking to him, asking him how he was. Typical Munson. "He'd try to distract you at the plate," Remy said. "He'd ask you how you were doing, and tell you how crappy he was doing." But Remy didn't engage; he felt the game's urgency, and he concentrated on Guidry. Remy appreciated this moment. With the Angels in Anaheim, where he'd spent the first three years of his major league career, the fans weren't passionate the way they were in Boston. The only time Remy got to play in front of a crowd with the Angels was when the already legendary Nolan Ryan was pitching. Either that, or when the Yankees or the Red Sox came to town.

The first pitch he saw was a fastball, inside, pushing him back off the plate a little bit. The next pitch was a slider headed toward the far side of the plate when Remy swung and pushed it in the air out to Roy White in left, not even close to the wall. An easy play. After six pitches, Guidry had two outs.

The man he faced next was having an offensive year comparable in its brilliance to the defensive season Guidry was having. Jim Rice was hitting .315, with 46 home runs and 138 runs batted in. He had accumulated over 400 total bases, the most in the American League since Joe DiMaggio's 418 in 1937. Rice never seemed to hit a single; he hit with power to all fields, line drives that thumped off the Green Monster, rockets to every part of the outfield that sent outfielders scurrying in pursuit. No one in the league had compiled numbers that even came close to Rice's, and it was clear that either he or Guidry would be voted the league's most valuable player at season's end. Most commentators thought it would be Rice; as great as Guidry had been, they argued, he pitched just once every five days. Rice was an "everyday" player, a cliché that was literally true in Rice's case. This was his 163rd game of the season.

The Red Sox fans gave Rice a standing ovation as he walked to the plate. As always, he looked supremely confident, with a commanding physical presence. He was about six feet two inches tall, a little over 200 pounds, and powerfully built. Rice's legs, forearms, biceps, and chest rippled with muscle, and the stories of his strength were frequently told—how he'd broken bats checking his swing, how even when he was a teenager, his line drives seemed to defy gravity.

Guidry, however, was also confident. He knew that Rice was a dangerous hitter, even, perhaps especially, in the first inning; fourteen of Rice's home runs had come in the first. Guidry was well aware that if you made a mistake with Rice, he'd punish you for it. Even if he didn't hit a pitch well, Rice was so strong he could power a ball out of the park. But Guidry thought that Rice had a weakness, a "hole," with fastballs that came in right over his hands. Rice swung down on the ball better than up on it, and a properly placed pitch could cause him trouble. Of course, Guidry knew, there was an important caveat. If you threw that pitch at 94 or 95 miles an hour, you could give Rice trouble. But if you threw it at 90 miles an hour . . .

Guidry made it look easy.

He threw a high fastball that Rice swung at and missed. Then he blew another fastball by him—same place, maybe a little farther inside. With the count 0–2, he threw a junk pitch in the dirt, to see if Rice would chase it, then missed again with a fastball on the outside corner, just getting him thinking that way. At 2–2, Guidry came with the slider. Rice swung where the fastball would have been, where Guidry's first two pitches did go—and, because the slider broke down and in on him, didn't even come close to making contact.

The first confrontation between dueling MVP candidates had gone to Guidry.

At the end of one inning, both pitchers had looked sharp, with perhaps a slight edge to Guidry. The Red Sox and the Yankees were tied at zero.

CHAPTER 5

The Season Begins

On April 5, 1978, the legend, Ted Williams, almost sixty but still looking strong and supremely confident, stood in front of the Red Sox and urged them to play hard from the very first game, to take nothing for granted, because while 162 games might seem like a lot, an infinity of summer stretching out from April through September, the games you won in the beginning counted just as much as the games you won in the end, and the games that you lost early could come back to haunt you. "I remember in 1949, on opening day, we had the Yankees, 9–0, and lost 11–10," he warned his audience. "That's right. And we lost by a game to them the last day of the season."

Williams's talk wasn't enough to save opening day, which came April 7 in Comiskey Park. Steve Stone pitched seven innings for the White Sox, and Mike Torrez, the Red Sox's prime off-season acquisition, went six. He was not sharp, giving up ten hits and four runs before leaving for reliever Dick Drago in the seventh. Torrez's so-so start didn't seem to matter. The Sox went ahead in the eighth when Rick Burleson singled, Jim Rice bunted for just the fourth time in his career, and Carl Yastrzemski singled to score Burleson. In the ninth, though, disaster struck. With one out, Drago threw a fastball to designated hitter Ron Blomberg, an oft-injured former Yankee who hadn't played since September 1976, and Blomberg crushed it into the right-field stands. The game was tied at 5. Then came a single by center fielder Chet Lemon, and Don Zimmer brought in relief ace Bill Campbell, who procured the second out on a fly ball. With catcher Wayne Nordhagen up, the White Sox called a hit-and-run. Remy broke to cover second, and Nordhagen dropped a pop-up into right center, just beyond where Remy had been standing, an easy catch if Remy hadn't shifted position. Sprinting from center, Fred Lynn couldn't reach it. Guarding against a ball being hit over his head, Dwight Evans was playing too far back. Rick Burleson, charging from short, probably came the closest. Lemon scored easily, and the Red Sox had lost one they could, probably should, have won. They'd been done in by a rinky-dink pop-up from the White Sox's number eight hitter.

Rick Burleson was furious. "I'm tired of seeing all the other teams get the breaks," he said. "We've let too many of these games get away in the past and we've got to stop doing that. We've got to win games like this." There was no suggestion that losing the first game of the season was hardly the end of the world. From the first day of the season, the Red Sox weren't just playing a single game, they were playing along a continuity of disappointment and frustration, with all the weight of the past on one collective shoulder and the expectations of the present on the other.

On April 8, with Dennis Eckersley pitching and Campbell relieving once more, the Red Sox lost again, 6–5, despite having led 5–0. Things were so grim that Carl Yastrzemski even dropped a fly ball, his first error in 201 games. "Doubts are creeping in," Peter Gammons wrote in the next day's *Globe*. After two games! On the other hand, three times in sixty years the Sox had lost the pennant by a game or less. In 1948, they lost an opening day doubleheader to the Indians, then, 152 games later, lost the pennant to Cleveland in the one-game playoff. In 1949, they had that 9–0 lead against the Yankees, blew it, and finished one behind them 153 games later. And finally there was October 2, 1972, when Luis Aparicio stumbled rounding third in a game against Billy Martin's Detroit Tigers and was tagged out. The Sox lost the game and the pennant to the Tigers—by half a game.

If the Red Sox started slowly, Gammons warned, Don Zimmer was in trouble. Everyone knew the level of talent on this team. The only weak link could be the manager. It wasn't fair, Gammons noted, for Zimmer to receive such scrutiny two games into the season. But such was the nature of Red Sox fandom; hungry, impatient, and sometimes unforgiving—especially when they could smell a pennant.

At long last, the Sox beat Chicago the next day when Bill Lee threw a seven-hit, complete game shutout, despite developing a painful blister on his hand. Finally Boston had played the kind of baseball everyone expected from the team. Jim Rice homered and had two singles. Jerry Remy beat out a bunt, then stole second. The defense was seamless, and Lee was at his crafty best, throwing with power before his blister popped, then resorting to his famous "junk" pitches, breaking balls and curves and off-speed pitches, gritting his way through the last four innings.

But then, tragedy: against the Indians the next day, rookie Allen Ripley went eight innings, and with the score tied, 4–4, in the bottom of the ninth, Dick Drago gave up another lead. "We should be 4–0," Carlton Fisk lamented. "Instead, we're 1–3 and everyone's sitting here going, 'What the . . . ? ' "

After just four games, the season was already so intense that *Globe* columnist Bob Ryan cautioned that the fans were forgetting to have fun. To them, Ryan wrote, "the only thing that matters is, 'How much does he make?' No longer does a fan grouse about a strikeout-prone slugger by saying, 'How can that bum strike out like that?' Now it's, 'How can that overpaid 400-grand-a-year bum strike out like that?' " The season had progressed from enthusiasm to fanaticism dizzyingly fast, Ryan argued, and in all their passion, fans were losing appreciation for the subtleties of the game, the pleasures of it that had nothing to do with who won. It wasn't Don Zimmer's fault if the Sox blew a one-run game, but Sox fans were blasting him anyway. "These people are saying, 'These guys had better damn well win this pennant,' rather than, 'I hope our team can win the pennant.'

"It all comes down to the individual's reason for attendance," Ryan concluded. "Is it to watch rich people at play? Is it to uphold the honor of the city of Boston? Is it to smoke pot without fear of harassment? Personally, I go in the hopes of seeing a good baseball game. Shows you how old-fashioned I am."

The times were indeed changing, and so was the atmosphere in Fenway Park. If the players were becoming more bottom-dollar oriented, the fans were becoming more insistent upon the bottom line: did their team win, and did their players perform as they were being (well) paid to? If fans were going to be digging deeper into their pockets to walk through the turnstiles, an inevitable consequence of free agency, then they wanted more bang for their bucks. The sport was becoming less sporting, all about winning and less about fun.

On the 14th, Dennis Eckersley pitched the Fenway day-game opener against Texas. He had pitched before 60,000 people at Cleveland on an opening day, but 34,747 in Boston almost seemed like more, Fenway Park was so intimate. In some ways, it was a typical Boston opener. The stadium was filled to standing room and beyond; the Sox had accidentally sold more tickets for bleacher seats than there were seats. Peter

Wolf, lead singer of the Boston-based J. Geils Band, sent a telegram saying, "We hope we both have a lot of hits this year." The fans were drinking and fighting and booing Don Zimmer before the third inning. A ferocious, winter's-tail wind caused the Rangers to drop fly balls like hot coals and actually bent the steel screen over the Green Monster. And the late afternoon sun made right field even more of a challenge as the game went into extra innings. "Right field here is the toughest sunfield in baseball," Dwight Evans said after the game. "On a day like this, with all that wind, you just have to play deep and not make a move on a ball until you're sure of where it's going. If you play in close, you're in trouble."

Eckersley pitched nine and two-thirds innings before leaving with the game tied at 4. The fans gave him a standing ovation. "A fucking standing ovation," Eckersley would recall almost thirty years later, still somewhat in disbelief. "You never forget that stuff." For Eckersley, who was going through a painful divorce—his wife had become involved with Eckersley's Indians teammate Rick Manning, and was staying in Cleveland with their two-year-old—it was a powerful and inspiring moment. When Boston took you to heart, you felt like you were home, even if your family was somewhere else. That, too, was part of playing for the Red Sox.

In the bottom of the tenth, with two outs and Butch Hobson on third, the Rangers' Len Barker threw Jim Rice a 2–2 fastball that looked headed for the bottom of his chin. Somehow, Rice not only connected with the ball but drove it to the opposite field, where it bounced off the bullpen wall. "All I was trying to do was fight it off," Rice explained. Hobson trotted home and the Sox were winners.

After that, the team started to roll. They won their next seven straight and finished the homestand with an 8–2 record. Though the Sox were traditionally a slow-starting team, this squad already looked formidable. Remy bunted and stole bases, Burleson played with his usual relentless hustle, Fisk threw out base runners, Rice and Hobson slammed home runs, and Yaz came through in the clutch. But it still wasn't enough for the fans to ease up on Zimmer, whom they booed every time he poked his head out of the dugout. Perhaps it was because he was following Darrell Johnson, the hero of 1975, or because he had clashed with the popular Buffalo Heads and traded all but Lee and Carbo. Pitcher Fergie Jenkins, now with the Rangers, sparked a controversy when he announced that as a Red Sox player, "I got shoved into the bullpen by a fat, ugly bald man who doesn't know anything about pitching." Zimmer responded, "He's right on three counts: I'm fat, ugly and bald." In any case, Zimmer said, "If he were still here, I wouldn't be."

Or maybe the fans worried that Zimmer had too much faith in certain players; he insisted on finding playing time for Bob Bailey, a past-his-prime right-handed hitter the Sox had bought from the Cincinnati Reds the previous September in an attempt to deepen their bench. "Sooner or later, Bailey'll win four or five games for us," Zimmer insisted. Bailey, who had hit .253 in 79 at-bats for the Reds in 1977, showed no sign of such promise.

In mid-May, the Sox were at 20–11, tied for first with Detroit at 17–8, two games ahead of the 16–11 Yankees. They had won 20 games earlier in the season than any Sox team since 1946. Starting pitching was one reason why. Mike Torrez began the year 5–1; Eckersley was, after several no-decisions, beginning to pitch brilliantly; and, after winning just 9 games in 1977, Bill Lee looked like he was once more the pitcher who won 51 games from 1973 to 1975.

Following the example they'd set with Eckersley, Fenway fans continued their new custom of giving starting pitchers a standing ovation with two outs in the ninth. They could do so because, as was customary at the time, Zimmer kept his starters in until they got knocked out or asked to be lifted, and few pitchers made that request. Going nine was a point of pride rather than a cause of concern. On May 6, Lee threw 146 pitches in a complete-game win against the White Sox, about 50 percent more than pitchers in today's game typically throw—too many pitches, some would later say, for a pitcher trying to come back from arm trouble. Two weeks later, against Detroit, Luis Tiant, recovering from a dislocated right index finger, threw 159 pitches. He won that game, 1–0, and would win his first seven decisions.

If the pitching was a pleasant surprise, the hitting was as awesome as expected—maybe better. In their first seven games at Fenway, the Red Sox racked up 93 hits and 60 runs. Two weeks into the season, they were hitting .315 as a team, despite the clammy weather. "If people think this is something, wait until the home run days" of warmer weather, George Scott said. "This place is going to look like Vietnam."

Jim Rice was already ripping apart opposing pitching as if every day was Christmas morning. On the first of May, Rice homered twice to help beat the Orioles, 9–6. A few days later, he had 5 hits and 5 runs batted in during a doubleheader against the White Sox. "I still don't think I'm swinging the bat properly," he said. Opponents begged to differ. Rice was hitting everything that came his way, and hitting everything with power; at the end of May, he had an astonishing slugging percentage of .686. When the Royals came to Fenway in the second week of the month, their manager, Whitey Herzog, shifted third baseman Jerry Terrell into left field and used four outfielders to defend against Rice. "What I'd like is a couple of guys on top of the fence in left," Herzog said. To make things worse for pitchers, they were reluctant to throw the brushback pitch to back Rice off the plate; he was so physically intimidating, few wanted to provoke him. When Royals pitcher Jim Colborn hit Rice with a pitch on the wrist, the slugger strolled to the mound and announced, "Do that again and I'll tear your head off." From the safety of the clubhouse, Colborn laughed off the episode, saying, "I asked him if he came out to get the ethyl chloride," a liquid anesthetic. But Whitey Herzog wasn't so blasé. "I'm just glad Rice wasn't that mad," he said after the game. "Colburn could have been killed out there."

The Sox were winning despite some nagging injuries. Bill Campbell, who had pitched in 69 games for the Sox in 1977, was clearly not the same pitcher he had been; he had soreness in his elbow that would not go away, and would pitch in only 29 games in 1978. Butch Hobson's deteriorating elbow hurt him every day; he hoped it was a result of the early season chill and would improve with warm weather. George Scott threw out his back. Yaz was hit in the right wrist by the Brewers' Mike Caldwell on April 26, and his arm swelled and developed a bump. Asked if Yastrzemski would need further treatment, trainer Charlie Moss said, "Further treatment? I'm going to let him have a few beers." But the injury, a deep bone bruise, would bother Yaz throughout the season. From time to time, the fingers of his right hand would simply go numb.

Nevertheless, after two months of baseball, the Red Sox looked unstoppable. They had a record of 34–16, a winning percentage of .680, and were on pace to win 110 games—more than any team had ever won in a 162-game season. And they actually seemed to be picking up steam: In May, they went 23–7. On the road they were average, with a record of 12–12, but at Fenway they were virtually unbeatable at 22–4. They led both leagues in hits, home runs, and runs batted in. Jim Rice was ahead of the home run calendars of both Babe Ruth and Roger Maris, and on track to drive in about 150 runs. "I'm better than anyone you put out there on the field right now," Rice declared. "I'm better than anyone on any team. If I wasn't, I wouldn't be here."

James Edward Rice—Jim Ed, to his family and childhood friends—had come a long way to make it to Boston. He was born on March 8, 1953, in Anderson, South Carolina, a town of about 40,000 near the Blue Ridge Mountains and the Georgia border. His father, Roger Rice, was a manager in a company that made antennae for CB radios. His mother, Julia Mae, helped raise their nine children.

Rice was such a gifted athlete that he was starting on his high school's varsity baseball team when he was in eighth grade. He was so good that his town bent the rules of segregation for him, redrawing the school district lines so that, instead of living in the area that would have him attending Westside, the black high school, Rice suddenly lived in the district which put him at Hanna High School—the white school— an hour's walk away. That year, Rice hit .500. He was said to have hit a home run that traveled 390 feet without ever rising higher than ten feet off the ground. That homer would become the stuff of myth; a writer for *Sport* magazine subsequently put it at 500 feet.

The Red Sox signed him in 1971 with a fourteenth-round pick, hoping that he wouldn't be snapped up before that and surprised that he wasn't, for a reported $45,000 bonus. Rice then spent four years in the minors, improving steadily every year. He was brought up to the majors in 1975 and had to compete for a spot against local favorite Tony Conigliaro; since Conigliaro had never fully recovered from the 1967 beaning, it wasn't much of a competition. Together, Rice and Fred Lynn put together two of the greatest seasons by rookies in baseball history. But Rice was hit by a pitch that broke his wrist on September 21 and missed the classic World Series against the Reds. Things might have been different for both the Red Sox and for Rice had that pitch been only an inch or so higher or lower. The Sox might have won the Series, and Rice might have earned a place in the fans' hearts that he never quite attained.

Physically, Rice was simultaneously handsome and intimidating. He had deep black skin and chiseled features with a winning, if rare, smile. He stood six feet two and weighed about 200 pounds, and his body was sculpted with muscle; while Carl Yastrzemski was always fit, no one on the Red Sox had a physique anywhere near as powerful as Rice's. On the field, it showed. In batting practice, Rice hit the ball so hard that he twice shattered the arm of a pitching machine. In June 1975, he checked a swing in Detroit and snapped his bat in half. No one had ever seen that before; Rice said he'd already done it twice. Eight years later, in 1983, he'd do it again in a game against Minnesota. The Red Sox had plenty of home run hitters: Fisk, Hobson, Lynn, Yaz, Scott. But Jim Rice was on a different level. When he connected, there was no doubt; his home runs rocketed over fences. The speed of his bat and the power of his swing were perhaps most reminiscent of Reggie Jackson, but he struck out far fewer times and hit for considerably higher average than Jackson did.

Rice was a complex and easily misunderstood man. He was shy, and that reserve could come across as arrogance. Sometimes, it was arrogance. He was a loner on the team, and he didn't have any close friends except for Cecil Cooper, who was traded after 1975. Some years before, Bill Russell, the great Boston Celtic center, had described the city as a "flea market for racism." Similarly, Rice was acutely self-aware of his awkward status as a black man from the South playing for the last team in baseball to integrate, competing for playing time against Carl Yastrzemski, a white legend and local favorite. He could be moody, and he worried that because he was black, he wasn't getting as much attention as some of his white teammates, especially Yastrzemski and Lynn. (Whether or not he was right, his sometimes surly demeanor made the prophecy self-fulfilling.) In 1975, a writer for the *Miami Herald* reported Rice saying that he thought Lynn got too much publicity. When the story came out, Rice denied having made the comments. Two years later, a writer for the *Boston Herald American* reported him saying that Carl Yastrzemski was an "old man" who should be used as a designated hitter while Rice played left. When the quotes were published, Rice denied them, too. "What I said," he claimed, "is that everybody knows what Yaz can do, but I've got to prove myself and I hope I get the chance."

He was better on the field than in the clubhouse, and he worked constantly to improve. Early in his career, he tended to swing at bad pitches, sliders down and away and pitches in the dirt. He practiced tirelessly to rid himself of those habits. Before games, he'd hit a couple of hundred balls, envisioning different game situations, hitting to various fields. When he came up from the minors, he was considered only a so-so fielder, certainly lacking the instinct and fluidity in the field of his contemporary, Lynn, who solidified that reputation in 1975 with an astonishing, running-into-the-wall catch in Game Six of the World

Series. But unlike Reggie Jackson or, say, Ted Williams, Rice dedicated himself to improving his defense, making himself into a more than adequate fielder. In left, he was no Yaz, but he played the Green Monster capably and had a strong throwing arm. It bothered Rice that he wasn't seen as a complete player, for the perception, while ubiquitous, was inaccurate.

In 1978, everything was coming together for Rice. The year before, he'd hit .320, with 39 home runs and 114 runs batted in. After two months of the '78 season, he was on track to pass those numbers comfortably. But he continued his prickly relationship with Boston, its media, and his teammates, who valued his contributions but didn't think of him as a team leader; Rice was too much of an island. "Rice was having an f'ing year, the greatest offensive year of its day," Dennis Eckersley would say. But "his personality wasn't the type to inspire the team."

At this point in the Red Sox's season, that hardly seemed to matter. Rice was carrying the Red Sox toward June, first place, and the team's first series against the Yankees.

New York, meanwhile, stumbled out of the gate.

The Yankees began their season on April 8 with Ron Guidry on the mound at Texas. To mark the occasion, the Rangers handed out "I Hate the Yankees hankies" to their fans, an act of officially sanctioned crudity that could not have happened without the social changes in language and tone inspired by Vietnam and the popular culture of the 1960s and 1970s; the handkerchiefs were a combination of a social nicety, the handkerchief, from a more rarefied era, mixed with the attitude of post-Vietnam America—baseball's version of, as Jimi Hendrix had put it, a freak flag. They were also an expression of hostility to the new paradigms of the era, George Steinbrenner and free agency. Already the Yankees had come to represent trends in baseball that were alienating fans around the league, especially those who rooted for small-market teams that couldn't afford to pay free agents what the Yankees were doling out. The Cleveland Indians had initiated the Yankee-hating handkerchiefs the previous Labor Day, and they would quickly travel to Boston.

Guidry should have had the victory; while the Yankees were leaving enough men on base to start a conga line, Guidry gave up a run in the first and nothing after that through seven innings, after which Billy Martin took him out. In the bottom of the ninth, however, brand-new,

$2.75-million relief pitcher Rich Gossage gave up a home run to out-fielder Richie Zisk and the Rangers won, 2–1.

That was the beginning of a mediocre start for the Yankees, who would lose four of their six to the Rangers and Brewers on that road trip, and a horrendous start for Rich Gossage, who three times gave up the winning runs to the opposition and was credited with three losses. As fierce as Gossage looked on the mound, the twenty-six-year-old, Colorado-born pitcher was, in fact, one of the friendliest men on the Yankees, an unexpectedly gentle soul, and the transition from success in Chicago and Pittsburgh to free agent wealth, and its attendant spot-light in New York, was not easy for Gossage.

Richard Michael Gossage was born on July 5, 1951, in Colorado Springs, Colorado, the fifth of sixth children. His father, Jack Gossage, worked as a landscaper, and his family struggled financially. Gossage grew up in a one-bedroom house. He and his siblings slept in the same room with his mother, while his father slept at the home of an aunt. Rich Gossage was always good at sports; he was a star in base-ball and basketball at Wasson High School. His father died when Gossage was a senior, and money in the Gossage household grew even tighter. Gossage was determined to chip in. On June 4, 1970, the eighteen-year-old Gossage ran home from a job interview to announce to his mother, Sue Gossage, "Mom, I've got a job working as a coun-selor at the summer camp!" His mother told him that something else had come up; they had a visitor, a representative of the Chicago White Sox, who had just drafted Gossage in the ninth round. Rich Gossage, fresh from high school graduation, was so overwhelmed that he bolted from the house, ran into the mountains behind his house, and broke down in tears.

He would pitch in the minors on and off for four years, starting in Appleton, Wisconsin, where he and Terry Forster, who would become a successful reliever with the White Sox, and a promising shortstop named Bucky Dent saved money by rooming together. "We had an old green '60-something Chevrolet and an apartment by a graveyard," Dent remembered. "Didn't have any money. Slept together on a mat-tress on the floor."

Gossage went 18–2 that season and joined the White Sox for the first time in 1972. He was making $12,500 a year. It was then that he picked up his nickname, Goose, the gift of fellow pitcher Tom Bradley, who rightly pointed out that, at the end of Gossage's delivery, his right leg driving forward, his right arm seeming to pull him off the mound, and his left arm thrown out behind him, Gossage did indeed look like a goose, albeit one in some distress. (Later, it would be suggested that the origin of the nickname had to do with Gossage's habit of putting goose eggs—zeros—on the scoreboard, but that was simply a fortuitous extension of the metaphor.)

Traveling back and forth between Chicago and the minors, Gossage had only middling success during his first years. His strength was his fastball, which he could consistently throw in the high 90s, sometimes reaching 100 miles an hour. That was pretty much all he had. In the minors, he worked on developing a breaking pitch, but it didn't come easily: when he once tried to throw one in a game, Gossage accidentally fired the ball into the visitors' dugout. The opposing team's manager, who was also coaching third, called time, trotted into the dugout, donned a batting helmet, and returned to the field. Gossage reverted to the fastball and struck out the side on nine pitches.

It took a while, but Gossage gradually honed his repertoire of pitches—though he would still throw the fastball about two-thirds of the time—and his control. Though Gossage might have looked like he was all over the mound, he had remarkable control for someone with such a live fastball, and gave up walks stingily. In 1975, White Sox manager Chuck Tanner used Gossage solely as a reliever and the pitcher bloomed, earning 26 saves and striking out 130 batters in 142 innings. The next year Tanner was gone and the White Sox turned Gossage into a starter. The move didn't take—Gossage couldn't go nine innings, throwing as hard as he did—and he went 9–17. At the end of the season the White Sox traded Gossage and his former roommate Terry Forster to the Pirates, who celebrated Gossage's arrival by acquiring a live goose, which was walked around the stadium outfield by a Pittsburgh "Pirette," a young woman in a tight t-shirt, short shorts, tube socks, and sneakers. Restored to his relief role, Gossage returned to form. Again, he saved 26 games—the same number, coincidentally, that Sparky Lyle would compile that season, though Gossage's 1.62 ERA was considerably lower than Lyle's 2.17—and Gossage struck out a National League record (for a reliever) 151 batters. Lyle, whose slider generated frequent ground balls, had only 68.

Gossage's numbers caught George Steinbrenner's eye; the owner liked that Gossage was just 26, and he knew that fans would come to the stadium to see the hard-throwing strikeout pitcher. On November 22, Gossage signed with the Yankees for six years and $2.75 million—a hefty raise from the $12,500 he was making just five years before, and more than triple the $135,000 that Sparky Lyle was being paid. Lyle would later say that when his wife heard the news, she started to cry; she knew it meant the beginning of the end of her husband's career.

Goose Gossage was, at heart, a small-town boy, in love with the space and beauty of his native Colorado, and unlike Reggie Jackson, he did not care for the lights and glamour of New York City. He chose to sign with the Yankees because he wanted to play for a winning team, rather than the lure of New York's ancillary benefits. He would quickly discover that the money of New York came with a price.

His trials began with Billy Martin in spring training. "Billy hated me," Gossage later recalled. Sparky Lyle—rowdy, old-school, veteran—was one of Billy's inner circle; Gossage was one of "George's boys." For that, Martin resented him, just as he did any player whom the owner signed in defiance of Martin's wishes. And so, in a spring training game against Texas, Martin decided to force Gossage to buckle to Martin's will. Before the game began, Martin told Gossage that he was going to use the pitcher at some point. He then instructed the pitcher that, when an African-American outfielder named Bill Sample came to the plate, Gossage was to hit him in the head. Only he didn't just identify Sample by name, he used a hateful two-syllable word to describe Sample, a word that was not part of Gossage's vocabulary.

"I thought he was kidding," Gossage said, "and then I knew he wasn't kidding. That was his way of testing my loyalty. I said, 'Billy Sample's never done anything to me.' " Gossage wasn't averse to a brushback pitch when appropriate, but hitting a man in the head? The way he threw, he said to Martin, he could kill the guy. "I don't give a shit if you do kill him," Martin answered.

"He screamed at me, he got in my face, and I thought we were going to fight right there," Gossage said. "He called me a cunt, a fucking pussy, a big fucking cunt. Every name in the book. Scared the shit out of me. I'm just there to help him win. But he put me in the game that afternoon to face Sample, and I didn't hit him. And from that time on he hated my guts."

"I didn't like Billy that much," Gossage said. "He drank too much, and he was a bad drunk. It was just the wrong way to test my loyalty, and I wasn't going to do that."

Gossage certainly had nothing against Sparky Lyle, who, after all, had won the Cy Young Award in 1977; between both men, there was respect. And when Gossage signed his contract with the Yankees, he came to New York hoping that the two of them would combine to form the greatest relief duo in baseball, Gossage from the right and Lyle from the left, an equal distribution of labor. Instead, Gossage said, "They gave me his job on a silver platter." Lyle had pitched in 72 games in 1977; he would pitch in 59 in 1978. But the numbers didn't tell the real story. He now pitched in less crucial situations, as a set-up man for Gossage, a mop-up pitcher in games the Yankees were winning easily, sometimes even a middle inning reliever. Along with the Oakland A's Rollie Fingers, Lyle had been one of the first of baseball's ace relief pitchers, the man who came in, day after day, when the game was really on the line. He thrived on both the pressure and the regularity of that routine. Now it was obvious that, at Steinbrenner's directive, Lyle had been relegated to secondary status, and he sulked and fumed and demanded more money—that, or be traded. The owner said no to both, telling Lyle, "How much market value is there in a thirty-four-year-old reliever?"

It was an unpleasant, uncomfortable situation for Gossage, and it couldn't help but affect his pitching. He was pressing, putting too much pressure on himself, as if his job weren't just to save games but to save the team. He lost on opening day, then did it again a few days later against the Brewers, entering the game in the sixth and giving up four runs. Rather than justifying his enormous contract, Gossage felt like he was only proving that he didn't deserve millions. And then came the fiasco on opening day, April 13, at Yankee Stadium. Before the game, as a slum fire burned somewhere in the Bronx and black smoke drifted across the outfield, New York mayor Ed Koch announced, "My fellow Yankees fans, happiness is a world championship," and the World Series trophy was presented to the team by Mickey Mantle and Roger Maris—the first time Maris had returned to Yankee Stadium since the team had traded him to the Cardinals in 1966. But when Gossage was introduced, the fans showered him with boos, both because of his recent pitching and because they liked Sparky Lyle. Gossage's confidence had been shaken by his poor previous performances. The boos added to the pressure he felt. As he stood on the field, fighting back tears, Gossage vowed that by the end of the season, he would turn those boos to cheers.

The Yankees faced the White Sox that day, and even though their season was just five games old, some of the New York team's challenges were already apparent. They had lost four of those five games, and the health of their pitchers was already a worry. Against Milwaukee on

April 11, Catfish Hunter lasted just two innings, giving up six hits and six runs in a 9–6 loss, an outcome that instantly made observers wonder if Hunter was simply finished—if age, or the previous season's shoulder trouble, or the diabetes he'd recently been diagnosed with had brought his career to an abrupt end. Hunter claimed his shoulder didn't hurt him, but the results suggested otherwise. Meanwhile, Don Gullett's right arm hurt so much Gullett would soon get his second cortisone shot of the season. Andy Messersmith was trying to come back from a shoulder separation he'd suffered in spring training. Trying, and failing—he would pitch only 22 innings all season. That left Guidry, right-hander Ed Figueroa, and Dick Tidrow, who was primarily a long reliever. The Yankees had two quality pitchers, Ken Holtzman and Rawly Eastwick, who were prepared to pick up the slack, but both were in Martin's doghouse; Eastwick, another free agent hire, was one of George's boys, and Holtzman—well, no one knew exactly why Martin didn't like the veteran lefthander. Veteran sportswriter Roger Kahn wondered if Martin was anti-Semitic; both Holtzman and another former Yankee, Ron Blomberg, were Jewish, and Martin had disliked both for reasons that seemed disconnected from the quality of their play. Team president Al Rosen denied the suggestion, saying, "I don't think Billy would have a bit of trouble managing a ballplayer he thinks is a winner, no matter what the guy's religion." But Kahn was unconvinced, writing, "I'd still rather play baseball for Joe Torre," who was then managing the Mets. Whatever the cause of Martin's antipathy, it was apparent that if the Yankees didn't trade him, Holtzman would spend the season riding the bench. At first, Martin put Holtzman on the disabled list, even though the pitcher loudly protested that there was nothing wrong with him. In June, the Yankees shipped Holtzman to the Cubs for a minor leaguer to be named later.

Though he gave up ten hits, Guidry went nine to beat the White Sox on opening day, 4–2, for his first victory. But the story of the game was Reggie Jackson. During the off-season, Jackson had signed a contract with a food manufacturer called Standard Brands to produce a chocolate and caramel confection called the "Reggie!" bar. To promote the Reggie! bar, Standard Brands gave all 52,000 fans on hand one of the squarish candy bars, wrapped in bright orange plastic. The company hired models and airline "stewardesses," as they were then known, to dole out 72,000 of the candy bars, which otherwise cost twenty-five cents apiece. "For reasons best known to themselves," the legendary sportswriter Red Smith would later recount, "recipients stowed thousands in pockets instead of stomachs."

Jackson must have been enjoying the moment, because when he came up in the bottom of the first against knuckleballer Wilbur Wood, with Willie Randolph and Mickey Rivers on base, he promptly smashed a floating knuckleball over the wall in right center. Combined with his heroics from Game Six of the 1977 World Series, Jackson had now hit four home runs in his last four swings at Yankee Stadium. The love—or at least the sugar—came pouring down. Before Jackson had finished rounding the bases, someone threw a Reggie! bar that landed near home plate. Then a second fan threw another. Within seconds, Sparky Lyle would later say, the rest of the fans realized "the beauty of the act," and Reggie! bars were raining from the sky like some high-calorie biblical plague. The square shape and two-ounce weight of the Reggie! bar, it turned out, made the candy an easily improvised projectile, especially if thrown sidearm, like skipping a stone. "They should advertise it as the candy bar made to throw," White Sox manager Bob Lemon said. Within seconds the field was littered with thousands of the candy bars, as if a piñata-blimp had been broken open, and dozens of quick-thinking boys scrambled over the fences and scurried onto the field to collect the loot. "Ladies and gentlemen, please stay in your seats," announcer Bob Sheppard instructed. The game was interrupted for five minutes while the grounds crew picked up the candy. Lou Piniella, who was waiting in the on-deck circle, took three practice swings with a Reggie!, thus proving that Piniella really would swing at anything. He whiffed twice before fouling one off. Hitting a Reggie! bar, Piniella concluded, was "very difficult. The flat bottom side makes it tough, and even if you'd meet one square, I don't think you'd drive it very far."

After the Yankees won, reactions ranged from thankful to comic to irritated. "It was a nice gesture," Jackson insisted. "It was a very thrilling moment for Reggie," Piniella deadpanned. "They wouldn't be throwing Yoo Hoo like that," coach and chocolate drink pitchman Yogi Berra said. "The people must have a lot of money here, to throw away all that food," Catfish Hunter concluded, noting that, to his great regret, he couldn't try a Reggie! bar because of his diabetes. Hunter seemed to be enjoying the whole thing. "When you unwrap a Reggie! bar, it tells you how good it is," he added. "In Boston," Billy Martin pointed out, "they throw metal objects. In our park they throw candy bars, which only proves that we have sweet fans."

The only person who seemed annoyed was White Sox manager Bob Lemon, whose team, after all, had lost the game. "I thought it was horse manure," Lemon said. "People are starving all over the world, and there's thirty billion calories laying on the field. . . ." Besides, Lemon added, what if someone had gotten hit?

The slightly silly, slightly surreal incident was typical of the Yankees. Was it a sign of the fans' ardor for Jackson, a sarcastic commentary on his celebrity, or both? Or just another symptom of the nuttiness that had pervaded Yankee Stadium since George Steinbrenner and Billy Martin arrived? Whichever the case, the players were blasé. Candy bars could shower from the sky, and the Yankees were, well, bemused; it was just one more curious spectacle in an endless pageant of the bizarre.

For someone like Gossage, however, adapting to the circus took time. On April 17, against the Orioles, Catfish Hunter got shelled again, going only four and a third innings while throwing 89 pitches— once what he might have required to go nine—while giving up six hits, five walks, and five runs. Gossage entered the game in the fifth and promptly gave up a two-run homer to third baseman Doug DeCinces, basically putting the game out of reach for the Yankees. Settling down after that, Gossage stayed in until the ninth, but in the seventh he threw a pitch that soared over Oriole catcher Rick Dempsey's head. Manager Earl Weaver stormed onto the field and persuaded home plate umpire Joe Brinkman to warn Billy Martin that subsequent brushbacks could bring ejections. If not, Weaver said to Thurman Munson, "I'm going to get you." Martin apparently heard the remark, because he rushed to home plate and engaged in spirited conversation with Weaver and Brinkman. He returned to the dugout only after saluting the Orioles manager with his middle finger.

After the game, Martin was livid. "Weaver got the umpire to warn me," he fumed. "Can you believe that? And the umpire was stupid enough to do it. Weaver said if he didn't warn me, his pitcher would throw at Munson. . . . If one of my hitters goes down tomorrow, I'm going to personally beat the living hell out of Weaver. If he says one word out of line, I'll deck him right at home plate." For good measure, Martin dubbed Weaver "the little midget."

Over in the Orioles locker room, Earl Weaver was also in high dudgeon. "I couldn't hear nothing [Martin] said," he contended. "It looked like he gave me the finger, and naturally, being the better person,

I gave him the thumb." As to the question of his height, Weaver said, "I would rather be small in stature than a mental midget."

Asked for comment, Thurman Munson, who was smart enough not to get in the middle of a pitched battle between Billy Martin and Earl Weaver, announced, "I'm just happy to be here."

The incident overshadowed Gossage's continuing struggles, but two days later, at Toronto, nothing could obscure the fact that the relief pitcher was in a bad way. With the game tied 3–3 in the bottom of the ninth, Gossage—who'd already pitched three and two-thirds innings in relief of the rarely used Ken Holtzman—gave up a no-out single. When Blue Jay catcher Rick Cerrone bunted over pinch runner Garth Iorg, Gossage tried for the force at second, but almost threw the ball away, and Iorg was safe. The next hitter, second baseman Dave McKay, also bunted, and this time Gossage went to Chris Chambliss at first— only he threw the ball a yard over Chambliss's outstretched glove, and Iorg trotted home for the game-winning run. A single, two throwing errors, and Gossage had single-handedly lost the game. His record was now 0–3.

Back in the locker room, Gossage collapsed into his locker so hard that he broke its seat. "I just began to cry like a little baby," he said. "Just bawling, distraught. I didn't know which way to turn. I'd tried to keep a good attitude and perseverance and all that, but this was the last straw." For the first time, Gossage felt like quitting baseball. "I must have stayed there another hour," he said. "The clothes were draped down, hanging off my hangers over my head." Suddenly someone pushed the clothes away. Gossage looked up to see Piniella, Hunter, Nettles, Jackson, and Munson standing in front of him. "Come on," Munson said. "We're going to dinner, and you're coming with us."

Things picked up after that. In Baltimore, a few days later, Gossage came on in relief of Ron Guidry, who had accidentally swallowed his chewing tobacco and become nauseous. Despite being pelted by the fans with ice cubes, half-eaten pieces of fruit, and a full beer—retaliation for the Dempsey incident—Gossage finished out the win. At the beginning of May, the Yankees won six out of seven, capping it off with a twelve-inning, 3–2 victory against the Rangers in front of 53,829 fans at the stadium, the season's largest crowd to date. Following up rookie Jim Beattie and Sparky Lyle, who carried the Yankees through eight innings, Gossage pitched the next four, striking out five, not giving up a run, and getting the win when Chris Chambliss homered in the bottom of the twelfth. Goose Gossage was getting his groove back, and he credited his new teammates.

"They stuck with me and helped me through those hard times," Gossage said. "They kept my confidence up until I worked my way out of it. And that's the fine line we walk between a good career and a great career—those teammates of mine sticking with me."

One in particular helped: Thurman Munson. In a sense, Gossage had known Munson for years. Back in 1976, when he was starting for the White Sox, Gossage had drilled the catcher with a fastball on the elbow. "You had to pitch Thurman inside or he'd kill you," Gossage said. This pitch was a little too inside. "I hit him as good as I ever hit anybody, and he had to leave the game." Afterward, Gossage was standing in front of his locker when a bat boy from the Yankee clubhouse brought him a note from Munson. "I took your best motherfucking shot, you fucking cocksucker," it said. The note was signed, "The White Gorilla," one of Munson's self-deprecatory nicknames.

That was classic Munson—all bluster and bravado on the outside, mixed with pride that he had, in fact, taken Gossage's best shot and could still joke about it, all the machismo cloaking the thoughtful message to Gossage that he hadn't been injured by the pitch—as if the more considerate the gesture, the more Munson felt he had to obscure its decency with tough talk. When Gossage came to the Yankees, Munson continued that sarcastic ribbing. He knew that Gossage was psyching himself out; better to get mad at his catcher than to get mad at himself. So when Gossage entered games during those early rough days, Munson would stroll to the mound, looking to all the world like he wanted to talk strategy. "How you gonna lose this one?" he'd ask Gossage. The reliever would reply, "I don't know, but get your little ass back there and we'll find out." It helped. "I never had as much fun with any other catcher as I did with Munson," Gossage said. And when you had fun, you played better, and you won games.

The Yankees were like that; they knew how to enjoy themselves, despite, or perhaps because of, all the pressures pushing in on them— Billy Martin's mercurial behavior, George Steinbrenner's intemperate words, the relentless media and demanding fans. In another game, outfielder Mickey Rivers prepared for Gossage's first pitch by turning his back to the mound and dropping into a sprinter's crouch. Gossage, oblivious, looked to Munson for the sign, but the catcher was, as Gossage put it, "laughing his ass off." Munson shouted, "Hey, check Rivers out." Gossage turned around, and "all I could see was his ass headed toward the wall, waiting to chase the balls that they were going to hit off me."

Of course, the laughter wasn't always easily maintained. By mid-May, the Yankees had a record of 17–12, matching their 1977 pace, but signs of dissension were cropping up in the Yankee clubhouse. Munson wasn't talking to the press about much, certainly not the pain his right knee was giving him. (Asked if it would require surgery, he said, "No, I'm too ornery.") Frustrated with his lack of playing time, Roy White asked for a trade with uncharacteristic emotion. "Get me the hell off this team," he shouted in the dugout one day, after Martin ordered him to bunt and he popped out to the catcher. "I can't play two days a week!" Rivers was angry that Martin benched him on May 15 for an apparent lack of hustle. "If I'm not in the lineup for a day or two, I'll ask to be traded," he said. Even the usually quiet Willie Randolph popped off to the press. At $70,000 a year, Randolph was the lowest-paid Yankee, and he wasn't happy about the honor. "I feel I'm not respected," he said. "I'm overlooked." Ken Holtzman had pitched credibly twice, but Martin benched him anyway in favor of rookie Jim Beattie. "It must be something that's not happening on the field," Graig Nettles said. "It must be something, because he should be pitching."

Billy Martin was trying to be on his best behavior, but he found it hard to contain himself, particularly when he'd been drinking. After the May 14 game, Martin was particularly upset. The Yankees had lost to Kansas City, 10–9, when Rivers trotted after a line drive to center and didn't even try to throw out a runner at home. Bad enough that the Yankees lost, but when a player didn't hustle, Martin took it personally; it made him feel, as many things did, that he was losing control of the team. The manager drank before getting on the Yankees' flight to Chicago, and he drank onboard the plane. He promptly yelled at Lou Piniella for playing cards with Rivers—though he said nothing to Rivers himself—then returned to his first-class cabin and issued an edict that the players were not to play tape recorders without headphones.

For whatever reason—perhaps either to tease Martin, or because he was irritated by Martin's tirade against Piniella—Munson defied the order, repeatedly removing his headphones from their jack, letting his music blare, then reinserting the headphones. After the plane, a commercial flight, landed, Martin returned to the coach cabin to yell at Munson, calling him a bad influence. When Munson responded, "The only reason you're saying this now is because there are nine guys between us," Martin went beserk and tried to attack Munson. The team's coaches prevented him from doing so.

Martin later apologized to Munson for the incident, which received widespread newspaper coverage, though the Yankee management tried to pooh-pooh it. "A ship that sails on a calm sea gets nowhere," Steinbrenner said. "You've got to have a little turmoil." Team president Rosen echoed the suggestion that a little chaos was standard operating procedure. "Ballplayers always bicker and curse and shout and call people names," he insisted. "What do you think our ball club is, the New York Choirboys?"

Such protestations aside, it was obvious to anyone with eyes that Martin was deteriorating physically and emotionally. Though the Yankees were within shouting distance of the Red Sox—no small feat considering how well the Sox were playing—the manager reacted to every loss as if it were a season-ender. He was eating too little and drinking too much, and he would show up before games clearly hungover, sometimes wearing dark glasses to hide his bloodshot eyes. On May 16, Martin almost passed out in the middle of a game against the White Sox. Martin told Murray Chass of the *New York Times* that he hoped to transition from manager to management one day, always with the Yankees. "Someday I'd hope they would say, 'You've done a good job. Come upstairs. There's a job for you.' " It sounded as if Martin were preparing for the afterlife. Still, Steinbrenner downplayed Martin's condition, claiming that Martin had settled down, become a calmer person. "He may say he hasn't changed, but he's changing," Steinbrenner said. "He really is. He's becoming a better man, a better organization man, a better business man, and a better manager because of it."

At the end of May, the Yankees were a more than respectable eleven games over .500 at 29–18, just three games behind the Red Sox. But injuries, unhappiness, and Martin's troubles started to kick in. Beginning June 2, they lost two out of three to Oakland, two out of three in Seattle, two out of three to the Angels, then won four straight against the A's and the Mariners before losing another two out of three to the Angels. The team's savior was Ron Guidry, who simply did not lose. "As the season was progressing, we started slowly," Guidry said. "Every time that I went out to pitch, it seemed like we had lost one or two games prior. I wasn't thinking as much that my season was special, I was thinking, I need to stop this streak right here—we need to win one game out of four, instead of losing four out of four."

But Guidry's season was special. He beat the A's, 3–1, on June 2, striking out eleven. Five days later, he beat Seattle, 9–1, going nine innings and striking out ten. Five days later, another win, 2–0, against Oakland. His consistency was remarkable; he had lost his last game on September 30, 1977, and since August 3 of that season he had won 20 of 21 decisions. It got to the point where he and Munson developed a ritual. When Guidry walked in from the bullpen before a game, the catcher would ask, "How many runs do you think you're gonna need tonight?"

"It started out as a joke," Guidry remembered. "You're saying something you shouldn't be saying, you don't want to upset the baseball gods by being cocky. But he asked me that one time, and I said, 'Gimme two.' And they get two and you win 2–0, and the next time you come in and say, 'Gimme two,' and you win 2–1—it becomes a routine now."

No one else would ever dare pose the question to Guidry; it was Munson's job. "And he'd just look at everybody down the dugout and say, 'He just needs two,' and then, boom, the game plan was formed," Guidry says. "I don't know if I ever said three."

On June 12, he beat the A's again, 2–0, striking out eleven batters; in the first inning, he struck out the side on ten pitches. Guidry was now 10–0, with eight of his victories following a Yankee loss. Then, on June 17 against the Angels, Guidry threw one for the ages; he struck out 18 batters, an American League record for a left-handed pitcher, as the Yanks won 4–0. The fans in New York were so excited about the way Guidry was pitching, they started a new tradition that eventually spread around both leagues; when Guidry reached two strikes on a batter, they stood and applauded before each subsequent pitch, trying to will a strikeout to happen. Guidry never let on, but he liked the clapping; the fans got him pumped up.

The day after Guidry's 18-strikeout gem, Ed Figueroa (at 7–5, the Yankees' second-best starting pitcher) would get beaten by the Angels, 3–2, when the pitcher gave up a home run in the top of the ninth. In the dugout, Martin, who had wanted Figueroa to pitch around the batter, erupted, screaming, throwing helmets, and slamming bats to the ground. "The pitcher was told by [pitching coach Art Fowler] to walk the guy that hit the home run," a furious Martin told the press. "That's how we lost the game."

The next day, the Yankees would head to Fenway for their first series against the Red Sox, trailing Boston by seven games. They were a battered group: Hunter's arm remained painful, Gullett was an ongoing question mark, Dick Tidrow had a jammed thumb on his pitching hand, Munson's right knee ached constantly, Bucky Dent had reinjured his hamstring, and Willie Randolph had torn cartilage in his right knee.

It wasn't exactly how the Yankees wanted to head into a series against a hated rival, a three-game matchup that some were already saying could determine the outcome of their season.

CHAPTER 6

THE SECOND INNING

Reggie Jackson had flied to Carl Yastrzemski in left to end the Yankee half of the first, but the ball he hit might well have carried over the Green Monster if the wind, blowing from left to right, hadn't knocked it down. Now, as Graig Nettles approached the plate to start the top of the second, the wind changed direction 180 degrees, and was blowing from right to left. That was good for right-handed hitters hoping to take advantage of the short left field, but bad for the left-hitting Nettles.

Curly-haired and handsome, the thirty-four-year-old Nettles, a native of San Diego, had been drafted by the Twins in 1965. He played for the organization, both at Denver in the minors and in Minnesota with the Twins, under Billy Martin. "For the first three weeks, I hated him," Nettles would say. "I didn't like his style. He was loud and nothing like the first two managers I played for. But in three weeks, he turned the club around. He started us winning, and the more I played for him, the more I liked him."

Apparently thinking that Nettles was a subpar fielder, the Twins traded him to Cleveland in December 1969—Martin had been fired by that point—where in 1971 he set a league record for most assists in a season, 412. But after absorbing Billy Martin's passion to win, Nettles found the Indians a letdown. "Cleveland," he once said, "was the type of place where everybody was thrilled if we finished at five hundred." Nettles played well for the Indians, but in 1972 he clashed with Cleveland manager Ken Aspromonte and had an off year, and the Indians sent him to the Yankees. Nettles called the trade "a new lease on life." When the Indians announced that they had 75,000 fans at opening day in 1973, Nettles joked, "If they had 75,000 for the opener in Cleveland, they had to give away 300,000 free tickets." Indians owner Nick Mileti responded, "That's the reason we got rid of Graig. He's not a positive thinker." It was probably just as well for Nettles that he rarely spoke to the press; when he did, he couldn't help but be sarcastic, funny, and candid, which fans appreciated but owners did not. "If you haven't got a sense of humor, you're dead," he would explain.

You needed humor to survive on Steinbrenner's Yankees. Nettles agreed with Martin: the new owner valued publicity and controversy more than skill on the field, and that could wear you down. Nettles didn't get a lot of publicity, but his play had improved steadily since he arrived in 1973. At the plate, he was a powerful hitter with a smooth home run stroke. His 32 homers led the American League in 1976; the next year, he hit 37 and finished second behind Jim Rice, who had 39.

And in the field, Nettles was a marvel, a third baseman with fantastic range, quick reflexes, and a powerful arm who constantly endeavored to improve by studying hitters, observing their habits, and positioning himself accordingly. Yes, he was quick, but because he knew where to play hitters, he looked even quicker. When Guidry was pitching, he and Dent had a system worked out. Because right-handers would invariably pull Guidry's slider, Nettles had to play closer to the line than when Guidry threw his fastball, which they rarely pulled. But from his angle at third, he couldn't see the sign that Munson was putting down. Dent, however, could. So when he saw Munson call for the slider, he'd call out "Puff," Nettles's nickname, and Nettles would know. Dent was an excellent fielder, but Nettles played on an even higher level. The third baseman was renowned for his acrobatic leaps, his body parallel to the ground, glove arm outstretched. "I never saw him miss a ball when he dove at it," Dent would remember. "Other guys would knock it down, but he always caught it."

Off the field, Nettles was less fluid, and could come across as aloof and distant to those who didn't know him. He was uncomfortable with the press, and disliked being interviewed. His teammates called him Puff because he got dressed and left the locker room so quickly after games. "I don't seek publicity," he said in 1977. "I think the more interviews you make and the more you get your name in the paper by saying things, the more pressure you put on yourself." At the same time, after a contract dispute with Steinbrenner, he had come to believe that not being outspoken was costing him money—that Steinbrenner had actually created an economic incentive for his players to stir up trouble in the press. "In dealing with our owner, you have to be flamboyant, you have to make headlines, to make money," he said. "You can't expect to just do a good job and be paid for it. You have to do a little something extra. George Steinbrenner doesn't pay you for doing a good job, he pays you for being controversial."

That was primarily a reference to Jackson, whom Nettles thought talented but obnoxious. "Reggie came to New York to make himself into a star," Nettles would say. "He knew how to play the game of baseball, and he knew how to play the game of publicity, too." It wasn't so much the value of Jackson's contract that caused dissension, Nettles explained, but his ego. "Some players will not respect the manager, no matter who he is," Nettles said in 1984. "Reggie is one of those players." Catfish Hunter had also signed a huge contract, yet he was quickly accepted by the Yankees. "He didn't want to create a lot of hoopla around himself," Nettles explained. "He wanted to fit in with the guys right away, and he did. He was a very easy guy to like."

Nettles would not say the same about Mike Torrez. He had been irritated by Torrez's derogatory postseason comments about the Yankees, and when interviewed by ABC before the playoff, he said so. "I had a lot of respect for Mike last year, and I lost a lot of respect for Mike over the winter," Nettles explained. "He had some bad things to say about us as a team and individually, too. Rather than thanking us for the job we did for him in getting him a nice contract with the Red Sox, he turned around and badmouthed us. It really hurt a lot of the guys on this club. They lost a lot of respect for him that way. But we know he's a good pitcher and we'd like to beat him more than anybody on that club."

As he watched Nettles come to the plate, Torrez hadn't heard those remarks. He was cautious about pitching to Nettles, who was having a fine season, batting .278, with 27 home runs and 93 runs batted in. He also led the Yankees with 13 game-winning base hits. Like most left-handed hitters, Nettles liked the low fastball, so Torrez didn't want to give him one. If he threw him a fastball at all, he would keep it away from Nettles, a pull hitter. Torrez wanted to throw breaking balls, and if he got two strikes on Nettles, he'd come with the curve as his out-pitch. "I didn't want to make a mistake because he loved the ball in the middle of the plate and down," Torrez would say. "You had to throw him breaking pitches, get ahead of him."

His first pitch was a fastball shoulder-high and inside, well out of the strike zone, pushing Nettles off the plate. Torrez didn't want him to get comfortable. The next pitch, a breaking ball, fooled Nettles, who swung, tried to check his swing, and popped the ball up to Rick Burleson. Slightly struggling with the sun, Burleson made the catch without flipping up his sunglasses.

First baseman Chris Chambliss was the sixth batter. Along with Willie Randolph, Roy White, Bucky Dent, and to some extent Nettles, Chambliss was part of the Yankees' quiet constituency. He rarely spoke to the press, and when he did, his remarks were so carefully chosen that they never produced any uproar. Like Nettles, Chambliss was another lefty—the Yankee lineup was designed to take advantage of the short right field fence in Yankee Stadium—brought over in 1974 by Gabe Paul from the Indians, where he had been rookie of the year in 1971. The trade, in which the Yankees sent four pitchers to the Indians for Chambliss, Dick Tidrow, and pitcher Cecil Upshaw, had been deeply unpopular with the Yankee players, who grumbled that they'd lost half their pitching staff. But Chambliss was a modest and hardworking man who soon won over his new teammates. Then, in 1976, he etched a place for himself in Yankee history by hitting a bottom-of-the-ninth, game-winning home run against the Royals in Game Five of the playoffs. Chambliss's shot put the Yankees back in the World Series for the first time since 1964, and so many jubilant Yankee fans poured onto the field that Chambliss never even got to round the bases.

Torrez thought Chambliss a typical left-handed hitter, with one caveat: he liked the ball up in the zone more than most lefties did. So Torrez would spot his fastball on the outside corner, and mix up his pitches, making sure to keep the fastball low. Chambliss had more than respectable numbers for the season—a .274 batting average with 12 home runs and 90 runs batted in—but Torrez knew that he had been slumping the past few weeks and hoped to keep him off balance. Chambliss was 3 for his last 24, singles all.

Torrez and Fisk went to work. The first pitch was a slider inside for ball one. Then came a breaking ball, which Chambliss swung at and missed. A fastball was barely inside, 2–1. Fisk called for the same pitch again, and Chambliss jumped on it, pulling a vicious line drive down the line. But first baseman George Scott reacted so quickly, it took the crowd a half second to realize that he'd speared the ball. Chambliss shook his head in frustration and trotted back to the Yankee dugout.

Batting seventh, switch-hitting Roy White approached the plate from the left-hand side. Once, White had been a Yankee star. In 1968, he replaced Mickey Mantle as the team's cleanup hitter. In 1971, when he was making $50,000 a year, he was the highest-paid Yankee but for pitcher Mel Stottlemyre. Seven years later, he was a consistent and good player who was either overlooked because of his mild demeanor or faulted for his ineffectual throwing arm. An arm like Venus de Milo's, *Sports Illustrated* had said, which bothered White deeply, and he did everything he could to compensate for his soft tosses. White learned to charge balls hit to him in left, to put some momentum on his throws. He practiced in the outfield every day, backing up and throwing, hoping to strengthen an arm that was never going to match that of, say, Reggie Jackson, who never had to work at it and didn't. "Roy was underrated," Gene Michael would insist. "He was a complete player except for the arm strength, and that's a nice asset, but it isn't something you can't live without." White did everything else well, just not exceptionally well. "I don't have the power to hit 30 home runs, but I can hit 20," he said in 1976. "I can steal 20 bases but not 50, and I've hit .290 four times, but not .300 even once."

Born December 27, 1943, White, a light-skinned black man, grew up in Compton, California, and had he been one of the sport's greats his story would be the stuff of myth. As a boy, he came down with polio and survived. He was small but tough. Playing in his backyard, he'd hit stones with his bat, pretending to be Stan Musial batting lefty or DiMaggio batting righty. He and his friends would play ball by wrapping tape around an old sock. His yard wasn't very big, so White pretended that it was Ebbets Field, legendary home of the Brooklyn Dodgers. A friend's yard was larger; it became Yankee Stadium.

The Yankees drafted White out of Compton's Centennial High School in 1961, and he spent four years in the minors, mostly as an infielder. Later, when his arm was doubted, White would remind people that he wasn't playing his original position. The team called him up in late 1965, and at spring training the next year White got the seal of approval from Yankee greats. "I like that nice, smooth batting stroke he's got," Joe DiMaggio told reporters. Yankee press reports touted him as the fastest player on the team, although that wasn't saying a lot at the time. The Yankees had always been a team built around power, not speed.

White was a good player on a bad team. In 1965, the Yankees finished sixth; in 1966, tenth; in 1967, ninth. He was quiet, diligent, constantly trying to improve his game, but he would never be great, and while the Yankees promoted White as a star at a time when they were in desperate need of one, they didn't always treat him correspondingly. In the spring of 1967, the team actually traded White to the Dodgers, only to get him back in August to fill in for a hurt starter. This time, he stuck with the Yankees, and over the years, White improved. He made the All-Star team in 1969 and 1970, seasons in which he hit .290 and .296 respectively, with 7 and 22 home runs. Always he would do what the team asked of him—playing left, first base, third. But he never felt appreciated or secure, and after Martin became manager, White saw less and less playing time. "Billy was just playing me against left-handers, but my left side was really my most productive side at the plate," White recalled. Martin blamed it on Steinbrenner. The owner, he said, just didn't like White. "I remember going into Billy's office one time and complaining about not being in the lineup," White said. "He put the blame on George—'You're one of my guys, I know you play hard for me, but the Boss is against you being in there.' " Perhaps the hardest part of hearing that excuse was not knowing if it was true. Martin had a reputation for being evasive and dishonest when confronted by someone who didn't like one of his decisions; he could have been pinning the blame on Steinbrenner. On the other hand, Steinbrenner might have been to blame, because White was the type of player Steinbrenner didn't like—too quiet, didn't put fannies in the seats—but Martin usually did: a veteran who could lay down a bunt, ran the bases well, knew how to advance the runner—the fundamentals about which Martin cared so deeply.

White would hit lefty against Torrez. He didn't have much power, but he liked fastballs over the plate to slightly inside. Torrez started him with a fastball too far inside to hit. White spun back away from the pitch, which was a replica of the first pitch Torrez threw to Nettles. Establishing territory was worth the ball one; it would keep the hitters from getting too comfortable in the batter's box, and set them up for the outside pitch.

Torrez followed with his slider, which White swung over. White fouled off the next pitch, a curve on the outside corner. The count was 1–2. So far, Torrez had gone inside and high; inside and low; outside and low. The variety was an excellent sign for him; he couldn't do that if he wasn't locating the ball well. The nerves that caused him to walk Mickey Rivers on four pitches were gone.

Now, on his fourth pitch to White, he came back with the slider again. White swung. He didn't come close.

It was a one-two-three inning for Torrez, who required just nine pitches to get through it. Except for Chambliss's line drive, the Yankees appeared overmatched.

He looks tough, White thought. *He's hitting his spots*. If Torrez could keep pitching like that, the Yankees were in trouble.

Ron Guidry would, in the bottom of the second inning, face the fourth, fifth and sixth batters in the Red Sox order: Carl Yastrzemski, Fred Lynn, and Carlton Fisk.

As thirty-nine-year-old Carl Yastrzemski walked up to the plate, the Boston fans stood and applauded in appreciation. Their cheering was not just for his season numbers, which were good but not great: a batting average of .275, with 16 home runs and 79 runs batted in. Nor was it simply for his toughness: with his wrists taped almost to the elbow, Yastrzemski looked like a burn victim. Underneath his jersey, he wore a brace to protect grinding vertebrae in his spine. It didn't matter: at an age when most players were long retired, Yastrzemski had played 144 games that season, dividing his time between left field, first base, designated hitter, and even center field. At five feet ten and 180 pounds, Yaz was still remarkably fit.

The Boston fans cheered because, after some years of skepticism, they had come to appreciate Yastrzemski. Even as the world of baseball was changing in ways that seemed to sever its present from traditions both bad and good, he had become the embodiment of Red Sox history. When Yaz joined the team in 1961, an astonishing seventeen years earlier, he was hailed as the next Ted Williams. The comparison would hound him for most of his career, because Yastrzemski was not Ted Williams. (Who was?) Yaz had his own virtues, and by 1978 they had become clear. He was not always friendly or social or good with the press. (Williams was even less so.) But he was competitive and determined, he was a better outfielder than Williams had ever been, and he had become a fixture of the Boston landscape, an avatar of all the intense and often conflicting passions felt by the team's supporters. Yaz had shared moments of delirium with the Red Sox fans, as well as crushing disappointments. He was like Fenway Park itself—aging, imperfect, a little cranky, but idiosyncratic and rare and wonderful. Now, at this moment when success was again so close, home against the hated Yankees on this glorious day, the fans were with him.

He had grown up in a family and a community that themselves felt like part of a vanishing America. He was the son of a potato farmer and his wife, and grew up in Bridgehampton, Long Island, then a working-class town with a year-round population of about 3,000. While most of his teammates were baby boomers, born in the postwar 1940s and '50s, Yastrzemski was born August 22, 1939—a child of the Great Depression. His family lived in a six-room house a couple of miles away from their farm. The house sat on about three acres of land. Maybe half of that was occupied by a garden, since the Yastrzemskis grew their own vegetables, canning and jarring what they needed for the winter. They slaughtered and butchered their own cows. Afternoons when he wasn't in school, Carl would help on the farm, lifting bags of potatoes onto tractor carts. "I used to love those little sacks," he would say. "Christ, I was like twelve years old, picking those things up. Seventy-five pounds. I kept saying to myself—and this is why I loved it—this is going to help me get strong, help me make it to the big leagues. It was going to help me in baseball."

For baseball was his passion, just as it was his father's. As a boy, he was a Yankee fan. There were the Giants and the Dodgers to choose from as well, and some of his cousins and uncles rooted for them. Not Yastrzemski. He and his dad would make the two-hundred-mile roundtrip into the city to watch DiMaggio and then Mantle at the stadium. In the summer, when he was on the farm, he'd bring his bat, and when he had a break, he'd fill a bushel basket with rocks. At almost the same time that, on the other side of the country, Roy White was hitting stones in his backyard in Compton, Yastrzemski would swing away in his boyhood fields. He'd stand in the warm dirt, crouch low, and swing lefty, like Musial, or reverse himself and hit right-handed, pretending he was DiMaggio. When he ran out of rocks, he'd go pick up more. Fill the bushel basket. Do it again.

He invented contraptions to help him practice. He'd drive a nail through a ball, tie a string to the nail, and hang the ball from the ceiling of his garage up a hill from the house, practicing his swings with a lead bat. He'd get his uncles to pitch to him with a tennis ball while he batted with a stick. They'd throw as hard as they could—twenty-five feet away, fifteen feet away. They couldn't strike him out. When it was warm, he would tie a ball to a thirty-foot cord and hit it off a tee. That way, he could see if he was hitting line drives. And when winter came, he'd put on a heavy parka and go out to that garage. Before dinner, he'd take his lead bat and swing at the ball dangling from the ceiling, seeing his breath in the cold air. His mother would call him inside to eat. When the meal was over, he'd go back to the garage. Swing. Swing. Swing. One hundred times. Two hundred.

He played football and baseball at Bridgehampton High, until his father found out about the football and stormed onto the practice field. *Take those goddamn pads off! You're not going to break your collarbone playing football!* When Yastrzemski was a senior, the Yankees came calling. They offered him $60,000. Yastrzemski wanted to take it. He thought about that short fence in right field in Yankee Stadium, how the power alleys to right center and left center suited his hitting strengths. Carl Yastrzemski, Sr. wanted no less than $100,000. When the exasperated Yankee scout threw his pencil in the air—*the Yankees will never pay that!*—Mr. Yastrzemski threw the scout out of the house.

At the strong suggestion of the family priest, Carl was soon bound for Notre Dame. He didn't stay long. After his freshman year, Yastrzemski was in demand. The Reds wanted him. So did the Phillies, the Tigers, the Dodgers, the Giants, even the Yankees. Carl's father found a reason to object to every team but one; the priest wanted the Red Sox. During Thanksgiving break, sophomore year, the Sox brought him to Fenway. There was snow on the field. His father said it would be a great place for him to hit; Yastrzemski wasn't so sure. Carl Sr. told him to sign with the Red Sox or go back to school. On November 29, 1958, for a $108,000 bonus, $5,000 a year for two seasons in the minors, and money to finish college if he wanted to, he signed. The Sox brought him up in 1960, Ted Williams' last season, and gave him the locker next to Williams. The legend didn't talk much, could go for days without saying a word. But ask him about hitting and he'd deliver an encyclopedia. Yastrzemski was playing second base and thought he was playing pretty well. Then they sent him back down to the minors. "Bull, absolute bull," Yastrzemski said. They sent him anyway. Only when he arrived in Deland, Minnesota, did they tell him that he was there to learn left field—Williams's position. In 1961, Williams was gone and Yastrzemski was the Red Sox left fielder.

The great Williams had always been far more interested in hitting than fielding, and Yastrzemski would never be the hitter that Williams was, not even close. Williams had a .344 lifetime average, Yaz, .285. But he would come to roam Fenway's left field better than anyone before him. Playing left in Fenway meant, of course, playing the Monster—a thirty-seven-foot-high wall with a twenty-three-foot screen on top, old and unpredictable. The first twenty-five feet of it were concrete. Above that were sheets of tin, held together with two-by-fours and exposed rivets. When a batter hit a ball toward the wall, Yastrzemski had to judge how high up it was going to hit, because the ball bounced hard off the concrete, less so off the tin. The angles mattered, too. Balls hit by right-handed batters rebounded differently than balls hit by left-handed batters. And if a ball hit one of those rivets, or the tin in front of a two-by-four . . . you couldn't practice for that. You just hoped that instinct and experience would count for something.

Then, in Game Six of the 1975 World Series, Fred Lynn almost knocked himself unconscious chasing a Ken Griffey line drive into the center field wall, and Red Sox owner Tom Yawkey turned to scouting director Haywood Sullivan and said, "Those walls must be padded by next season." During the off-season, the Green Monster was rebuilt with fiberglass and padding, which gave balls hit off it a truer bounce. That made playing left a little easier—but only a little. That's because Yaz also had to play the Corner, where the wall met the left field seats. Making a play in the Corner was tough. The fans were just feet away, yelling, waving, grabbing for the ball with caps and gloves. But Yaz mastered that, too, learning how to play balls that rattled around in the Corner, pushing off the wall with his right foot to put added oomph into his throws. He knew that the grass at Fenway was immaculately maintained, and he could trust the bounce from it. He learned to deke runners, pretending that he was going to catch a ball that he knew would hit the wall, then trying to throw out runners advancing to third from first on a single off the wall, or trying to score from second. Other times, Yaz would drop his head as if to suggest that he was giving up, the batter had hit a home run, when he knew the ball was bouncing off the wall . . . and if the hitter fell for the head fake, went into his home run trot, Yastrzemski would catch the bounce and throw the runner out as he suddenly scrambled to get to second. Almost always Yastrzemski played a very shallow left field, not far behind the shortstop, knowing just how many steps he could come in and still retreat in time to make a play at the wall. That gave him an advantage catching shallow fly balls and throwing home. His arm was strong and accurate; Roy White thought it one of the most accurate in baseball. In 1977, the season Yastrzemski turned thirty-eight, he played an entire season in the outfield without making an error.

At the plate, he'd had great seasons. He'd won the American League batting title in 1963, 1967, and 1968. Still, for a time in the early 1970s, the Boston media and fans were down on him. The reporters said he quit playing hard when the team was out of contention; the fans booed. Once, it got so bad that Yaz ran into left field with cotton balls in his ears, then made a show of pulling them out in front of the fans. He was Mr. Red Sox, and if the team was bad, then the fans—and in Boston, that usually included the sportswriters—took their frustrations out on him. When the team got better—certainly when the Sox went to the Series in '75—that went away. And as free agency kicked in, fans came to realize that having a player who'd played for one team only since 1961 was special. If Reggie Jackson epitomized what many fans didn't like about modern baseball, Yaz stood for the virtue of constancy.

His hitting had tailed off somewhat with age, but in 1977 he had still hit .296 in 558 at-bats—remarkable for a thirty-eight-year-old. He'd always been primarily a fastball hitter. Now, he was almost exclusively so. "He was a dead fastball hitter," Fred Lynn recalled. "When he was older, against lefties, he wouldn't even swing at a breaking ball, ever. If you threw him three breaking balls in a row, he's out. He'd just sit there and wait for the fastball and yank it." Yaz himself would admit that he wouldn't swing at a breaking pitch unless he had two strikes on him, and sometimes not even then. Generally with two strikes, he'd look for a fastball, and if something slower was coming, he'd try to adjust. You could do that, go from fast to slow. But if you guessed breaking ball and the fastball came, you could never adjust in time. The pitch had already beaten you.

Yastrzemski knew Guidry well. The first time he'd seen the pitcher, late in the 1976 season, he'd homered off him. Of course, that was a different Guidry then, without the slider that was not only devastating on its own, but made the fastball less predictable and therefore more dangerous. Still, Yaz had seen the new, improved Guidry plenty of times in 1977 and 1978.

He's going to throw me high, Yaz thought as he approached the plate. He wanted to hold back on that high fastball. *If it's up around the letters, that's the pitch you have to lay off, because it will go out of the strike zone.* Yastrzemski normally used a 35-inch bat that weighed 33 ounces, but that day he had switched to a larger bat, one Jim Rice normally used, that was 36-inches long and weighed 35 ounces. *He'll supply the power,* Yastrzemski thought. *Get the head of the bat out, get the head on the ball, let him take care of the power.*

Yastrzemski didn't usually get nervous before games, not after all these years. But before this one, he was, he would admit, "damn scared." It was the biggest game of his career, "without a doubt." He was thirty-nine years old, playing on a team at its peak. Who knew what could happen next season? The Sox could lose players to injury, to free agency. Carl Yastrzemski had been trying to win a World Series for seventeen years. Twice his team had lost in the seventh game of the Series. This season might be his last, best shot; this Red Sox team may have been even better than the Impossible Dream team of 1967 or the underdogs of 1975. If they made it into the playoffs, they would face Kansas City, a team that had won seven fewer games than Boston had despite its presence in a weak division. And if the Red Sox made it to the World Series, there was no Bob Gibson to face three times, no Big Red Machine looming ahead. They could end their seventy-year World Series drought, and Yaz could get his World Series ring.

But first, they had to beat the Yankees.

As a younger man, Yastrzemski had held the bat up high, so that his hands were behind his left ear. From there, the bat had farther to travel to make contact, particularly when Yaz was swinging at low pitches. When he was young and quick, that didn't matter so much. But starting in 1974, Yaz had dropped his hands to chest level, gaining a fraction of a second to compensate for the quickness that he'd lost as his body slowed. A hurt shoulder in 1975 had made it virtually impossible for him to hit to the opposite field and almost as difficult to hit to center. Now Yastrzemski's power zone was strictly waist-high or higher, the middle of the plate or inside; the bad shoulder made it impossible for him to hit opposite-field home runs. If a pitch came low and inside, and Yaz was looking to drive a ball, he'd generally let it go. Age had made him more selective, more patient. That was how Yastrzemski had stayed in the game for so long; by realizing what he could no longer do, and adapting.

For his part, Guidry was confident about how to pitch to Yastrzemski: get ahead of him with the fastball, then throw the slider. He knew that Yaz would guess fastball almost all the time, so if you could set him up with inside fastballs, he'd swing on the slider breaking late and outside. The only problem would come if you hung a slider or missed your spot with the fastball.

Munson called a slider. It was outside, for a ball.

Be disciplined, Yastrzemski reminded himself. *You don't hit it out against Guidry. Up the middle, up the middle, up the middle.*

He knew how hard it was to pull Guidry. "His ball," he would say, "just exploded on you," as if a rocket booster kicked in a split second before the ball reached the plate. Guidry came next with the fastball, hoping to jam Yaz. But the ball wasn't inside enough—Guidry missed his spot. The pitch was heading across the plate when Yastrzemski swung and connected. The ball rocketed off the bat, a line drive pulled sharply down the left field line. As a hopeful Yaz toted his bat more than halfway toward first, the only question was whether the arcing ball would stay fair. Not by much, it did. First base coach Johnny Pesky jumped in the air, the fans roared, and Yastrzemski jogged quickly around the bases.

The Sox led, 1–0. Yaz had pulled a home run off a pitcher who almost never gave up home runs—just 12 in 269 innings up to that point, and only one of those home runs had been hit by a left-handed hitter. Players on both sides knew what that meant: Guidry's fastball wasn't up to par. That short rest might be hurting him already, and he'd only faced four batters.

Yankee second baseman Brian Doyle thought, *Uh-oh. He better do some pitching now. He doesn't have his great stuff.* The Yankees would have to step up their defense too, Doyle knew. If Guidry wasn't throwing with his usual power, the defensive players would have to make adjustments.

In right field, Lou Piniella, playing in place of the defensively challenged Reggie Jackson, took note. If Yaz had been able to homer off a Guidry fastball, the Red Sox might all be pulling the ball a little more than usual. He resolved that when left-handers came to the plate, he would play a few steps closer to the left field line than he normally would.

On the mound, Guidry chewed his tobacco, held his glove against his chest, and looked as unfazed as he did after any other pitch. Inside, he was ticked off. He felt he was throwing as hard as always. The pitch had just been a mistake—too hittable. That was the disadvantage of being a power pitcher, he would say later. "The harder you throw, the harder the ball goes when someone hits it well."

Carlton Fisk was up next. With a .283 average, 20 home runs, and 88 runs batted in, he was a dangerous hitter, and he looked like it, tall and strong, leaning in so that the top half of his body was almost on top of the plate. But Guidry thought Fisk's height was a weakness; Fisk had trouble reaching low pitches. So Guidry liked to bust him inside once in a while, just to keep him honest, then go away with the fastball. And once he got ahead of the count, Guidry would use the downward-dropping slider to finish Fisk off.

But his pitches weren't cooperating. Guidry threw a fastball high and outside, not even close to the strike zone. His second pitch was a slider, low for ball two. Falling behind made it harder to throw a slider, so next came a fastball on the outside corner of the plate. Fisk swung and pulled the ball to left, but the pitch had been just outside enough that Fisk couldn't decisively drive it; Roy White made the catch at the warning track.

Fred Lynn, another left-handed hitter, came to the plate. He'd had a fine year: a batting average of .296, with 22 home runs and 81 runs batted in. Guidry threw him a slider, which Lynn smacked to dead-center field. Mickey Rivers had to race back to make the play at the warning track. There were two outs, but the Red Sox had driven three hard balls in a row off Guidry.

I hit the ball right on the screws, Lynn thought. *This is looking pretty good—our two lefties, me and Yaz, hit the ball hard the first time up.*

Guidry, however, was not all that worried. He was throwing strikes, which was more important to him than blowing the ball by people. If the Red Sox had hit the ball hard, that didn't much bother him. The Red Sox always hit the ball hard. It was better to get them to put the ball in play, let your defense do its job, than to walk men and lose control of the game.

Third baseman Butch Hobson came up, another Red Sox right-handed power hitter. He'd hit .250 for the season, with 17 home runs, and 80 runs batted in, and he'd have hit more if it weren't for the bone chips in his right elbow, the one that provides most of the force for a right-handed swing. As the season had progressed, the elbow problem had gotten worse, and Hobson's offensive production had fallen. Hobson quickly fell behind 0–2 on the count, and after that, he was easy. Guidry threw him two fastballs on the outside corner. Hobson let the first go for a ball, but guarding the plate, he swung at the second and hit an easy bouncer to Nettles at third. Guidry was out of the inning. Still, the Red Sox were winning, and the fans roared their approval.

CHAPTER 7

The Origins of a Rivalry

There were certainly rational reasons why the first series of the 1978 season between the Red Sox and the Yankees mattered so much to both teams. Despite Boston's strong start, they had not put the Yankees entirely in their rearview mirror, and the three games against New York represented an opportunity to extend their seven-game lead over the world champion Yankees. The Yankees needed a credible performance because they looked like a team with more at stake—a team already afflicted with more dissension and pressure than were present in Boston. The Red Sox gave every indication of being a team playing up to its potential, with perhaps a smidgen of room to get even better; the Yankees looked close to the brink of a fatal downward slide.

But not all the reasons for the intensity of emotion surrounding the upcoming series were rational. In addition to the pressures of the moment, this first New York–Boston series mattered because, to these teams and their fans, every game against each other mattered. The Red Sox and the Yankees were baseball's oldest and most impassioned rivals, and there could be no such thing as a casual meeting between them. "When you play the Yankees," Butch Hobson said, "it was going to be war, both on the field and in the stands."

For the first twenty years of the twentieth century, the Red Sox had been the better team. But steadily, over the course of the century, the advantage had tilted to the Yankees and stayed there. In 1903, the Red Sox, then known as the Americans, won the first World Series against the Pittsburgh Pirates. The next year, the two teams met on the last day of the regular season to determine the pennant winner. The Sox beat the New York Highlanders, as the Yankees were called at the time, that day, but because of a dispute with the National League no World Series was played. Still, the Sox were the dominant team, and between 1912 and 1918, they won four more World Series. But then, in 1920, came the disastrous trade of Babe Ruth, followed in short order by the awesome, overpowering Yankee teams of the 1920s, which would then be followed by decades of frustration for the Red Sox. Boston would win the pennant just three times in almost six post-Ruth decades. Each time the Sox lost the World Series four games to three. The Yankees, however, won pennants again and again and again, including that devastating year of 1949, when New York beat the Red Sox twice the last two days of the season—October 2 and 3—to win the pennant by a game. But as intense as the competition was, it was still civil. "There was respect" between the two teams, Red Sox legend Johnny Pesky recalled. "It seemed every time the Yankees needed a great player, they found one. Joe DiMaggio, one of the finest players ever created—you had to respect Joe DiMaggio. Billy Martin, he was a rascal but he was a good player. If you didn't like Mickey Mantle, you didn't like your wife, and if you didn't like Yogi Berra, you didn't like your sister. Those Yankees were good guys and great players. That's the way I looked at it."

The 1950s were dominated by New York just as the 1920s had been, but both franchises fielded competitive teams. In the 1960s, the intensity of the rivalry dimmed somewhat, largely because, for much of the decade, the two teams simply weren't very good, or when one team was strong, the other was weak. "When we played back in those days against Boston, it was a rivalry, but we just weren't good enough to be the top two teams," Yankee shortstop Gene Michael would recall. In the first half of the decade, the Yankees appeared in the World Series from 1960 to 1964, winning in 1961 and 1962. "When I first came to the Red Sox in 1961," Carl Yastrzemski said, "it wasn't much of a rivalry. They had Mantle, Whitey Ford, Moose Skowron, Elston Howard. The Yankees just pounded us all the time."

But after CBS bought the team in 1964, the Yankees disintegrated fast, the result of aging stars, a barren farm system, and poor management. In Boston's miraculous 1967 season, the Yankees were never a factor; they finished next to last, barely edging out the Athletics. In 1968, things were back to mediocre for both teams, as the Sox finished fourth and the Yankees fifth. "As our broadcasters always used to say, 'Plenty of good seats still available,' " former Yankee public relations man Marty Appel recalled.

In the 1970s, however, the Yankees and the Red Sox not only improved, but began competing—fiercely, intensely, angrily competing—against each other for dominance in the American League. A central element in each team's rise was the introduction of a new catcher. For the Yankees, it was Thurman Munson; for the Red Sox, Carlton Fisk. The two men would come to embody the rejuvenation of their teams, and because each developed a smoldering, furious dislike of the other, they came to personify the reinvigorated rivalry between Boston and New York. By 1978, the hostility between Fisk and Munson had spread more generally between the two teams, so that the games the Yankees and the Red Sox played weren't just about the standings or about money or statistics—they were blood feuds.

"I respected the Yankees," Carl Yastrzemski said. "Respected 'em, but didn't like 'em. You wanted to beat the Yankees more than any other team. Not only did you want to win, but you wanted to grind 'em into the ground."

"We did not want to lose to the Boston Red Sox," Bucky Dent said. "You knew the history. You knew the two teams don't like each other. They hated the Yankees and we hated the Red Sox."

"These players really didn't like each other," Red Sox team historian Dick Bresciani said. "They had disdain for each other."

Munson was slightly older than Fisk and the first to make it to the major leagues. He was not a glamorous man, not the kind of ballplayer that George Steinbrenner hired to put "fannies in the seats," as Steinbrenner had said of Reggie Jackson. He was, much of the time, stubborn, sullen, rude, grumpy, and moody. In May 1978, Dave Anderson of the *New York Times* said of Munson that he was the kind of person who "didn't know how to say hello until it was time to say goodbye." And yet, on a team filled with veterans and athletes of enormous talent, Munson was the undisputed leader. By 1978, even Reggie Jackson seemed to accept that fact, and was trying to take a lower profile than he had the previous season. "If you had to say who was the one leader on the club, it was Thurman," Lou Piniella would say. Probably no Yankee was more respected by opponents. "He was just full of life," Orioles pitcher Jim Palmer said. "A consummate professional. He always used to give you a little wink and then just go to war." Even Red Sox pitcher Dennis Eckersley found it hard to dislike Munson. "He was a guy's guy," Eckersley said. "Kind of a sloppy guy. Everything was nonchalant with him. But meanwhile, he's sly as a fox."

Thurman Munson was born in Akron, Ohio, on June 7, 1947, the youngest of four children, to Darrell and Sue Munson. His father was a truck driver, frequently gone, driving from Canton where the family lived, to both coasts. Darrell Munson was a hard man. "When Dad was around," Munson would later recall, "everyone in the house, including Mom, was intimidated. It seemed as though her chief responsibility was to keep us out of trouble so that Dad wouldn't get mad at us."

Darrell Munson was a ballplayer, convinced that he could have made the majors if war, work, and responsibility had not intervened, and he made sure that Thurman played baseball from an early age. When he was back from the road, he'd practice with Thurman, hitting ground balls to his son for hours at a time, and if one kicked up and bloodied Thurman's nose or jaw, so be it. You wiped the blood dry, and you got ready for the next one. No matter how good Thurman was— and he was good, better than good, that was clear early on—he could never please his father, because the better Thurman got, the more Darrell seemed to resent his son for it. "To my face, he would ridicule me," Munson later recalled. "But to everybody else, he would say, 'Hey, that's my son.' " The mockery the boy heard shaped him far more than the compliments he did not.

At Canton Lehman High School, Munson was captain of the football, basketball, and baseball teams. He was proud of that trifecta, but he was just as proud, he would later insist, of the fact that he wrote poetry. "I'd write about children, or God, or things that required some sensitivity," Munson would say in his autobiography. Munson didn't look like a poet, but neither did he look much like an all-state shortstop, the position he played most frequently in high school. He had a heavy face and a stocky frame. His forehead was broad and flat, his eyes small and set deep in his face, and his hairline receding by the time he was twenty. Thurman Munson would have looked at home slicing up meat behind a deli counter or pulling the tap in a barroom, or, like his father, driving a truck—but on the diamond, he would never prompt comparison to Mickey Mantle or Ted Williams. "Munson was the Pigpen character," said Marty Appel, who helped write Munson's book. "The little squatty body, that's what they called him. He'd get dirty and grimy."

"Munson just didn't look like a player," Fred Lynn recalled. "He looked like he should be smoking a cigar, playing pool or something."

"You'd look at him in his underwear and you'd think, 'He's a professional athlete?' " teammate Brian Doyle said. "He looked like everything but an athlete."

Munson was well aware that he was less than statuesque. "I'm little, I'm pudgy, I don't look good doing things," he once told a reporter. "Those big tall guys look super."

At least one person liked the way Munson looked. When he was twelve, he met Diana Dominick, his future wife; they were both on "junior patrol," helping younger kids cross the street. The two hit it off immediately. "She was the only one who would play catch with me," Munson said. In sixth grade, Diana would practice writing "Mrs. Thurman Munson." She'd bicycle along with him when Munson went out on his paper route, delivering the *Canton Repository* after school. When training for baseball, Munson would run a mile from his house to Diana's, give her a kiss and catch his breath, then run back home. They were the only girlfriend and boyfriend that each ever had, and in 1968 they were married.

If Munson had wanted to continue playing football after high school, he could have gotten a scholarship virtually anywhere; football scholarships were far easier to come by than baseball ones. But he wanted to play baseball, and so he picked Kent State, one of the three schools to offer him a baseball scholarship. It also happened to be the closest to his home. Eventually giving up football and basketball, Munson became a full-time baseball player at Kent State, and a full-time catcher. As a senior, he was named all-American, which he would later say was one of the proudest moments of his life. He was competing against athletes from five thousand major colleges, he explained, and he was the catcher they chose to single out.

He was the Yankees' top pick in the 1968 draft, but even then Darrell Munson wasn't satisfied. The two, never close, had grown steadily more distant over the years, and Darrell's resentment of his son's success seemed to have overwhelmed the pride he once took in Thurman's accomplishments. When a Yankee scout came to Canton to offer Thurman a contact, he found Darrell lounging half dressed on the living room sofa. Thurman Munson's father looked at the scout and said, "He ain't too good on the pop flies, you know."

Signed for a $75,000 bonus and a $500-a-month salary, Munson would spend the 1968 season in the minors at Binghamton, New York, hitting .301. In 1969, he moved up to Triple A at Syracuse, where he hit .359 before joining the Yankees at the end of the season.

(The team was winding down the season, going nowhere.) Joining the Yankees for good in 1970, Munson got a salary increase to about $15,000 a year. "I always liked the Yankees," he said at the time. "They were cocky without being overbearing. I like to think I'm that way."

It had been some time since the Yankees had had a strong catcher; Munson was competing for a job against Jake Gibbs, who had been with the team since 1962 and in his ten-year career would compile a career batting average of .233, with totals of 25 homers and 146 runs batted in. The job was quickly Munson's. "I hope to be around for fifteen years," he said in an early interview. "I'd like to hit .300, but don't quote me and say I would." He quickly showed that he had grounds for a little cockiness. Hitting .302 on the season, he was chosen rookie of the year, the first American League catcher ever to win that honor. Meanwhile, the Yankees were improving: they won 93 games. But the Baltimore Orioles won a remarkable 108 that season, and New York finished second, fifteen games out of first. Even so, after just one season Munson had helped restore credibility to a struggling franchise.

It wasn't just his hitting that made Munson such a valuable addition. He was an outstanding defensive catcher, skilled at calling a game, quick to win the pitchers' trust, a student of the strengths and weaknesses of hitters around the league. Behind the plate, he was constantly chatting with the batters, always amiable, but trying to get into their heads. He'd tell them what pitch was coming, and sometimes he'd even be telling the truth. It kept the hitters off-balance. He'd say that he'd heard they were in a little slump, or that, well, they looked a little tired today. And Munson was even good at managing his manager. When Billy Martin joined the Yankees, Munson would make sure to indicate the location of close pitches to Martin, so that the manager wouldn't start screaming at umpires undeservedly, thus costing the Yankees more close calls.

In 1971, Munson played in 125 games and committed only one error, and that came at a play at the plate in which Andy Etchebarren of the Orioles knocked him unconscious, at which point Munson dropped the ball. His teammates joked that Munson woke up in the ambulance and tried to tag everyone in sight. But Munson took pride in his toughness; Darrell Munson had taught him to suck it up, to shut up about the pain and play on, and so he did. In another 1971 game, Charlie Spikes of the Indians slammed into Munson at the plate. The next day, you couldn't see the bone in Munson's right knee; the joint had become a swollen balloon of blood and pus. Two days later, Munson was behind the plate again.

But for all his success, all the awards he had won and would win, Munson still wanted more approval than he got—though he didn't like to admit it. At some point early in the 1970s, Darrell Munson simply disappeared; no one knew where he ran off to. After Thurman won the rookie of the year award, the only member of his immediate family to congratulate him was his sister Janice, who sent him a pair of cufflinks. By 1978, Janice would be the only member of his childhood family with whom he regularly spoke.

The family that he and Diana were creating mattered more to him. They would have three kids, girls Tracy and Kelly, and then a son, Michael, and when he was with them, their father, so tough on the field and surly in the locker room, was a changed man. He had no model of a loving parent, but he found within himself the ability to be a father in ways that Darrell Munson never could. Michael was a hyperactive boy who exhausted Diana by waking up ten, twelve times a night. But when Thurman was home, he would put his son to bed and say, "Michael, I don't want you getting up at night and calling Mommy." Michael would sleep through the night, and in the morning, when he woke up he would call for his father. "When I see that," Diana said at the time, "I know we need Thurman around."

With his teammates, Munson could be mischievous. "A lot of times, Thurman was devilish," Cliff Johnson remembered. "We'd be in batting practice in spring training, and cameramen and writers would be standing around watching, and he would be hitting balls in the cage like he was trying to hit those guys, just laughing and having fun and cracking up. Just being devilish. Just being Thurman."

Munson had a favorite t-shirt that epitomized his contrarian sense of humor, Bucky Dent recalled. It bore a picture of the cartoon character Yosemite Sam, with his long beard and his two smoking pistols, and it read, "I *hates* baseball," just the way Yosemite Sam used to say, "I *hates* rabbits."

"That t-shirt used to tickle me," Dent said. "Because that was his image. He reminded me of that—the guns smoking, that kind of thing. And when I think of him, that's how I think of him, in that t-shirt he used to wear."

When Munson felt slighted, he could respond with gestures of defiance and anger. Sometimes he simply seemed to want attention. After the 1972 season, Munson grew a mustache, later explaining, "The whole world was turning hippie, why shouldn't I?" (Some years later, in the 1977 season, Munson would extend that mustache to a beard, despite the fact that George Steinbrenner had forbidden his players to grow beards. At Martin's request, he shaved.) Munson could be testy with fans when he thought they didn't appreciate his contributions. In a 1976 game against Oakland, Munson hurled a ball into center field that allowed a runner to score from second. The next inning, he struck out. When some fans booed, Munson gave them the finger. At the plate the next day, Munson was greeted with a huge round of nonironic applause. New York fans appreciated a guy who told them where to go—at least when he was right—and they remembered what the Yankees had been like before Munson arrived. So the guy could be crude and rude. New Yorkers knew that you needed a tough exterior to survive in their city, and with Munson, they suspected—suspected, but never knew—that the shell was so tough only because the inside was so sensitive. He may have come from Ohio, and he was always longing to return home to his family, but Thurman Munson was a New Yorker through and through.

It would have been unthinkable for Carlton Fisk to salute Red Sox fans with an obscene gesture. Even during his contract holdout of 1976, when fans heaped abuse upon him, Fred Lynn, and Rick Burleson, Fisk kept his feelings to himself. Lynn didn't. He flipped the fans the bird more than once. Burleson would swear at them under his breath. But Carlton Fisk saved his emotions for umpires, pitchers, and opponents. He couldn't lash out at the New England fans. They were his people, and as disheartening as their opprobrium was, he could not turn against them. Doing that would be giving the finger to the world that shaped him.

He was born on December 26, 1947, in Bellows Falls, Vermont, but grew up across the Connecticut River in neighboring Charlestown, New Hampshire. His parents were Leona and Cecil Fisk, a machinist. The Fisks had six children, all of them athletic. Young Carlton played basketball and baseball; his heroes were the Celtics' Bill Russell and, of course, Ted Williams. It could be hardly otherwise, living in such a classic New England milieu. "Growing up where I grew up," Fisk once said, "you learned to hate the Yankees early."

Like Munson, Fisk was not at first a picturesque athlete, although he would become one. In fifth grade, he stood four feet eleven inches and weighed 120 pounds, and for that he earned the nickname Pudge, which would endure even after he had grown into his more imposing six-feet, 210-pound frame. Through high school, he gravitated toward basketball; Charlestown was not an ideal place in which to hone one's baseball skills. It had cold weather and snow for much of the year; when he could play baseball, Fisk played in sandlots and cow pastures. Baseball season was short in New Hampshire, never longer, according to Fisk's high school coach, than twelve games. In wanting to play professional baseball Fisk was competing less against other New Hampshire athletes than he was against boys from sun-drenched states such as Florida, Arizona, and California. In his entire amateur career, Fisk played in just 96 games, what one of those boys from the baseball states might rack up in a single year.

So for most of Fisk's youth, basketball was his priority—he played guard—and as hard as he worked at it, his father always pushed him to work harder. In one high school basketball game, Fisk scored 40 points and had 36 rebounds. "You missed four free throws," Cecil Fisk told him after the game. Asked about that comment some years later, Cecil was unapologetic. "In a close game, it's often decided by free throws. You've got to hit them."

In high school, Fisk was mostly a pitcher, but after starting at the University of New Hampshire on a basketball scholarship, he shifted to catcher. He just didn't have the metabolism for pitching. "I don't want to knock another guy's job, but I couldn't stand working only every three or four days or accept the uncertainty of the bullpen," he explained. "My temperament is such that I have to be in there every day." He was a terrific athlete, but not much of a student. "I'm one of those guys who doesn't like school," he said. He would not have to endure it for long. He was scouted by the A's, the Indians, the Reds, the Mets, the Orioles, and the Washington Senators, but all held back; it was well-known that there was only one team Fisk wanted to play for, one team for which he seemed destined to play. So when, in 1967, the Red Sox asked Fisk if he would leave college if they made him their top pick, he leaped at the chance. "I was delighted," he said. "I was going to leave school anyway."

He did minor league stints in towns from Greenville, South Carolina, to Waterloo, Iowa. While his defense was strong, his offense was erratic; Fisk blamed nagging injuries. In 1972, he started the season with the Red Sox as the team's third catcher, behind Duane Josephson, a .258 hitter with 23 home runs in eight seasons, and Bob Mont-gomery, who would hit 23 home runs in ten seasons. Josephson got hurt, and Montgomery, who had come up to the Sox in 1970, took over the job. Fisk would give him an occasional breather, until one day he beat the Yankees with a triple and it became apparent to everyone that the catcher of the future had become the catcher of the moment. In their entire history, the Red Sox had never really had a catcher who could anchor the team with both offensive and defensive prowess. "Until Carlton arrived," one local sportswriter wrote, "you could mail a ball to second base faster than you could throw it."

For a rookie, he had remarkable self-confidence, perhaps even cock-iness. The 1971 Sox had finished third in the American League East with an 85–77 record, eighteen games behind Baltimore but (and this mattered) three games ahead of the Yankees. They hoped to do better in 1972, but started slowly. In the pages of the *Springfield (Mass.) Union,* Fisk chastised Carl Yastrzemski and right fielder Reggie Smith for not showing more leadership. "When Yastrzemski and Smith don't show desire in the outfield, the whole team droops," Fisk said. "Maybe a goal has been taken away from them by obtaining security. Maybe huge salaries have something to do with a player's attitude." Since few baseball salaries beyond those paid by Tom Yawkey could be consid-ered huge, Fisk's remarks constituted an implicit criticism of the owner. To his dismay, the comments got play all over New England, leading to a meeting of the three players and manager Eddie Kasko at which Fisk apologized. But his words actually seemed to have an impact. Yaz and Smith both went on hitting streaks, and the Sox went from playing .500 ball to going 15 games over .500, finishing just half a game behind the Tigers. (If only Luis Aparicio hadn't slipped . . .)

When he approached the mound, Fisk was often similarly blunt. "Fisk is not the type to stand on the mound listening," reliever Bob Veale said. "He just marches up to you and tells you, 'Get the lead out of your butt,' and then stomps back to the plate."

"Some pitchers respond to a verbal butt-kicking out there," Fisk would explain.

He took charge on the field, developing a slow, meticulous style of calling a game, directing pitchers and defenders like a stage manager, which could slow the pace of a game like a driver's ed teacher instruct-ing a student to ride the brake. He was constantly trotting out to the mound to talk to the pitcher, sometimes to buck him up, sometimes to talk strategy, sometimes, it seemed, because he was just enjoying the

moment. Not every pitcher appreciated Fisk's methodical approach. "I liked to work fast," Mike Torrez would say. "Let's get the ball, let's go. And Carlton loved moving guys around. By the time he got down, fixed his mask, and got his body settled, I was like, 'I'm ready to go, ready to go.' I used to say, 'Carlton, let's speed it up a little bit, I want to get going.' " Fisk would grumble, "All right, all right."

In his rookie year, Fisk made his presence felt. He impressed at the plate, hitting .293 with 22 home runs—the most ever for a Red Sox catcher—with 61 runs batted in. Defensively, he showed poise beyond his years. In a September game against the Orioles, Fisk made a rare and exciting play. When one Oriole tried to bunt home a man on third, Fisk quickly fielded the bunt, jumped backward, tagged out the runner trying to score, then threw to first to complete the double play. The Red Sox hadn't seen a catcher like Fisk before, and the rest of the league also took note; Fisk was the American League rookie of the year by unanimous vote, the first time that had ever happened.

Baseball's sportswriters weren't the only ones to notice Fisk's arrival; so did Thurman Munson, who didn't take long to commence disliking Fisk. "It was kind of a territorial demand," Fisk said. "He was the reigning catcher in the league and I was the new kid on the block."

Fisk's analysis was probably charitable, because Munson's sentiment may have been more base. Something about Fisk—his looks, his swagger—either exacerbated Munson's insecurities or irritated his sense of baseball decorum. The catcher who never thought he got the attention he deserved was being eclipsed by a younger catcher who, in Munson's opinion, was earning more praise than he merited.

"Munson really created this rivalry between him and Fisk, because he was jealous of the attention Fisk was getting," biographer Marty Appel explained. At the time, baseball fans across the country got to see a national game every Saturday on NBC's *Game of the Week,* and for the first half of the decade NBC's play-by-play announcer was Curt Gowdy, who had been a Red Sox announcer for fifteen years before moving to the NBC broadcast. "To Munson's thinking, Curt Gowdy was always building up Fisk, because of his Boston connection," Appel said. "It would annoy Munson because Munson was accomplishing really good things and Fisk was always getting hurt. And still Gowdy was always going on about Carlton Fisk."

Of course, it wasn't just what was written and said about Fisk that irritated Munson; just as noxious were conflicts that developed on the field. In a 1971 game, Fisk embarrassed Munson, who was hitting, by beating him down the first base line on a ground ball Fisk was backing up. Two years later, on July 31, 1973, the Yankees and the Red Sox were playing at Fenway when Roy White tried to score on a play at the plate. Confident that he was comfortably ahead of the incoming throw, White remained standing as he neared the plate. But as the ball neared his glove, Fisk stretched his left leg backward and tripped White, who went airborne and missed the plate entirely—giving Fisk time enough to tag him. The Sox won the game and moved into a tie for first with New York. In the locker room later, Yankee manager Ralph Houk reminded his players that it was better to run into the catcher than to be tripped, fall over, and get tagged out.

The two teams met again, the next night with John Curtis on the mound for the Sox and Mel Stottlemyre pitching for New York. In the second inning, Stottlemyre zipped a pitch past Fisk's head, a notice that the events of the previous night had not been forgotten. The game was tied at 2 when the Yankees came up in the top of the ninth. After Munson doubled, Graig Nettles grounded out, moving Munson to third. First baseman Felipe Alou then walked. With light-hitting shortstop Gene Michael coming up, Ralph Houk called for a suicide squeeze.

On the first pitch, Munson broke for the plate and Michael pivoted to bunt. But Michael missed the pitch, and Munson barreled toward home looking like an easy out. So Munson did what Houk had suggested; he slammed into Fisk with all his force. Fisk held on to the ball, and as Felipe Alou headed toward third, Munson lay on top of Fisk. The Red Sox catcher kicked Munson off him; Munson promptly jumped up and punched him. Then Gene Michael got into it, and suddenly Fisk was fighting both Munson and Michael at the same time, and holding his own. (Michael was a better shortstop than fighter, and Fisk was strong.) Within seconds the field was flooded with players from both dugouts. When Munson, Fisk, and Michael were separated, Fisk went back to the dugout bleeding, his face slightly swollen. An angry Bill Lee asked if Gene Michael "had scratched [Fisk] with his purse." Later, Lee would tell reporters that the Yankees were like "a bunch of hookers, swinging their purses." The Yankees would remember that insult. "Ask [Fisk] who won the fight, he knows," Munson would say.

When play resumed, the Sox went on to win the game, 3–2, in the bottom of the ninth. They would finish second in 1973, eight games behind the Orioles but nine ahead of the fourth-place Yankees. Fisk, meanwhile, was earning a reputation as a player with a knack for getting on opponents' nerves. "If a fight starts, Fisk is sure to be in it," the *Sporting News* said. Shortly after the Yankee incident, Fisk got embroiled in another home plate altercation with the Angels' Alan Gallagher, and then days later nearly landed in another with the Angels' venerable Frank Robinson. "Tell him that people don't like him in this league," Robinson said afterward. "He's got a lot to learn." From Fisk's point of view, he was not merely defending his turf, but was also sticking up for a certain way of playing the game—tough, physical, relentless, old-school. If Fisk had been a Yankee, Billy Martin would have loved him. But Carlton Fisk could never have been a Yankee. Perhaps even more than Carl Yastrzemski—who, after all, had hoped to play for the Yankees before his father told him otherwise—Fisk personified the Red Sox.

The years after 1973 were difficult for Fisk, who suffered a string of demoralizing injuries. While catching in spring training in 1974, he was hit in the groin by a foul ball from Met Joe Torre, and for two months afterward suffered nauseau and cramps. As Bill Lee would later describe the incident, "From the mound, I could see that one of his nuts was hanging out, pinched between his thigh and his cup. The ball nailed it. . . . Carlton went down as if he'd been shot." Then, in a June 28 game in Cleveland, outfielder Leron Lee slammed into Fisk at the plate, tearing tendons in Fisk's left knee. Fisk would miss the rest of the season, and the injury prompted him to reconsider the cost of fearlessness. "I did a lot of thinking that winter," he would recall. "If I closed my eyes, I could see Lee running into me again. I began to wonder: what comes first, your body or one lousy run?"

By the spring of 1975, Fisk was ready to return. Luck was not on his side. On March 12, in his second spring training at-bat, Fisk was hit by a pitch that broke his left arm. The injury devastated him. After all the time he'd missed, and all the desire he had to get back onto the field . . . Sixty-three games later, an impatient Fisk was finally healed. Within a few games, a play at the plate forced him to confront fears he'd never had before. Baltimore's Don Baylor was at third base when the next batter hit a slow ground ball; Baylor, who was not a small man, charged toward the plate. Fisk had to reach for the throw, just as he had with Leron Lee the previous year, and Baylor slid between his legs. "I was shaking so badly, I had to call time out," he said later. "All the time I was waiting for the throw, I kept telling myself how hard Baylor slides." But Fisk didn't flinch. He knew fear now, the visceral knowledge that an athlete's hopes for a great career could be wiped out in just one play, and he refused to flinch.

Still the rivalry between Munson and Fisk simmered, and again it was driven largely by Munson's conviction that Fisk was getting more credit than Munson and more credit than he deserved. In four of the six seasons in which the two players overlapped, from 1972 to 1978, Fisk was voted the All-Star starting catcher, a fact that drove Munson nuts. In 1973, for example, Fisk collected half a million more votes than Munson did; Munson wound up hitting .301 for the season, Fisk .246. "Fisk is a big, tall, good-looking guy," Munson said. "He looks like what an All-Star catcher should look like. I'm short, I'm pudgy, I don't look good in a uniform." In 1975, Fisk was on the cover of *Sports Illustrated* twice, Munson not at all. And as good as Fisk's numbers were that season—a batting average of .331 with 10 home runs and 52 RBI's—Munson hit .318, with 12 home runs and 102 runs batted in, while playing in 78 more games than Fisk's 79. "Compared to him, why should I be so overlooked?" Munson said in July 1975. "He's a good ballplayer, but I don't think he's as much of a threat in other parks as he is in Boston. He might be a better ballplayer than I am, but he has never done the things I done. . . . In six and a half years in the big leagues, how many games have I missed?"

For a player with a reputation for treating sportswriters as if they were contagious, Munson could give startlingly honest and personal quotes when he did speak, and that was probably one reason why, as the years went on, Munson's shell grew thicker, his interactions with most writers more curt. "Thurman didn't like people delving into his private life, and so he came across as gruff to people in the media," Graig Nettles said. His old roommate, Gene Michael, suggested that Munson's brusqueness stemmed from an awareness of his vulnerability. "It wasn't that he didn't like the media, it was that Thurman had a kind of mistrust until he knew people," Michael said. "There were certain media members that he knew he could say things to and relax—he knew that they weren't going to write 'em. But if he let them *all* in"— if Munson opened up to everyone who asked him to—"someone was going to mess it up. And he didn't want that."

Michael knew Munson well enough to tease him about his fixation with Fisk. "Thurman was a great athlete but didn't necessarily look like it, while Carlton was a good-looking guy who looked more athletic than Thurman, but wasn't. So I used to gather magazines that had an article about Fisk, or a picture. I'd put them in his locker or on his stool in front of his locker, and Thurman just threw them aside. Soon there was a big stack in there. And one day, he was irritable, and I put a couple of new magazines in the stack, and he came out of there just firing a whole pack of 'em, shouting, *Someone's gonna pay for this!* And he still didn't know who was doing it."

While it was unfair of Munson to fault Fisk for his injuries, it was certainly true that Munson was spending more time on the field. From 1972 through 1977, Munson averaged 148 games a season. During the same period, Fisk averaged 114. Those numbers didn't mean that Munson was healthy. While Munson managed to avoid the type of season-ending injury Fisk had suffered, his body was beaten down by catching. He had aching knees, a bad right hand from being hit by a bat, a bad right shoulder from another collision—a wealth of small wounds and everyday indignities inflicted upon his body from crouching behind the plate or standing in the way of sprinting two-hundred-pound men. His shoulder was so bad that after about 1975 Munson could no longer throw overhand. Instead, he developed a sidearm motion that looked awkward but was surprisingly effective. "Throwing to second, he was mechanically horrendous," Brian Doyle said. "He had very quick feet, but he never threw the ball over the top. A lot of the time, he couldn't get his arm up, his shoulder was hurting so much. But he was quick, and the ball would be there."

"He played with a lot of pain," Doyle said, "and he never complained, and if someone did, and he heard it, he said one word: 'Retire.' "

When Cliff Johnson first arrived in New York after being traded by the Astros in June 1977, Munson had stitches on one finger of his throwing hand. Johnson expected that he'd have to start the same day he arrived. "I'm going, 'My goodness, you're telling me I gotta come over here and jump in like this?' " Johnson recalled. But Munson had no intention of skipping a game just because of stitches. "He played through it," Johnson said. "He was not a guy that relished sitting around watching the ball game. I don't know what the heck he would have done if he had to do that—climbed the stadium and jumped off the walls or something."

As with everything else, Munson was proud of his durability, proud of his better-than-you'd-expect speed, proud of his ability to do the small things, like hitting to the opposite field to advance the runner. It infuriated him when Rick Burleson told one newspaper in 1975 that the position of catcher was extremely difficult, "unless you're a guy like

Munson, who doesn't worry about his defense. He just goes up there and hits."

The truth was, Fisk and Munson had some physical differences, and some stylistic ones as well. But underneath their divergent exteriors, they were both fiercely competitive players who distrusted the changes occurring in the game and valued baseball's traditions and history. "They both had the same instincts and baseball knowledge," said Mike Torrez, who pitched to them both. "They both wanted to outdo each other."

Nineteen seventy-five was, of course, a magical year for the Red Sox, and upon his return from injury Fisk contributed immensely to the team's push for the World Series. Then in October came that iconic home run in Game Six against the Reds. Fisk's wishful leaping would forever endear him to Red Sox fans and become one of baseball's most memorable images. Though it was well past midnight when Fisk drove the ball into the stands in Fenway, his hometown residents rushed to the local church and rang its bells, as if Fisk were Paul Revere. But Fisk irritated the Yankees, and so did his heroic moment. As a general matter, "the Yankee players thought Fisk just sort of pranced on the field," Marty Appel recalled. "Even when you see the replay of him with the home run, there's something delicate and dainty about him. The players had very little use for that."

Nor did Fisk have much use for Munson or the Yankees. When asked how he and Munson got along, Fisk would say, "He's not one of my best friends, nor is he my worst of enemies." Asked what exactly that meant, Fisk said, "It means I don't like him worth a damn."

It didn't take long for the next conflagration between the two teams to erupt. On May 20, 1976, Bill Lee, hardly a Yankee favorite, was pitching to New York designated hitter Otto Velez in the sixth inning at Yankee Stadium. With two out, the Sox were leading, 1–0. Lou Piniella was on second and Graig Nettles on first. Velez hit a line drive single to right, and as Piniella came rounding third, Dwight Evans fired the ball in to Fisk. Though Piniella was easily out, he nonetheless plowed into Fisk, who managed to, in short order, flip Piniella over, tag him, and punch him.

Instantly, the two men were fighting, and instantly the two teams swarmed around each other, a full-out brawl around the mound. Most baseball fights are pretty tame stuff, with more players milling around looking for something to do than fighting. Not this one. Bill Lee, who'd been backing up the play at home, tried to tackle Velez, only to be slugged from behind by Mickey Rivers. Then, suddenly, Nettles yanked Lee out of the pile and threw him to the ground—trying, he later said, to disentangle Lee from the melee. But Lee landed hard on his left shoulder, his throwing shoulder, and when he finally managed to stand up, he knew there was something wrong with it; he couldn't feel his arm. In his fury and disbelief, he screamed at Nettles and lunged after him. Since he had only one operable arm, that was a mistake. As one *Sports Illustrated* reporter later put it, Nettles "opened up with both fists, and Lee was hammered into a bloody pulp."

Nettles and Lee were both thrown out of the game, though Lee couldn't have continued even if he were allowed to; he would spend the next six weeks on the disabled list. The next day, Lee talked to reporters and called Billy Martin a "Nazi." The Yankees, he added, were George Steinbrenner's "Brown Shirts." The Yankees were unrepentant. Asked what happened, Nettles said, "He shouldn't complain. I hurt his shoulder. He earns his living with his mouth. It would have been worse had I broken his jaw and it had to be wired shut for a few days."

When the Sox came to Yankee Stadium in 1977, Billy Martin would respond to the Nazi references by sending a clubhouse boy to the Red Sox locker room with a dead mackerel and a note for Lee. Depending on whom you believe, the note (sadly lost to history) read either, "Stick this in your purse"—a reference to Lee's earlier remark regarding Gene Michael's fighting prowess—or, "Stick this in your pussy." Lee said he doubted Martin would write that, because he didn't think Martin could spell *pussy*. He also said, "If this is one of his illegitimate kids, I don't want to accept the burden."

Referring to Lee's injury, Thurman Munson's response was short, to the point, and wholly evocative of Munson's sarcastic personality. "I guess Graig hit him with his purse," Munson said.

The 1976 season should have been a great year for the Yankee catcher; so, for that matter, should 1977. Yet both seasons were unexpectedly difficult for him. In Martin's first full season with the team, 1976, the Yankees won 97 games, beating the Orioles by 10½ and the Sox by 15½, then advanced to the World Series after edging out the Kansas City Royals in an exciting five-game playoff determined by Chris Chambliss's home run in the bottom of the last inning. But against the Reds in the World Series, the Yankees were manhandled, losing four straight and only once coming within one run. Munson himself had an excellent series, hitting .529 and setting a World Series record for consecutive hits with six. And he'd had an excellent season, hitting .302 with 17 home runs and 105 runs batted in—his second consecutive .300/100-RBI season. But those numbers didn't change the fact that his team had just been humiliated.

After the last game, Munson walked into a mandatory press conference to hear Reds manager Sparky Anderson replying to a question asking him to compare Munson with Reds catcher Johnny Bench. "Munson is an outstanding ballplayer and he would hit .300 in the National League," Anderson was saying. "But don't ever compare anybody to Johnny Bench. Don't never embarrass nobody by comparing them to Johnny Bench."

No matter what Munson did, it seemed, it wasn't enough. As he took the microphone, he was fuming. "For me to be so belittled after the season I had, and after the season I had . . . it's bad enough to lose, but worse to be belittled like that. To lose four in a row and rub it in my face—that's class."

The incident left a bad taste in Munson's mouth heading into the off-season, and 1977 brought more bitterness and frustration. When George Steinbrenner signed Reggie Jackson, Munson was incensed over the fact that Jackson was being paid more than he was, despite an earlier promise from Steinbrenner that he would be the highest-paid Yankee. (As Catfish Hunter once said of Steinbrenner, "He's a man of his word. You just have to get it in writing.") Steinbrenner would eventually agree to renegotiate Munson's contract, but not until months later, months during which Munson fumed and sulked. Then came Jackson's "straw that stirs the drink" interview, followed by months of tension within the team whose excellence had only begun to develop when Munson arrived in 1970.

Again, Munson and the Yankees were successful. Munson hit .308, with 18 home runs and 100 runs batted in, his third straight .300/100 season. (Meanwhile, Fisk had his best offensive year ever, with a .315 batting average, 26 home runs, and 102 RBIs—the first time he'd driven in 100 runs, and the first of only two times in his twenty-four-year career he would hit that mark.) The Yankees, of course, won the World Series against the Dodgers. But the joy of the victory was dimmed for Munson by the pain of the season, the constant bickering between Martin, Jackson, and Steinbrenner, the sense that the man at the heart of the team, Munson himself, had been eclipsed just as the Yankees finally achieved greatness.

In the off-season, Munson demanded to be traded to the Indians;

Cleveland was about a forty-five-minute drive from his home in Canton, and Munson hated spending so much time away from his family. The 1977 Indians had finished fifth in the division with a 71–90 record, and their attendance hadn't even hit the million mark—despite George Steinbrenner's concerns about whether fans would come to the Bronx, the Yankees' was over twice that, passing two million for the first time since 1950—but Munson insisted he would not return to New York. Trade me or I'll quit, he said. When Murray Chass of the *Times* reached Munson at home in February 1978, he asked Munson what he thought he'd be doing during the upcoming baseball season. "I'll probably play baseball," Munson said. For whom? "I'm still a Yankee at this time."

The Yankees had no intention of trading Munson, who was at the beginning of a three-year contract, and simply waited him out. "He'd miss being on a winner," Billy Martin said. "You don't appreciate being on a winner until you're not on a winner." Martin, who knew what that was like, may have been right; Munson would probably have been miserable playing for a bumbling team. On the other hand, Munson was a family man, and Martin would never have understood how family could matter more than baseball.

Munson did, of course, return to the Yankees in 1978, and though his relations with reporters were as testy as ever, he showed glimpses of happiness, or at least begrudging contentment. His knees were as sore, perhaps more so, than ever, and the cumulative effect of having caught, by this point, over 1,000 games was catching up to him. At times Martin would use Munson as a designated hitter, and he even briefly tried him in right field, to give the catcher a break. Munson himself was coming to accept that the time when he would be physically unable to catch was imminent, and he pondered what other positions he could play—designated hitter, the outfield (probably not), first base (more likely). In the meantime, he hoped to hit .300 and drive in 100 runs for the fourth straight year. The last man to reach that milestone was Ted Williams, who had done so from 1946 to 1949.

One change in his lifestyle helped relax Munson: determined to spend more time with Diana and the kids, he had taken flying lessons and earned his pilot's license. In a two-seater Beechcraft, he could make it from New York to Canton in a little over an hour, and he would often take off from a New Jersey airport after a night game, flying west to be with his family. The next day, he'd turn around and fly back to Yankee Stadium. He enjoyed flying, and even more, he loved the time at home that he'd been missing for the better part of a decade.

Halfway through the season, Munson would finish work on his autobiography, in which he talked about his new contract, the new home he had built in Canton, and his desire to forge a truce with journalists. "I'm actually enjoying the season as I used to," Munson said. "Why not? I may be around here a long time after all."

The Red Sox began their series against the Yankees on June 19 having won 9 of their last 10, and the loss had only come the day before, 3–2 to the Mariners. Judging from the pitching matchups, they seemed poised to extend their winning ways. For one thing, Ron Guidry would not face the Sox because he had just pitched. "We've tried him on three days before, and it hasn't worked," Martin explained. In the first of the three game series, Luis Tiant (6–0) would face rookie Ken Clay, who was 1–3. The second game would see Mike Torrez, with 10 wins and 2 losses, facing Don Gullett, whose arm troubles were sabotaging his season; Gullett's record was 1–0. And in game three, Dennis Eckersley, 6–2, would face another Yankee rookie, Jim Beattie, whose record was 2–2.

The Yankees were hurting. Andy Messersmith was trying unsuccessfully to recover from a separated shoulder. Hunter was trying to save his career. Dick Tidrow had a bad right thumb. Bucky Dent would miss the series with that hamstring pull. Willie Randolph had a badly bruised knee, Mickey Rivers a hairline fracture of his right hand.

The Red Sox had a problem of a different sort, one more often associated with the Yankees: controversy. On June 16, general manager Haywood Sullivan sold backup outfielder Bernie Carbo to the Indians for cash, though the team wouldn't say how much. Carbo, one of the team's two remaining Buffalo Heads, was another hero from 1975 and hugely popular with Boston fans. But Don Zimmer had grown tired of his free-spirited behavior—Carbo griped if he wasn't playing, and there was reason to believe that he had not infrequently soothed his pain with the solace of at least one recreational drug— and the Sox essentially gave Carbo away. The last Buffalo Head, Bill Lee, was incensed. On hearing the news, he said, "I wanted to kill Haywood Sullivan, that gutless. . . . They trade away all the genuine personalities. . . . If Tom Yawkey were still running this club, it wouldn't be like this." Lee promptly cleaned out his locker and went home. He was back a day later, and would pay a seven-hundred-dollar fine for his absence. "A fine means nothing," Lee said. "I don't play for money. They shouldn't pay me in the first place."

Almost as quickly as that incident settled down, a perhaps more serious one hit the Red Sox: a *Sport* magazine profile of Jim Rice reported that the outfielder had accused the team's management of racism. "Race has to be a factor when Fred Lynn can hit .240 in the minors and I can hit .340 and he gets a starting job before I do." Lynn was also "the more natural press favorite: He's white. . . ." The story broke on the eve of the Yankee series, and Rice was quick to disavow it, saying, as he had in the past, that he had been misquoted. "Why would I want to say anything while this club is going so good? . . . There may have been a time when race was an issue on this team, but it certainly doesn't exist today."

The Lee and Rice controversies suggested that while the Yankees' troubles might get more attention, lines of division crisscrossed the Red Sox as well. But the Yankees were coming to Fenway, and the players focused on the arrival of their archenemies. "It seems that we always keep one eye on each other, no matter how far apart we are," Carlton Fisk said. "And by the time we meet, there's tension unlike anything I've experienced anywhere in my life." Tensions between the teams certainly hadn't dissipated since the 1976 fight. The previous season, when the Sox were playing at the stadium and Reggie Jackson was at the plate, the Yankee scoreboard had started blinking, "REG-GIE, REG-GIE," and shortstop Rick Burleson had turned to face the scoreboard and literally screamed at it, a primal shout of frustration and anger and, Burleson would say later, hatred. All the emotions, it seemed, were coming to a head in 1978.

The first game was a Boston blowout, 10–4. The Yankees had gone up 4–1 against Tiant on home runs by Munson and Roy White, but then Clay started getting pounded and Goose Gossage relieved in the bottom of the fourth. Still pitching in the eighth, he tired, and the Sox poured in six runs. Gossage's loss put him at 3–7 on the season and 2–5 career against Boston. After the game Reggie Jackson said, "If they keep playing like that, we won't be able to catch them with a race car."

The next night, however, the Yankees stormed back to win, 10–4, soundly beating their former teammate, Mike Torrez. Don Gullett, who had lasted only eleven innings in his three previous starts, threw 154 pitches for his first complete game of the season. After Torrez intentionally walked designated hitter Jim Spencer with two men on in the fourth, utility infielder Fred Stanley, playing in place of Dent, hit a grand slam. After the game, Stanley took a moment to remind the world of Torrez's off-season claim that his new team was better than his old one. "It's nice to beat Torrez, and it's nice to beat the Red Sox," he said.

In game three, Dennis Eckersley, who had never beaten the Yankees, earned another ninth-inning standing ovation, beating the Yankees, 9–2. "I was all jacked up, I wanted to win," he said. "I had pitched well against a lot of teams, but not against New York." The Sox scored six runs in the third, sending Jim Beattie packing, and after the game, a furious George Steinbrenner did the same, ordering the rookie pitcher dispatched to Tacoma, Washington, as soon as he was showered. "That kid pitching for us tonight looked scared stiff," Steinbrenner fumed. "The other young pitcher [Ken Clay, in game one] had a three-run lead the other night and he blew it. Why aren't our young pitchers coming along like other young pitchers? What's holding them back? Who's handling them wrong?"

The first series between the two teams had proved inconclusive and atypical—three lopsided victories, two by the Red Sox, didn't much feel like the tight competition both teams had expected. With about two-fifths of the season gone, the series felt more like two teams feeling each other out, sizing up strengths and weaknesses, preparing for future battles.

But the Sox were rolling, eight games ahead of the Yankees now, and New York was worried—or at least Steinbrenner was. And the more Steinbrenner fretted and fussed, the more pressure he put on Billy Martin, and the more everyone in New York City wondered just how long it would be before one of the two men couldn't take it any longer.

CHAPTER 8

THE THIRD INNING

Substituting for regular second baseman Willie Randolph, twenty-three-year-old Brian Doyle came to the plate to start the third inning. By any reasonable expectation, Doyle, a clean-cut rookie from Cave City, Kentucky—"The Gateway to Mammoth Cave," as the town Chamber of Commerce put it—should have been nervous: he was by far the least experienced player on the field. Doyle had batted only 50 times for the Yankees in 1978, with just 10 hits, all singles. That made for a .200 average, with no walks and no runs batted in. To add to the pressure, he'd endured a season that would have bruised the confidence of the most secure athlete: Starting on June 15, the Yankees had called Doyle up from their minor league team in Tacoma five separate times. Five cross-country flights from Tacoma to New York, then four flights back. For this stint he'd come up just days before, after Randolph had pulled his hamstring playing against Toronto. The loss of Randolph was a serious setback for the Yankees. A speedy contact hitter, Randolph batted second; he and Mickey Rivers could create havoc on the base paths. Instead, Brian Doyle found himself starting at second base against the Red Sox in a game that made even Carl Yastrzemski nervous. On top of that, he was playing in Fenway Park, where his older brother Denny had played the same position for the Red Sox until the previous March, when the Sox had released Denny Doyle after acquiring Jerry Remy.

Brian Doyle was a quiet, modest man who didn't fit in with the Yankees' hard-bitten, big-city culture. Married to his high school sweetheart, he had found God in the minor leagues and was now a born-again Christian. And Doyle was nervous, at least during the pregame warm-ups, wondering how he would do, hoping he wouldn't screw things up for his team. But then everyone stood for the national anthem, and the butterflies in his stomach just disappeared. His baseball instincts kicked in. Doyle knew that the Yankees weren't expecting him to hit; that was the job of Jackson, Munson, Piniella, Nettles, and the rest. His role was to field, and fielding was his passion, his gift, the only reason he'd ever make the majors. After he retired from baseball a few years later, he would open a school to teach young players how to field. A few years after that he would become an ordained minister.

Despite the hostile environment, despite the trade of his brother, Doyle loved playing in Boston. Baseball mattered in Boston. The fans were true believers. When the Yankees were in town, the players could expect fire alarms in their hotels, smoke bombs rolled down the hallways—crazy stuff like that, anything to mess up their routines, leave them a little tired at game time. Doyle appreciated the intimacy of Fenway Park, the way the fans were right on top of you. That was the way baseball should be. But once the game started, he didn't hear them; he just shut them out. It was a talent he'd developed. It also helped that he was surrounded by such veterans as Munson, Piniella, and Nettles. Their poise calmed him. Before the game, they didn't reach out to the rookie, give him any special advice or reassurance. They just treated him like he belonged, and that made Doyle believe in himself.

On the mound, Torrez wasn't particularly worried about the rookie. Though he hadn't seen much of Doyle, who was 0–3 to that point against the Red Sox in 1978, everyone knew the second baseman was all field, no hit. So Torrez challenged Doyle, throwing him a fastball in on the first pitch. Doyle swung late and hit a looping fly ball toward right field, the kind that can plunk in just beyond the second baseman and in front of the right fielder. But Jerry Remy sprinted backward, stretched out his arm at the last possible moment, and caught the ball. Torrez was still rolling.

Shortstop Bucky Dent, hitting ninth, approached the plate. Dent had been slumping the past few weeks, and his season numbers—.243, with 4 home runs and 37 runs batted in—had suffered as a result. But even during the best of times, the right-handed Dent was not much of a hitter. In his best season, 1974, he hit .274 with the White Sox, but only once during the next decade would he hit over .250. He didn't have much power, either; in 1977, he'd hit 8 home runs for the Yankees, and in the three years before that, just 10 total. Most years Dent hit about .250, and in those pre–Cal Ripken days, that was what you expected from your shortstop—reliable fielding, endurance, hitting that wasn't abysmal. And Dent was a fine defensive shortstop. With Nettles at third, Randolph, usually, at second, and Chris Chambliss at first, he was part of a tight infield, certainly a stronger group defensively than were the Yankee outfielders.

Still, Dent was frustrated with the way he'd been playing; that was typical of him, to beat up on himself. In the last weeks of the season, with the Yankees locked in a tight division race, he had wanted desperately to contribute. For most of the previous month, he really hadn't—at least, not at the plate. And even though the Yankees were the kind of team where some player was always picking up the slack, Dent's inability to hit the ball was weighing on him.

It had been a tough season for Dent, and a tough couple of seasons since he'd come to the Yankees from the White Sox in April 1977, traded for outfielder Oscar Gamble, pitcher LaMarr Hoyt, and a minor leaguer named Bob Polinsky, plus $200,000 cash. (Gabe Paul was determined to land a shortstop for the Yankees.) Coming to New York was the fulfillment of a childhood dream for Dent. Growing up in Florida, he'd idolized the team and dreamed of playing for them. The Yankees had that tradition of excellence. Who wouldn't want to be a part of that? Their players took the field with a confidence, an awareness of being part of a history, that no one on any other team could really understand. They knew their place in the world. Dent felt the weight of that history as soon as he arrived at Yankee Stadium. "When I walked in and sat down at my locker and put the uniform on, *as* I was putting it on—it sounds kind of kooky, but it goes through your head," he said. "All the great players that have come through here, the tradition, the history. Then you walk through that tunnel and you step onto that field and *you're a Yankee*. Like Mantle and Maris and Berra . . . it starts to sink into you. *Hey, I got a responsibility here.*"

Dent was a low-key man who never felt comfortable with the Yankees' locker room flare-ups. "Bucky just went about his business in a real quiet manner," Graig Nettles recalled. "He didn't say much, but he was a very steady shortstop."

"Bucky was so consistent," Brian Doyle said. "He didn't do anything spectacular, never did anything spectacular, but he made every routine play, and I saw the same thing in my role—if that's how Bucky performed, that's how I'm going to, too."

From the start, though, Billy Martin had never warmed to Dent. Maybe the problem was that Martin made every new player prove himself. Maybe it was that Dent was someone whom Gabe Paul wanted, and he would be starting over Fred Stanley, a hardworking player of limited talent whom Martin liked. Maybe it was that Dent was too handsome, almost pretty. With shaggy black hair and twinkly eyes and a movie-star smile, Dent looked like the all-American kid, the high school hero, the kind of self-confident, popular-with-cheerleaders, easygoing guy that Martin never was and never considered himself to be. The realities of Dent's life and identity were considerably more complicated, but Martin couldn't see that.

"It was like, the guys that were with Billy, those were *the guys,* and the new guys that came in . . . He used to like to mess with us," Dent said. Dent had been a popular player with the White Sox, and he wondered if Martin didn't feel the need to take him down a peg. "I think he was kind of jealous of the popularity, where I was in Chicago," Dent said. If Martin had really known Dent, he'd have known that Dent struggled with a lack of confidence, and that he needed to be supported more than challenged. But that was Martin. He wanted to break players, to grind down their egos and purge them of past influences so that he could remake them into tough, gritty players like the one he had been. "He used to mess with us," Dent said. "Because Billy wanted to be *the* guy."

In Dent's case, that meant showing the shortstop that Martin had no confidence in his hitting. So when Dent came up to bat in run-scoring situations, Martin almost invariably made him bunt, or simply pinch-hit for him and yanked him from the game. At times, Martin would instruct Dent to sacrifice in the early innings of a game, not even giving Dent a chance to drive in a run when there were five or six innings left to play. That was how Dent and Reggie Jackson became friends in 1977. "They'd take Reggie out for defense in the seventh inning, and they'd take me out" for hitting, Dent recalled. "We'd be in the clubhouse together, kind of in the same boat, and we became good friends."

Martin's disrespect depressed the twenty-six-year-old shortstop. "In Chicago, they pinch-hit for me only when a home run or something like that was needed to win a game," Dent said. "Because I was pretty good at driving in runs—I could put the ball in play. But after I came over from New York, literally from the first game I played in, Billy pinch-hit for me late in the game. Then he told me, 'I won't be doing this for you once you get your feet on the ground.' Well, it didn't happen that way."

Martin's attitude toward Dent didn't change in 1978. In a game against the Blue Jays on May 27, Martin pinch-hit for Dent with the Yankees losing, 4–1, in the bottom of the ninth. Instead, he sent Dell Alston, a career .238 hitter, to the plate. *A career .238 hitter.* Alston had

had just 40 at-bats in 1977, and would have only 2 others with the Yankees in 1978. Dent didn't have a huge ego—in fact, he might have been well served if he had a slightly larger one—but like any professional athlete, he did have pride, and insults like that stung. "That really got to me," he said. "Out of all the things . . . that got to me."

Dent grew so frustrated, so demoralized, that he started tensing up before he got to the batter's box. Late in the game, rather than approach the plate, he'd linger in the on-deck circle until he was really sure that Martin wasn't going to yank him. Just a few extra seconds . . . But those moments of hesitation weakened his concentration and sapped his confidence.

So Thurman Munson reached out to him in the catcher's typical way—empathy hidden under layers of tough-guy sarcasm. Munson noticed how Dent had begun second-guessing himself, and late in games, when Dent was on deck, he started whistling at Dent from the dugout. "Like I was being called back," Dent explained. Dent would turn around to head back to the dugout, but then he would see Munson. "And he'd start grinning. He'd start laughing. I'd go, 'Thurman . . . ' " Dent would get so pissed off at Munson, he'd forget about his anxiety.

Dent's season had been challenging not just mentally, but physically. In the fifth game of spring training, batting against the Orioles, he had fouled a ball off his left shin, just below the knee. He developed a painful bruise about the size of a fist, as well as a blood clot that required minor surgery. After that injury, Dent started using a homemade foam pad that he strapped onto his left shin every time he batted. He would wear it all season long, for Dent had a distinctive swing that aggravated the problem. Dent did not hit inside fastballs well, and consequently pitchers threw him a lot of them. To make better contact with the pitch, Dent choked up high on his bat, leaving a good six inches of handle sticking out from beneath his bottom hand. "Bucky choked up so much, sometimes you couldn't tell which end of the bat he was holding," Fred Lynn would say. Sometimes, when he made contact on inside pitches, Dent chopped the ball down and in, toward his left leg and foot. And even with the pad, whenever one of those foul balls hit his leg, the leg would swell up just the way it had the first time.

Then in June, Dent pulled a hamstring and would miss around 35 games. He'd never been injured before, and not being able to play drove him crazy. He tried to come back in early July to play in a series against the Red Sox, but it was too soon—he pulled the muscle again. Finally, "they just shut me down completely," Dent said. "They told me that if I did it again, it would be really bad." So Dent went home to Florida, and for about ten days, every day, he would slowly wade through the shallow surf near his home, trying to strengthen the muscle. His improvised rehab worked, and Dent returned for July, August, and September. But he'd already missed more games than he ever had before. For the three previous years, Dent had averaged 158 games a season. In 1978, he played in only 123, and in many of those, he just didn't feel fully himself.

It was a tough season, and for Dent that was unusual. Baseball had always been an outlet for him, a reprieve from the problems and tensions of an unusual childhood. For while you'd never know it to look at him, with that sweet smile and those sun-fed good looks, Dent had had, in one profound way, a difficult life: he was the product of two bitterly divided parents, although for years he didn't even know it.

Dent was born on November 25, 1951, the son of Denise O'Dey and Russell Stanford, a young, unmarried couple in Savannah, Georgia. Denise and Russell had a rocky relationship, and the two broke up, angrily, months before Bucky was born. Denise took her baby to Hialeah, Florida, where her sister and brother-in-law, Sarah and James Earl Dent, lived. She gave her son, Russell Earl O'Dey, to the Dents to raise as their own, and they did so with love, but also with secrecy. As the baby became a little boy, he never had the slightest hint that the Dents were not his biological parents. They even changed his name on his birth certificate: Russell Earl O'Dey became Russell Earl Dent, later nicknamed "Bucky." No one told the boy that the people he considered his parents were, in fact, his aunt and uncle.

"They just didn't want me to know," Dent explained. "It was too complicated. They wanted me to have normalcy."

But Denise O'Dey didn't like the notion that her son would never know his real mother, and that she would never be able to call Bucky "son." She was not a woman who spoke of her feelings easily, but the pain of seeing her son grow up with another family, never knowing that she was his mother, ate away at her. So she arranged with the Dents to have Bucky visit her in Savannah during summer vacations as soon as he was old enough to travel. Bucky was told that he was visiting his aunt, who would pick him up in Hialeah and bring him to Savannah, then travel south with him when it was time for Bucky to return.

"Every summer, I had to get on this bus to go to Georgia," Dent recalled. "I couldn't figure out, 'Why am I getting on this bus to go to Georgia with this lady?' "

When Dent was ten, one mystery ended and another began. Denise O'Dey had grown increasingly anxious about her relationship with her son, almost bitter that the boy didn't know her true identity. "My mother had started to get a little edgy," Dent said. Every time she had to return the boy to the people he thought were his parents, the departure pained her. So on their annual bus ride—they were up around Jacksonville, headed south—Denise abruptly turned to Bucky and said, "Do you know who I am?"

No warning. Just . . . *Do you know who I am?*

Ten-year-old Bucky said, "Yeah, you're my aunt."

Denise shook her head. "No-no-no-no-no. I'm your mother." Those people Bucky thought were his parents? "They're your aunt and uncle."

And then she turned away and said nothing further. What was going on inside her head, Dent would never know or understand. And, of course, he had enough to think about without trying to figure out what she was thinking—why she chose that moment to tell him, why she couldn't have done so more gently. She sat next to him and said nothing more.

Bucky was reeling, trying to take in the implications of what this woman—*his mother*—had told him. It made sense in a way; now he knew the reason for these odd summer visits. Still, it was a hell of a lot for a little boy to absorb. And almost immediately he thought, *Wait a minute. If you're my mom, who's my dad?*

The answer to that question was not forthcoming, not on this bus ride, not for years; Denise's anger at Bucky's father hadn't diminished. "They would never tell me," Dent said. Not his mother, not the Dents, not anyone else in the family. "They just didn't want me to know."

For years, Dent lived, unhappily, in ignorance, wondering why his family wouldn't share such vital information with him. He longed to know the identity of his blood father; no one would tell him anything. In the meantime, his relationship with Denise, which had never been easy, was increasingly strained. He hadn't grown up with her, never felt any real emotional connection to her. Once she came to pick him up from school and he ran away, jumping over a fence and hiding out on a nearby Indian reservation. "I said, 'I'm not going,' " Dent recalled, "and I ran." The people who had raised him, they were his real mom and dad, and Dent kept calling them that. But still . . . it was a painful and confusing situation. Sometimes at family gatherings, Dent hesitated before using the word *mom*, because he didn't know which woman would respond.

As he progressed through high school and junior college, Dent was growing into a thoughtful young man and a talented baseball player. On the field, he could set aside the pain he lived with; baseball was a great distraction, and Dent loved it and excelled at it. But the gap in his life nagged at him. *Who is my father?* Not just his name, but what kind of man was he? What did he do? Was Bucky like him? Was he such a bad person that Bucky could never know him? Or did his mother insist on the separation for selfish reasons, because she was still angry at the man? In 1970, when Dent was 18, he even made a road trip to Savannah by himself to try to find his father. But without a name or a picture, he didn't get very far.

At least Dent was enjoying more success in baseball. The White Sox signed him in 1970 and, after a couple of years in the minors, he became their starting shortstop. He wasn't a flashy player, and he didn't speak much to the press. Yet he was quietly consistent both on the field and at the plate. From 1975 to 1977, he averaged 158 games a year. In 1975, he hit .264 and made the All-Star team. From the outside, Dent seemed to be living a charmed life.

But he still felt incomplete. He never gave up searching for his father, and he even got counseling to know what to expect if and when he found the man. "This counselor gave me a whole thing to say" to his father, Dent recalled. " 'You've got to be careful, you've got to assume that he doesn't know that he has a son. So you have to ask him some questions, and if he answers them, you know where to go from there.' "

In the fall of 1976, Dent called his mother and demanded to know. He wasn't going to accept no for an answer any more, he said. She had to tell him.

He'd made similar calls before, to no avail. But for some reason, this time his mother gave in. Finally, she told Bucky that his father was a man named Russell Stanford and that he lived in Savannah. But she couldn't resist trying to throw him off the scent; Stanford lived in a nursing home, Denise O'Dey said. It wasn't true. But perhaps if Dent looked in Savannah's nursing homes and still couldn't find his father, he might assume that the man had died and give up his search.

Dent traveled to Savannah and looked in the phone book. Fourteen

Stanfords were listed there. One of them had a first name, "Russy," close to his own name. Dent wrote down the address and drove to the house, but nobody answered the door. As he turned to walk away, he saw a next-door neighbor watching him. "Does Mr. Stanford live here?" he asked the woman. She hesitated before saying yes. "Do you know where he works, or when he's coming home?" Dent said. She shook her head no. "Listen," Dent implored. "He's my father. I'm looking for him, and I'd like to find him."

The woman gave Dent a close look, then told him to wait and went inside her house. When she opened the door again, she held a business card in her hand—Russy Stanford's card. It listed the address of an upholstery company in town. Clutching the scrap of paper, Dent went to the small shop.

"I walked in and saw him standing in the back, and he looked at me and he turned around real quick, like he saw a ghost," Dent said. "I asked the lady at the desk, 'Is Mr. Stanford here?' "

The woman called to the man, who had retreated into a back room, and he returned, his face expressionless. Dent said to him, "Do you know who I am? My name is Bucky Dent."

And his father looked at him and said, "Russell Earl"—the name that Bucky had been given at birth.

"I've been looking for you for almost twenty-five years," Dent said, and his father answered, "Well, I've been living in the same damn house for twenty-five years."

"And so it went from there," Dent would recall. That night, the two went to a gathering of all the Stanfords, and Dent kept looking around the room in wonder, seeing all these people who looked like him.

Over time, Dent would get to know his father somewhat. He would learn that though his father had married once, he had never had any other children. Meeting Bucky had moved him deeply, and when the Yankees won the World Series in 1977, the son had felt a deep satisfaction that he could bring such happiness and excitement into his dad's life. That was another reason why he wanted to do well in 1978: to make his father proud. To make up for lost time. When the season was over, Dent would start writing a book about his family journey, an inspirational book for kids to show them that they could come from broken homes, painful situations, and still make it. The book never got published, because, thanks to the huge success of Jim Bouton's *Ball Four* back in 1970 and Sparky Lyle's *The Bronx Zoo* in 1979, publishers were in the mood for gossip and insider revelations about baseball.

"They wanted bad stuff," Dent said, but dishing dirt wasn't his style. He wanted to call his book "American Dream."

Still, the time Bucky and his father spent together as grown men couldn't replace the time they should have shared as father and child. And some years down the road, another of life's hard knocks would separate them again. Dent's father, who had become a trucker in the meantime, grew tired while driving a truck through a snowstorm in North Carolina. To be safe, Stanford pulled off the road and went to sleep in the truck cab. He didn't know that the truck's tailpipe had come loose and some of what he was breathing was carbon monoxide. When he woke up—it was something of a miracle that he did wake up—much of his memory was gone. He would spend a year in the hospital, and when he came out, he was really never the same. Something was wrong with his speech, for one thing. His words sped up and tumbled together, so that it was difficult to understand him. "I'd call and say, 'Hey, Dad, how you doing?' " Dent said. "And he'd go, '*Realgoodhowyoudoing?*' " Dent, who had had to work to get to know his father, now had to work just to understand what the man was trying to say.

So as he entered the batter's box to hit against Mike Torrez, Bucky Dent carried within him a personal history that shaped the way he played baseball. He was thoughtful, reliable, and consistent, qualities you might expect from a guy who'd been methodically searching for stability all his life. Dent was religious, and wore a Saint Christopher medal around his neck. He could be one of the guys—the night before, he'd gone out to Daisy Buchanan's for beers with his teammates—but he would never be one of the loud and raucous personalities on the Yankees; Dent had too much heaviness in his life for that. And today, he was feeling more than the usual intensity. This—going into Fenway, playing one game to determine your future—was more pressure than he'd felt during the '77 World Series. "We did not want to lose to the Boston Red Sox," Dent said. "That was the last thing we wanted to do."

Despite his low batting average, Dent had hit Red Sox pitching hard: over the season, he'd gone 11–35 against Boston, a .314 average. Even so, Torrez felt comfortable pitching against Dent. He liked to pitch aggressively against the shortstop, who was, after all, the team's number nine hitter. Generally he'd try to get ahead on the count with fastballs, jamming Dent inside, then mix it up with a curveball, and, if he got two strikes on Dent, he'd use the slider as his out pitch.

This time, he started with a breaking ball, high, then followed that with a fastball. Dent swung awkwardly and missed. Another ball high was followed by a slider away. Dent swung and hit a sinking line drive into right-center field, similar to the ball hit by Brian Doyle but this time clearly out of Remy's reach. For a second, as Remy and Fred Lynn raced from their positions, the ball seemed certain to drop for a hit. But Rice, who had gotten an excellent jump, caught it while sprinting in the direction of second base.

I just missed it, Dent thought as he trotted back to the Yankee dugout. *I took a pretty good swing and just missed it.*

With two out now, Mickey Rivers quickly smacked a line drive past Scott at first base. Rice retrieved the ball near the right field line, but Rivers zipped into second easily. Twice now in three innings, Mickey Rivers was edging off second base, the only Yankee to get aboard against Torrez.

Thurman Munson, who had struck out in the first inning, came up again. In left field, Carl Yastrzemski moved in, hoping to throw Rivers out at home on a single. It wouldn't be necessary. Munson fouled back a slider, then watched a fastball that bounced about three feet in front of the plate, which Fisk nicely blocked. With the count 1–1, he lined another slider foul into the stands along first base—a classic Munson swing, an attempt to drive the ball to the opposite field to increase Rivers's chances of scoring. With Yaz playing in, a single to left might not score Rivers.

Torrez gave him a high fastball next, and Munson awkwardly checked his swing to make the count two balls and two strikes. On the next pitch, a breaking ball that also hit the dirt before home plate, Munson couldn't hold up; he swung and missed. When Fisk couldn't hold on to the ball, Munson dashed for first, but Fisk jogged up the line and tossed the ball to George Scott for the third out.

Mixing location and speed, Torrez had struck out Munson a second time. While the Red Sox batted against Guidry, he would retreat to the locker room. Torrez sweated so much when he pitched that after three innings, his jersey would be soaked with perspiration, and in a typical game he would change shirts twice. (In one 1977 game, Graig Nettles had switched Torrez's jersey as a joke, so that, without realizing it, the pitcher started the seventh inning of a game with a different number than he'd worn in the sixth.) Torrez had shut out the Yankees for three innings, settling down fast after starting the game by walking Rivers on four pitches. Now he seemed to be cruising. Shutting out the Yankees in Fenway Park, even if only for three innings, was no small accomplishment.

Ron Guidry now started the bottom of the third determined to keep pace; he could afford no more mistakes like the home run pitch to Yaz. Guidry would begin by facing George Scott, the big, right-handed-hitting first baseman known as "Boomer." Scott had had a poor season; in 119 games, he'd hit .230, with just 12 home runs and 54 runs batted in. Over the course of his thirteen-year career, Scott had won eight Gold Gloves at first base and, as his snare of Chris Chambliss's line drive in the top of the second showed, he could still field. But Scott, whom the Red Sox had originally drafted, then traded, then reacquired, had had an off year that would mark the beginning of the end of a career that never quite lived up to its potential.

Born on March 23, 1944, in Greenville, Mississippi, Scott came from a poor family; as a six-year-old boy, he was picking cotton from six in the morning till six in the evening, for which he received the sum of $1.50. Little League baseball was his escape, though he was so good at it, and so much better than his peers, that for some years his coach asked him not to play; his presence made games too uneven. The Red Sox signed Scott in 1962, just three years after Pumpsie Green desegregated the team. He played his way through the farm system and joined the team in 1966. Scott was strong and quick and, at six feet two inches and 215 pounds, a powerful home run hitter. He was a flamboyant personality, known for his colorful language and clothing; on his first road trip with the Red Sox, he wore a brightly colored ascot instead of a tie. "George could be the biggest drawing card in Boston in many years," one *Sporting News* writer said, "and the Red Sox certainly need one."

But Scott had a strong personality—some would call it arrogant, others just proud—and an unfortunate habit of striking out with prodigious frequency. He also had a weight problem. The Sox listed him at 215, but that was wishful thinking; he left that weight in the rearview mirror soon after reaching the big leagues. In 1967 and 1968, he'd feuded with manager Dick Williams, who decided that Scott was fat and dumb, and didn't hesitate to say so. After Scott went 1–8 in an extra-inning game in 1967, Williams declared, "Talking to Scott is like talking to a cement wall." Williams seemed to think that such criticism would motivate Scott, but the opposite occurred. The next season, Scott developed a flaw in his swing and had a miserable year, batting a lowly .171 in 350 at-bats. He and Williams fought again, and near the end of the season, Scott announced that "I'd rather pick cotton than play for him again."

Both were soon gone, Williams fired by Tom Yawkey in September 1969 after feuding with Carl Yastrzemski, and Scott sent to Milwaukee in October 1971 as part of a ten-player trade. Scott played well for the Brewers. In 1975, he hit 36 home runs with 109 runs batted in. But he clashed with his manager and teammates in Milwaukee as well, developing a reputation as a selfish player who didn't appreciate coaching well. "If I wanted to be a puppet," he said once, "I could still be in Boston." As it turned out, in December 1976, the Brewers sent him and outfielder Bernie Carbo back to the Sox for first baseman Cecil Cooper—yet another in a history of bad Red Sox trades. Cooper would go on to a far more productive career than Carbo and Scott combined had in their remaining years. Several Brewers were glad to see Scott go. "He was a bad influence on the club," infielder Don Money said. With Scott gone, "It's quieter here now. There's more of a team atmosphere."

Scott was supposed to be the Red Sox's answer to Reggie Jackson. "If you look it up, Scott has almost as good and in some cases an even better record than Jackson," Red Sox general manager Dick O'Connell said. But Scott wasn't the same player he had been when he'd first come to Boston. He was heavier, for one thing—around 240, 245 pounds. Scott's ballooning midsection led to criticism from the fans that was thought by some observers to have racist overtones. "Enough already with the tired chicken-wing and racist watermelon jokes," *Boston Globe* columnist Ray Fitzgerald warned.

Scott had hit 33 home runs and driven in 95 runs in 1977, but he would not come close to matching those numbers in 1978. In April he'd broken a finger trying to catch a pop-up, and a bad back plagued him for much of the season. Through most of his career, Scott would have been insulted to be batting eighth, and would have made his displeasure known. But in this lineup, and with Scott's numbers, he couldn't argue. Scott could still be a threat, but he was unquestionably a fading one.

Guidry started Scott with a fastball, high. His second pitch looked like a slider, but Scott swung and smashed it deep to center. For a second, Rivers hesitated. He couldn't see the path of the ball; for some reason, he wasn't wearing sunglasses. The drive bounced low off the wall, where Rivers, who had given up trying to catch it, fielded it cleanly. As Rivers pivoted and threw, Scott lumbered toward second, a matchup of a slow runner versus a weak thrower. The former slid into second and won—barely. With no one out, Scott was in scoring position, an excellent opportunity for the Red Sox to add to their 1–0 lead. Rivers, meanwhile, trotted off the field and toward the Yankee dugout, where someone handed him a couple of pairs of sunglasses to consider. He angrily tossed one back into the dugout, took the other, and trotted back to his position in center field.

Third baseman Jack Brohamer, another right-handed hitter, came to the plate. The previous November, the Sox had signed the twenty-eight-year-old, a light-hitting infielder with the Indians and the White Sox, for three years at $100,000 a year. The team had originally thought he would take over second from the even lighter-hitting Denny Doyle. Brohamer was an improvement, but not a huge one, and he was honest about his status in the game. "I'm the first to admit that my range isn't all that good," he said when he was playing for Cleveland. "I'm not the best, but I'm not the worst in the league either." But a week after signing Brohamer, the Sox traded for Jerry Remy, and Brohamer was quickly relegated to the role of utility infielder. "Being a utility player is fine with me," he said. "When I was with Cleveland and Chicago, I knew the season was going to be over for us by July 1. Over here, I know we have a chance at winning." Now, he was starting at third in the most important game of his career because of Butch Hobson's chronically hurt elbow.

It almost didn't happen that way, though. The night before, Don Zimmer had called Carl Yastrzemski into his office to talk about the upcoming game. Zimmer mentioned that he planned to start Brohamer, even though Brohamer was a left-handed hitter and another substitute infielder, Frank Duffy, hit right-handed. That didn't make sense, Yastrzemski argued. Duffy stood a better chance of being able to hit the lefty Guidry. "Brohamer's not going to have a chance against this guy." And if right-hander Goose Gossage came in to relieve Guidry, then Zimmer could always use Brohamer as a pinch hitter. But the manager wouldn't change his mind. Brohamer had been playing well in relief of Hobson the past couple of weeks, and for Zimmer, you stuck with the guys who got you there.

Zimmer was playing one run at a time against Guidry; he didn't expect to get many, so he would scratch them out wherever he could. On the first pitch, Brohamer bunted perfectly down the first base line—a deeply conservative play given that there were no outs and a man on second. But Scott wasn't a sure run on a single, and who knew if Guidry would give up another hit?

Munson fielded the ball, glanced toward third, saw that he had no play there, pivoted, and threw Brohamer out at first. One down, but Scott stood large at third. Brohamer had executed his job perfectly.

Rick Burleson, who had been called out on strikes in the first inning, now came to the plate. He took two fastballs low; Guidry wasn't going to give him anything he could put in the air for a sacrifice fly. The third pitch was a slider that Burleson swung on and bounced to Nettles at third; right-handed hitters had hit just that kind of ground ball off Guidry's slider all season, and just as he had done all season, Nettles threw the batter out easily. Two out, and the situation was a little safer for the Yankees.

It was up to Jerry Remy, who had previously flied out to Roy White in left, to drive Scott home. Guidry started him with an inside fastball for a strike. Then he put the slider on the opposite side of the plate, but just missed, making the count 1–1. Remy sat on the third pitch, which looked like it hit the exact same spot as the previous slider. This time, Denkinger called it a strike.

Behind on the count now, 1–2, Remy had to protect the plate. So when Guidry spotted a fastball on the outside corner, Remy had little choice but to swing. He drove another soft fly ball to left field, where Roy White caught it easily for the third out.

Guidry had defused the threat of the leadoff double. Still, the Red Sox had hit some hard balls off him, and it seemed only a matter of time till they added to their 1–0 lead.

CHAPTER 9

BILLY MARTIN FEELS THE HEAT

There is a story, perhaps apocryphal, about Billy Martin: In the summer of 1978, he was filming a commercial with a six-year-old boy. When the child shook hands with the Yankee manager, the first thing he said to Martin was, "My grandfather told me to be very polite and nice, or you'll kick the hell out of me."

Martin wouldn't have beaten up a six-year-old, unless perhaps the boy played for an opposing team. But Martin was a fighter in every sense of the word, and unapologetically so. "My temper has not been a detriment, it's been an asset," he insisted. In some ways, that was true. Martin's emotion kept his teams from growing complacent, and some players responded well to his pushes and shoves, whether physical or figurative. Yet Martin's temper came with other emotional millstones: He could be evasive, passive-aggressive, manipulative, childish, and uncommunicative. When he was feeling hurt or threatened, he reacted badly, alternating between lashing out and sulking. He refused to take responsibility for problems of his own making. No one who ever played for Martin would have questioned his knowledge of baseball, his feel for strategy, his gift for anticipating the moves of other teams and making just the right calls in return—or, just as often, in advance. Only a handful of other managers could lead a team as Martin could when he was at the top of his game—Sparky Anderson, Earl Weaver, Dick Williams, perhaps. But it was only a matter of time till Martin's toxic personality infected a clubhouse and the arc of his players' performances began to curve downward. In combination with George Steinbrenner's obsessive desire to involve himself in the Yankees' daily conduct, and Steinbrenner's bullying management style, Martin's various ailments, both physical and mental, began to take their toll on the Yankees in June and July of 1978.

To be sure, the owner wasn't helping matters. In the Boston series,

Steinbrenner had ramped up the pressure; whispers that Martin might get fired if the Yankees didn't sweep started to drift through the pages of the New York newspapers like gossip over clotheslines. (Only on the Yankees could a manager's fate hinge on the outcome of a single regular season series, or even a single game.) One rumor, probably true, held that the Yankees were considering swapping managers with the Chicago White Sox, firing Martin so the White Sox could hire him while the White Sox fired Bob Lemon so the Yankees could hire him.

"Billy, being a professional manager, knows what happens to managers who are supposed to win who don't win," said team president Al Rosen. After the Yankees lost the first game against Boston, Steinbrenner reminded the public that Martin "understood at the start that I wasn't particularly happy when we left spring training. I didn't think we stressed fundamentals enough and I didn't think we were ready, and I said that at the time. . . . I told [Martin and Rosen] that and let it be. I said, 'You've heard how I feel, that's all I'm going to say. You guys run the club. That's how you guys want it. If you win, you deserve all the credit; if you lose, you're going to get the full blame.' "

In later years, such edicts would become numbingly familiar to Yankee players and their fans, but in 1978, they were still relatively new, and thus their impact was greater than in the years to come, when Steinbrenner's patterns and techniques of suasion had grown more transparent. The logic behind Steinbrenner's stratagems was not easily deciphered. First was the dubious wisdom of making such a statement publicly; Steinbrenner genuinely believed that deliberating in the press about Martin's job would somehow cause Martin to manage more effectively, as if he were currently going through the motions. It was a wildly counterproductive measure; no one put more pressure on himself than Martin did, or was more disappointed when the team lost.

Then there was Steinbrenner's insistence that he had empowered Martin and Rosen to do whatever they wanted, and that any unfortunate results were consequently their fault and their fault alone. The premise was absurd; not even when Steinbrenner was banned from running his team had he ceded the running of it, and free agents such as Jackson, Gossage, and reliever Rawly Eastwick had been signed by Steinbrenner against Martin's will. The conclusion was equally hollow; it did not follow that, if the Yankees weren't in first place, the fault was inherently that of the manager and team president. Wins and losses were rarely that simple. Three days later, however, Steinbrenner would reinforce the theme: Martin's fate, he said, "was Al Rosen's decision, but I'll tell you one thing, I won't put up with this much longer." The line showed how maddening Steinbrenner could be: he began by saying something that was patently untrue, then flatly declared the untruth of it, never acknowledging that he had contradicted himself within the span of a single sentence. Martin's fate clearly was not Rosen's decision, except when Steinbrenner was saying so either to pressure Rosen or to distance himself from an unpleasant situation. But whenever Steinbrenner wanted to intervene, whether Martin stayed or went would be his decision.

And finally there was the accuracy of Steinbrenner's charge that the Yankees were losing because Martin had insufficiently schooled them in baseball fundamentals. The idea that Steinbrenner knew enough to lecture Martin about the fundamentals of baseball was laughable, as was the notion that a Billy Martin–managed team failed to execute the basics of the game with precision and consistency. The Yankees were not missing cutoff men or failing to execute hit-and-runs or forgetting to cover a base. There were two primary reasons why the team was not in first place: the fact that the Red Sox were extremely good, and the number of injuries the Yankees had endured, particularly to its pitching staff, a fact of life about which Steinbrenner was particularly unsympathetic. After rookie Jim Beattie was shelled by the Sox, and very shortly after Steinbrenner dispatched him across the country to the minors that same night, Steinbrenner declared, "He looked scared," which couldn't have been helpful to anyone. In the ensuing days, Steinbrenner floated a plan either to fire pitching coach Art Fowler or send him to the minors. Since Fowler was a close friend and drinking partner of the manager's, most observers thought that the move was an attempt to force Martin to resign. All the twisting in the wind was torturing Martin. Sometimes he sounded petulant. "It hurts me," he said of the firing talk. "I get tired of it. After winning two straight pennants and a World Series, why should I have to be on the block all the time?" Other times Martin came across as angry and defiant. "I'm sick and tired of hearing about being fired," he would say. "There are managers all over baseball who have never won and you never hear about them being close to being fired." Martin had a point: no manager in baseball history had ever lost his job the year after winning consecutive pennants.

While he lambasted his own team, Steinbrenner overlooked the fact that the Red Sox were playing better than any other team in either league. On the day Steinbrenner made his remarks, Boston had a record of 46–21 and a winning percentage of .687, which would have put the team solidly in first in any of baseball's four divisions. At that rate, the Red Sox would finish the season with 111 wins, which would have made them one of the most successful teams in the history of the sport. The Yankees were nine games above .500 at 38–27. Their winning percentage of .585 would have put them first in the American League West, over Kansas City, and in the National League East, over the Cubs.

Martin did not handle Steinbrenner's manipulations well; he wanted to be listened to, to be understood and sympathized with. He wanted, even, to be loved. And so he pled his case before an audience always willing to listen: the press. "Next year, I'm not coming to Boston," he told a reporter for the *New York Post*. "Every time I come here, I get fired"—a reference to his dugout fight with Jackson in June 1977. "I'm on George's side. I'm trying to win. . . . You see this uniform? It says 'Yankees.' We're all Yankees. We're all trying to win." There was something plaintive and wistful in Martin's lament, a call to an era when Yankee pride had more romance, more coherence to it than it had had since 1973. *Let's stop fighting with each other. We're Yankees!*

With a two-game series coming up against the Sox in the stadium starting on June 26, and then two more games in Fenway on July 3 and 4, the Yankees insisted that there was plenty of time, plenty of reason to hope. "Sure, they beat us two out of three," Lou Piniella said. "But when we threw one of our better pitchers at them"—Don Gullett—"we beat them." Just thinking about the Red Sox seemed to irritate Piniella. "Boston's no damn cinch, I don't care what anyone says," he declared. Martin agreed: "When we start winning the way we should, and we will, we don't have to worry about the Red Sox."

But in the days between the two series, Boston certainly looked like a cinch. Behind the pitching of Bill Lee, Luis Tiant, and Mike Torrez, they swept the Orioles handily, stopping a seven-game winning streak by Jim Palmer. Lee's win was the first since his one-day strike following the trade of Bernie Carbo, and he seemed back to form in more ways than one. "I have to compliment my tenacity on this one," he admitted after his 5–2 victory against Palmer. On the way to the showers, Lee shouted to the press, "Remember—no nukes is good nukes!"

When the series was done, Orioles manager Earl Weaver insisted that the Sox could be beaten. "They can't play all year without playing poorly," he said of the Sox. "They're going to hit a stretch where everything goes against them, as individuals and as a team." Don

Zimmer disagreed. "I don't think we're going to win every game," he said, "but we're not going into any tailspin."

In Boston, the fans were responding with an enthusiasm perhaps greater than any the team had seen. They poured into Fenway Park. On June 25, the Sox reached the million mark in attendance—1,010,061, to be exact—the earliest in the team's history. In 1977, Boston had hit the 2 million mark in attendance for the first time; now they were on track to top 2.2 million. The last team to reach that number was the 1949 Yankees.

On television, the Red Sox were equally successful. Sox games were earning almost a 50 percent share of the New England television audience—and this was for games in June, long before the high-stakes contests of September and October. What made that number especially impressive is that Sox games were carried on Channel 38, WSBK-TV, a UHF station with a weak signal. Snowy reception and all, fans tuned in. On a Sunday afternoon against Baltimore, the Sox scored a 76 percent television share, the highest in their history. Sox fans sensed that the World Series victory that had been denied them for so long felt more plausible this year than it had in '67, more than it had against the Big Red Machine in '75, more than it had in decades. They wanted to see history in the making and years of frustration come to an end.

On the afternoon of June 26, Billy Martin, Al Rosen, and George Steinbrenner met to try to resolve their differences. For two and a half hours, they talked, and when they were done, Steinbrenner released a statement saying that Martin's job was secure for the rest of the season. "It was a solid, air-clearing session," the statement read. "Everything was discussed in considerable detail, and I think Billy and Al got a lot of things ironed out." (After all, Steinbrenner—wise, benevolent, above the fray—couldn't have been part of the problem.) "In fairness to Billy, I think this commitment to him is warranted in view of his cooperative attitude at the meeting."

Later, Steinbrenner would make his management manipulations still more explicit. "I know what I'm doing," he told the *New York Post*. "I know how to run a business, whether it's the shipping business or the baseball business. I didn't come into this town on a pumpkin. There is a lot of psychology involved in running a team. The manager was fighting with the players, the players were fighting with each other, the players were angry with the manager. Now they can take their minds off that, be mad at me, and play ball."

Unfortunately for the Yankees, it wasn't that simple. If Steinbrenner's intention had been to show the world that he was the boss, his public humiliation of Martin, and especially his patronizing praise of Martin's "cooperative attitude," backfired. When Martin brought out the lineup card for the game against Boston on the 26th, the 52,000 fans present stood and roared, and Martin tipped his cap, smiled, and looked like a man who's just been spared the guillotine. Perhaps they were all Yankees, after all; perhaps Martin could call on the glory of the Yankee past to rally the people around him in the team's tumultuous present. "This is worth all of it," he would say. Martin certainly needed the infusion of popular support. Before the game, he had faced twenty-six writers, two interviewers from ABC, which was broadcasting that night's game, and assorted photographers and radio reporters. Flanked by his lawyer and agent, Martin insisted that "our team doesn't worry about stuff like this."

That wasn't entirely true. While the Yankees had been hardened by the turmoil of the 1977 season, all the rumors, the reporters' questions, the newspaper headlines were distracting. Their on-field challenge was daunting enough; on June 26, Boston was at 50–21, a winning percentage of .704. The Yankees lagged 8½ games back, at 41–29 and .586. Meanwhile, all the tension was tearing up Martin, who looked awful—tired, pale, thin, exhausted, a man on the verge of a breakdown. He was drinking even more heavily than usual, and sometimes before day games he would show up in the clubhouse with just an hour or so to spare. The press room at Yankee Stadium had a liquor cabinet, and Martin had his own, oft-used key. There was talk that he had some ominous physical ailment, perhaps a mysterious spot on his liver. Whatever the cause, there was certainly reason to fear for the health of both Martin and his liver. Martin looked "about 90 feet from a collapse," the *Post*'s Henry Hecht said.

Dennis Eckersley beat the Yankees for the second time in a week on the 26th, 4–1. Andy Messersmith, still trying to come back from his separated shoulder, pitched valiantly, only to be undone by a novice mistake. In the fifth inning, rookie Damaso Garcia—yanked up from the minors to fill in for the hurt Willie Randolph—slammed into Fred Stanley, who was playing in place of the hurt Bucky Dent, while Stanley was trying to catch a Butch Hobson pop-up. Garcia knocked the ball out of Stanley's glove, Hobson wound up on second, and two outs later, Jim Rice slammed his 23rd home run, an opposite-field shot to right center. In the eighth, Carlton Fisk homered off a Rich Gossage fastball to make the score 4–1, where it would remain.

Headlines about the Martin-Steinbrenner-Rosen meeting blared the next morning, overshadowing the outcome of the game. A pattern was becoming established in the New York papers: the sports pages would banner the news of Yankee controversies, while stories of what happened on-field were relegated to smaller type. Perhaps there was a method to Steinbrenner's madness, because fans across the country were tuning in to the Yankees' drama and the rivalry of two teams: one the world champions but struggling, the other easy to like and ascendant. Broadcast by ABC, the Monday night contest earned a 28 percent audience share, meaning that some 26 million people in the United States watched the game. That was the highest share of any prime-time baseball broadcast since April 8, 1974, when Hank Aaron hit his 715th home run.

In the second game, Ron Guidry started versus a twenty-seven-year-old Sox rookie, Jim Wright. Guidry was not his sharpest; he looked tired, and in the seventh inning, with the Yankees leading, 3–2, he loaded the bases. Martin brought in Gossage, who promptly gave up a two-run single to Rick Burleson before closing out the side. In the eighth, Reggie Jackson drove in Thurman Munson to tie the game. Gossage then silenced the Red Sox for five innings before giving way in the twelfth to Sparky Lyle, who shut out Boston until Graig Nettles hit a two-run homer in the bottom of the fourteenth. The Yankees had earned a victory, but they'd made it look hard.

They didn't exactly come out of the two-game split with momentum. The next day, the Yankees, playing three games in a twenty-four-hour span, were swept by the Milwaukee Brewers, 5–0 and 7–2. (The Sox had the day off, then, on the 29th, resumed their domination of the Orioles.) New York was now 9½ games back, in third place behind Milwaukee, and Steinbrenner's patience was wearing thinner. He blasted the Yankee veterans, who, he said, had disappointed the team during the Milwaukee doubleheader. "The kids did all right," he said. "The veterans let us down. Jackson, the cleanup hitter, 0–7? Nettles, not playing?" (Claiming exhaustion, the third baseman had sat out the second game.) The owner questioned the toughness of players such as Munson, Dent, Rivers, and Randolph, all of whom were either not playing or playing below their potential because of injuries. "Maybe they don't play anymore because their agents tell them not to," Steinbrenner suggested.

Blood rivals: In one of numerous Yankee–Red Sox fights during the 1970s, Yankee Thurman Munson tries to tackle Red Sox catcher Carlton Fisk on August 1, 1973. Carl Yastrzemski holds Munson back as Yankee Gene Michael, Munson's roommate, and Red Sox players Doug Griffin and John Curtis look on. (Image by Bettman/CORBIS)

Red Sox third baseman Butch Hobson played like the former football player he was, but was hampered by bone chips in the elbow of his throwing arm.
(Image by Bettman/CORBIS)

With shortstop Pee Wee Reese looking on, Dodgers second baseman Don Zimmer jumps for the cameras during spring training in 1955. Zimmer was one of the Dodgers' most promising minor-league prospects before being twice hit in the head by pitches. (Image by Bettman/CORBIS)

In the Red Sox clubhouse, a dejected Don Zimmer searches for words after the Yankees won on October 2, 1978. (Image by Bettman/CORBIS)

"When everything was good in his eyes," second baseman Brian Doyle once said of Billy Martin, "he was fun to be around." (Focus on Sport/Getty Images)

Angry that the Yankees had not really tried to resign him after the 1977 season, Mike Torrez—here pitching against Cleveland on April 12, 1978—desperately wanted to beat his old team in October. (Ron Kuntz Collection/Diamond Images/Getty Images)

A swing powerful enough to break bats: With a batting average of .316, 46 home runs, and 139 runs batted in, Jim Rice had one of the greatest offensive seasons in baseball history in 1978. (Diamond Images/Getty Images)

In 1978, Carl Yastrzemski had been a Red Sox for 17 years, but was still capable of the form that had helped win him the Triple Crown in 1967, the last player in the sport to do so. (Rich Pilling/MLB Photos via Getty Images)

Better known as a hitter than an outfielder, Lou Piniella would make two outstanding plays in right field against the Red Sox that saved the playoff game for the Yankees. (Neal Preston/CORBIS)

Rich "Goose" Gossage joined the Yankees in 1978 hoping to relieve in tandem with Cy Young winner Sparky Lyle. Instead, Gossage said, "They gave me his job on a silver platter." (Image by Bettman/CORBIS)

Like Billy Martin, the man he replaced, Yankee manager Bob Lemon liked a drink. Unlike Martin, he didn't mix drinking and managing. (Image by Bettman/CORBIS)

"Nobody can tell me I'm not good enough to do something I want to do," Ron Guidry once said. "In one way or another, I will prove you wrong." In 1978, Guidry compiled an astounding regular season record of 25–3, with an earned run average of 1.74. (Barton Silverman/The New York Times/Redux)

In twelve pro seasons, Bucky Dent hit just 40 home runs. This one, however, would become an iconic moment in baseball history. (AP/World Wide)

After weeks of feeling that he was letting his teammates down, Bucky Dent is greeted at home plate by Roy White and Chris Chambliss after his seventh inning home run put New York ahead of Boston, 3–2. (Image by Bettman/CORBIS)

After his 8th-inning home run that gave the Yankees a 5–2 lead over the Red Sox in their October 1978 playoff, Reggie Jackson stopped to shake hands with Yankee owner George Steinbrenner. (Image by Bettman/CORBIS)

He's going to do it again, Graig Nettles thought when Carl Yastrzemski came to the plate in the bottom of the ninth. Instead, Yastrzemski popped up to Nettles, and the Yankees won, 5–4. (Image by Bettman/CORBIS)

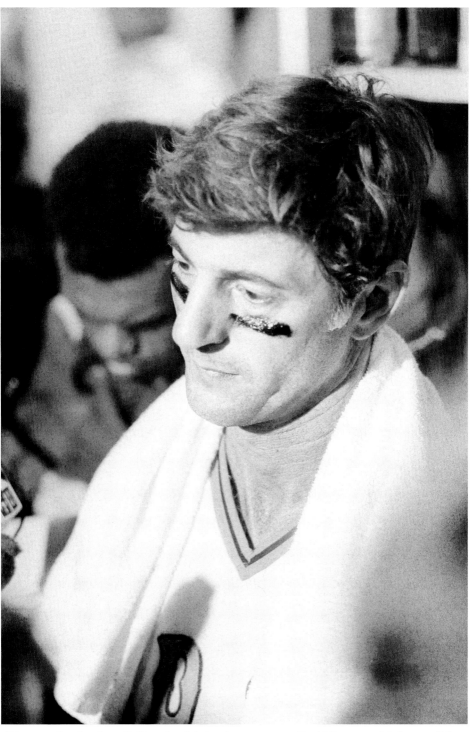

"I wanted to be there": Despite driving in two runs, Carl Yastrzemski, here talking to reporters after the game, felt like he'd let down "all of New England."
(Neal Preston/CORBIS)

"I'm just happy to be here," Thurman Munson repeatedly told reporters in 1978. Sportswriters rarely saw the funny, caring man who helped his teammates through hard stretches and learned to fly in order to spend more time with his family. While practicing landings at an airport near his Ohio home, Munson crashed his plane and was killed on August 2, 1979. The New York Yankees of that era would never really recover from the loss. (Photo by Ronald C. Modra/Sports Imagery/Getty Images)

Perhaps Steinbrenner was hoping to prick the players' pride, make them so angry at him that they'd show more life on the field. Again, though, there was more evidence that the strategy backfired than that it worked. Thurman Munson was livid about the suggestion that he wasn't giving his all. "I've got three years more on my contact after this one," he said. "I wouldn't count on my playing all three." Jackson, who had been markedly more reserved than in his first season with the Yankees, was starting to sound worn-down. "I'm tired," he said. "I make a lot of money, sure, but it's tough, the grind every day, the people after me, the booing." In Detroit, a fan had thrown a cherry bomb at Jackson, and the startled outfielder had played the rest of the game wearing a batting helmet in right field. "Tough, tough, tough," Jackson said. "Go out there someday, put on number 44, paint your face black . . . see what it's like."

On June 30, Jackson had five runs batted in against Detroit, including a grand slam, but he insisted that his output had nothing to do with Steinbrenner's goading. "That stuff is as weak as a five-cent pack of Kool-Aid in the ocean with two teaspoons of sugar," he said. "You know how weak that is." In speaking to the press, Steinbrenner hoped to demonstrate that he was the one in control of the club. But his comments prompted the players to bite back, and the resulting profusion of angry quotes created the impression that no one was in control. Such chaos boded poorly for Martin, as Steinbrenner was unlikely to blame himself for the unsettled state of affairs. Only Ron Guidry, who won his 13th straight game on July 2, seemed immune to the madness.

The Red Sox, meanwhile, were cruising, winning decisively not just in Fenway, but even on the road, where as of the 2nd they had won 16 of their last 25 games. That was unusual for the Sox. So was the fact that their pitching was superlative. Tiant, Eckersley, Torrez, and Lee were all comfortably on a pace to win more than the 12-game mark that Tiant had set the previous season. Torrez, who had already won 11 games, was proving to be a workhorse even when he didn't win. Against the Orioles on July 1, he lost to Jim Palmer, 3–2, but went eleven innings and threw 160 pitches. Pitching, hitting, and defense were all in sync, and the Boston media, which was consistently more boosterish than New York's, was getting excited. One *Globe* columnist suggested that the entire Red Sox lineup should start the forthcoming All-Star game. "Billy Martin and Reggie Jackson and George Steinbrenner and the Yankees can talk about sore arms being healed, about stretch runs that can be made," Leigh Montville wrote. "The Red Sox just keep rolling."

The pitching deficit was glaringly obvious as the teams faced their third matchup in two weeks, a two-game series at Fenway starting July 3. "We get a well-pitched game every day, while the Yankees get a new guy on the disabled list every day," Carl Yastrzemski said. The Red Sox would start Dennis Eckersley and Bill Lee, winners of 16 games between them. The Yankees would go with Ed Figueroa, although the pitcher was complaining of a sore forearm. Who would pitch the second game for the Yankees was anyone's guess. Don Gullett was pretty much finished for the season. So was Andy Messersmith, who had gone one and a third innings against the Tigers on July 1 before leaving the game in enormous pain. Ken Clay had pulled a chest muscle. The "gutless" Jim Beattie was in Tacoma. Billy Martin hadn't helped things by trading away Ken Holtzman on June 10 and Rawly Eastwick on June 14, largely because he didn't like them. The Yankees had signed Eastwick for $1.1 million, including a $350,000 bonus. They would receive for him outfielder Jay Johnstone, who would bat 65 times for New York that season, and a minor leaguer named Bobby Brown. In the past week, the Yankees had warmed up outfielders Jim Spencer and Paul Blair in the bullpen, just in case.

And then there was Catfish Hunter, whose status was uncertain at best. Once, "all you needed to win a game was to give him the ball," Yastrzemski recalled. "He could put it anywhere he wanted and change speeds." Not anymore. Hunter had pitched one inning against the Red Sox in the previous series, giving up four hits, including two homers. When Yastrzemski struck out with the bases loaded, some observers thought he'd done so on purpose, to take pity on a fading legend. "It's the kind of thing, [like] when you see a car coming, and it's gonna hit a small animal in the road," Don Gullett said. "You turn your head away. You don't want to see it happen."

There was one hope for Hunter: on June 27, he'd undergone a procedure in which he was put under general anesthesia and his shoulder was "manipulated." Team physician Maurice Cowen turned and twisted the shoulder to stretch the muscles, ligaments, and tendons, trying to break down lesions that caused Hunter immense pain whenever he tried to throw. "My arm hurt so bad, I told the doctor I didn't care if he cut this one off and glued another one on," Hunter said. The cracking of the lesions was so loud, for a second Cowen thought he had broken Hunter's arm. He hadn't—but it would take time to know if the procedure had worked, and even if Hunter's pain vanished or lessened, there would be no assurance that the relief was more than temporary. "I'll tell you one thing, the man don't have nothing to be ashamed of, no matter how he goes out," George Scott said. The Yankees were hoping that it was not yet Hunter's time to go out.

On July 3, for the third straight time, Eckersley beat the Yankees, throwing 128 pitches in eight innings. The score was 9–5. Graig Nettles, Gary Thomasson, and Bucky Dent all homered—Dent was back after missing 20 of the previous 34 games—but the game wasn't close, as Yastrzemski and Fisk each drove in three runs, knocking out Figueroa and beating up on rookie Bob Kammeyer, who was pitching in his first major league game. Still the Yankees didn't know who would start for them the next day. "You never know what's going to happen with our pitchers," Sparky Lyle said. "We're going to have to hire fourteen trainers. Make the place like *M*A*S*H*."

On July 4, however, the Yankees got lucky. It rained. And much to the frustration of the Red Sox and the relief of the Yankees, the game was postponed, tacked on to the beginning of a three-game series in Fenway in early September. The Red Sox were sure that they had been robbed of a victory—Bill Lee against some minor leaguer? That was a no-brainer—which would have increased their lead over the Yankees to ten games. "We were crushing them," Fred Lynn recalled. "I said at the time, 'We need to play this game. We don't want to be sending this game somewhere down the road when they're playing better. We *have* to play. Play in slickers, I don't care, get 'em out there.' The Yankees were down."

At the time, though, the consequences seemed harmless. The Yankees were down, and they showed every sign of staying there. Even Ron Guidry couldn't stop the bleeding this time. On July 7, he lost his first, getting pounded by Milwaukee, 6–0, lasting only six innings and giving up five runs. Guidry did not linger in the clubhouse for postgame interviews, and when reporters asked why not, Martin erupted. "There's only one man making the rules in this fucking clubhouse, and that's the manager," he shouted. "Do your fucking homework and don't ask stupid questions like that."

While the Red Sox swept a doubleheader in Cleveland, the Brewers proceeded to take the next two games from the Yankees, who were clearly demoralized. The *New York Times* quoted an anonymous Yankee saying, "This is a cancerous situation. Guys are just going through the motions. Nobody's doing anything." The news got worse still.

Bucky Dent hurt his hamstring for the third time and was put on the fifteen-day disabled list, and the Red Sox lead grew. As baseball shut down for the All-Star game on July 11, Boston was now 10 games up on Milwaukee, 11½ over New York.

Even the stubborn Lou Piniella had to admit that things didn't look good. "It sure doesn't look like we're going to catch them," he conceded. "But I don't think we'll give up. You can still finish a very respectable second."

Second place, however, was not something that either Martin or Steinbrenner would ever consider respectable.

The Fourth Inning

For Torrez and the Red Sox, the Yankee fourth was easy.

Lou Piniella, who had grounded to third baseman Jack Brohamer on his first pitch in the first inning, began the fourth inning by taking a fastball on the outside corner for a strike. Torrez followed with another fastball, this one on the inside part of the plate. Piniella chopped the pitch to almost the same spot he'd hit to in the first. This time, though, the ball was a couple feet farther to Brohamer's left, and scooted under his glove. Behind Brohamer, running to his right, Rick Burleson looked as if he had a play, but the ball bounced off the heel of his glove on the edge of the outfield. Piniella, who had now seen three pitches in two at-bats, was on with a single. Though Piniella was an unlikely candidate to steal, Scott played behind him at first, holding him to the bag.

Reggie Jackson, whose deep fly ball to left field had been knocked down by the wind and caught by Carl Yastrzemski to end the first, now came to the plate. Unfortunately for Jackson, the wind had changed direction entirely since the first inning; now it was blowing solidly out to left. Had that been the case in Jackson's first at-bat, his ball would almost certainly have hit the Green Monster, if not gone over, and with Mickey Rivers on second base, the Yankees would have been at least tied with the Red Sox.

Torrez threw Jackson his first curveball of the game, but it broke low and inside and Jackson laid off it. The second pitch, though, was a breaking ball that caught more of the plate, and Jackson whipped his bat around. The ball shot out to right field. Jim Rice, however, was playing Jackson perfectly, and with only a few quick steps toward the foul line, he caught Jackson's line drive. Rice quickly threw a bullet to first, looking to catch Piniella off the bag. He almost did; Piniella tagged first just a split second before George Scott caught Rice's throw.

In addition to his catch of Bucky Dent's sinking line drive the previous inning, it was Rice's second fine play of the game.

Graig Nettles, who had popped out to Rick Burleson on a check swing in the second, now stepped into the batter's box. Behind the plate, the late afternoon shadow was creeping toward the field now, creating a dark border that snaked from the left field foul line to the area behind home plate and out past the first base dugout. It wouldn't be long before the batters themselves were obscured by the shadow, meaning that the ball would leave the pitcher's hand in sunlight and, somewhere on its way to the plate, pass from a plane of light into one of darkness. That moment of visual shift would make it harder for the batters to pick up the ball and give the pitchers a significant advantage. As the game wore on and the shadow grew deeper, that advantage would grow, which was why even a 1–0 Red Sox lead mattered. The greater the shadow, the harder it would be to overcome a deficit.

Nettles, who wanted so much to beat Torrez, took a fastball outside. Torrez followed that with a breaking ball, which Nettles fouled behind home plate. With a 1–1 count, Torrez came back with a fastball low and away, which Nettles hit hard but foul into the left field stands. It wasn't a pitch the pull hitter would normally swing at, a sign that Torrez was successfully working all areas of the plate, keeping Nettles and the other Yankees off balance. His next pitch, though, was almost a mistake—a fastball waist-high and inside, close to Nettles's power zone. The third baseman swung hard and enthusiastically. But Torrez had put the pitch just a few inches above where Nettles swung most comfortably, and again the third baseman hit under the ball and popped it up. Trotting out into right field toward the third base line, Rick Burleson made the catch, the second time he'd done so against Nettles. With two outs, Lou Piniella was starting to look stranded at first.

First baseman Chris Chambliss came to the plate. In his first at-bat two innings previously, Chambliss had smashed a line drive right at George Scott. This time Torrez started him with a high fastball, which Chambliss, who liked high fastballs, fouled back. Torrez followed with a breaking ball in the middle of the plate. Chambliss bounced a ground ball toward Burleson, who caught it a step or so away from second base and gracefully touched the bag to force out Piniella, then continued on into the Red Sox dugout. Quietly, Burleson had made two of the three put-outs that inning and almost had a play on a third. Torrez, meanwhile, was challenging the Yankee hitters and getting away with it. Only Jackson had hit the ball hard. Otherwise, Torrez was cruising through the Yankee lineup, looking for all the world as if he was finally making good on his desire to demonstrate that he'd made the right move in the off-season, that the Red Sox were a better team than the Yankees, and that the subtraction of him from one team and his addition to the other was, perhaps, the difference in the balance of power between the two.

Ron Guidry would have to work a little harder to get through his half of the inning—and he was already pitching on three days rest to start with.

He began by facing Jim Rice, whom he'd struck out swinging in the first. In the batter's box, Rice looked confident, focused, and relaxed. He tapped its outer edge once with his bat, then took a few practice swings, and that was all; he simply waited. Rice had such quick bat speed that he could wait on most pitches, take a fraction of a second longer to watch the arc of the ball before swinging—and he was so strong and so fast that even on a late swing he could drive the ball anywhere in the park. With Guidry, however, Rice didn't have that option. The speed of Guidry's fastball negated Rice's ability to wait on a pitch, and his location was so precise, he was almost always ahead of batters. The combination put Rice at an atypical disadvantage. Rice had ended the regular season 0 for 8 against Guidry, which was remarkable, a sign of Guidry's awesome command.

Guidry came at him with power, just as he had in their first matchup. He began with a fastball right down the middle of the plate; Rice was late on it and fouled the pitch into the right field stands. Working quickly, his body motion as efficient as his speaking style was laconic, Guidry threw exactly the same pitch again, and again Rice could not catch up to it and fouled the ball into the right field stands. Munson and Guidry had a rhythm. The catcher called the pitch; the pitcher, supremely confident that he could put whatever pitch Munson wanted exactly where Munson wanted it, never shook his head, never stared back and asked for something else, just wound up and threw the ball.

Guidry's third pitch was another fastball, slightly lower than the first two but again right in the middle of the plate. Again Rice fouled it into the stands behind first base. Three fastballs against the best hitter in the major leagues, all of them down the middle, and Jim Rice hadn't been able to get around on any of them. And then came a fourth fastball, a slider maybe, but Rice interrupted the pitch by grounding it hard to Bucky Dent. The play should have been easy, but Dent threw high to first base and toward home plate. Chris Chambliss had to jump to catch the ball, and as Rice was running by him, Chambliss managed to swipe Rice with his glove. Dent was lucky; the play could easily have been a two-base error.

But Guidry had thrown four straight fastballs against Rice, a sign of the pitcher's confidence and of the confidence Munson had in him. Pitching against the man who led the majors in home runs, a right-handed hitter at Fenway Park, Guidry had challenged Rice on four straight pitches, and Rice had not come close to hurting him.

The next batter was Carl Yastrzemski, who had homered down the left field line off Guidry in the second, and the crowd greeted him with a standing ovation. That a a man who had started his career in Boston in 1961 was still playing was remarkable; that he had taken Ron Guidry deep was even better.

Guidry was convinced that he'd simply thrown a bad pitch against Yastrzemski. This time, he started Yastrzemski off with a fastball inside for ball one, then followed with a slider down and away, which Yaz watched for a second ball. Down 2–0, Guidry came with a fastball inside and above the belt, and Yastrzemski, expecting the pitch, swung so hard he fell to his knees, but only managed to foul it back. He swung again at a fastball on the outside corner, a little too far outside to be pulled, and fouled that off as well. Guidry had evened the count at 2–2.

Whenever Yastrzemski had two strikes on him, he looked fastball. If Yaz didn't guess fastball, he'd be hopelessly late on one if it came. And if it wasn't a fastball, he would try to adjust, hang in there until he got the fastball he preferred.

But Guidry surprised Yastrzemski by throwing a breaking ball, something he had in his repertoire but almost never used; that was the work of Munson, who knew that Yastrzemski had trouble with anything other than fastballs and certainly would not be expecting this pitch. Yaz, defending the plate, swung unconvincingly and barely managed to foul off the ball.

Let him hit that one out, Guidry thought. Last time up, he'd given Yastrzemski his power, the fastball. A great pitch, except if someone—Yastrzemski, say—managed to hit it squarely. This time, Guidry would make Yastrzemski generate the force.

Though the count was still 2–2, the balance of power between pitcher and batter seemed to have changed. Guidry came with another breaking ball, and again Yastrzemski swung awkwardly and fouled the pitch off. Yaz was set up now. Guidry followed with a slider, low and away, so low it almost hit the plate. Yastrzemski was badly fooled and swung; it was almost an impossible pitch to hit, and Yastrzemski didn't come close. Two down.

That brought up Carlton Fisk, who had a .235 career average (4–17) against Guidry. Fisk wouldn't see any breaking balls. He took a fastball down the middle for strike one; he fouled off another fastball right across the plate for strike two. More often than not, Guidry would throw the slider on a right-handed batter with two strikes. Instead, Munson called another fastball. Guidry put it on the far corner of the plate. Back in the second, Fisk had swung at exactly the same pitch, tried to pull it, and flew out to Roy White in left. This time Fisk swung and drove the ball to dead-center field; the location of the pitch had put it inches outside Fisk's ability to pull the ball. He'd hit it perfectly—but to the roomiest part of Fenway. The crowd roared, but Mickey Rivers easily tracked the ball down and caught it on the warning track.

Though Fisk's drive was well hit, Guidry wasn't worried. Except for one pitch to Yaz, he was pitching the game he wanted to pitch— throwing first-pitch strikes, not walking anyone, not letting the leadoff batter get on base, making the Red Sox hit the ball, not trying to blow batters away with a 95-mile-an-hour pitch, tiring himself out, if a 91-mph fastball would do the job. So the Sox had hit the ball hard a few times. It wasn't anything they hadn't done to any other pitcher all season. That's what you had teammates for—to make plays when the ball got hit.

Mike Torrez needed just ten pitches to shut down the Yankees, while Guidry required fourteen—still more than acceptable—to put the Red Sox out in order. After four innings, the Red Sox had 1 run on two hits, while the Yankees had two hits and 0 runs—a pitcher's duel. But this was a contest between two great offensive teams at hitter-friendly Fenway Park, and it seemed impossible that it could stay a one-run game for long.

Good-Bye for Now

On July 9, the day before the All-Star break, the Red Sox lost, 7–1, to the Indians. The game itself wasn't particularly meaningful. Elsewhere in the division, the Brewers beat the Yankees and Baltimore lost to Kansas City, so the Sox still held a 9-game lead over Milwaukee, 11 on the Yankees, and 13 on Baltimore. A play that was thought to be insignificant at the time would, however, matter more.

In the top of the first, leadoff batter Rick Burleson singled. With typical aggressiveness, Burleson promptly tried to steal second. But he timed his slide a fraction of a second too late, slamming into the bag with momentum that his left ankle had to absorb. Pain shot through his leg, and Burleson instantly knew that he couldn't continue. His replacement, Frank Duffy, acquired from the Indians in the off-season, had been considered a competent shortstop since coming to the majors in 1970. But the Indians didn't ask much for Duffy—they got Rick Krueger, a left-handed pitcher who'd pitched in two games for the Sox and would, it turned out, never pitch in any more, for any team—a sign that Cleveland felt Duffy's best years were behind him. After coming into the game to replace Burleson, Duffy would promptly commit three errors against the Indians.

Burleson's injury was at first thought to be minor: a bone bruise, a little swelling, pain that subsided when Burleson iced the ankle. But the pain kept coming back, and a subsequent examination revealed that Burleson had sprained his ankle and stretched ligaments surrounding it. He would need two to three weeks of rest and rehabilitation.

If one had to pick a moment in the 1978 season when the Red Sox faltered—when the rhythm of the team's sprint to the division title was shattered—Rick Burleson's departure from the lineup was it.

Burleson was never a natural player, smooth and graceful, like, say, Fred Lynn, who made everything look easy. "Everything [Lynn] does seems so fluid," Burleson once said. "I'm sure he could go out and hit a golf ball for the first time and hit it well. I'm not like that. I can't just pick things up like that."

His first year in the minors, at Winter Haven, Florida, in 1970, Burleson hit .220 and committed an error every three games. He would spend parts of five seasons in the minors, during which time he never hit more than .274 and averaged .250. But he was stubborn and tough, and no one would work harder. He'd always been that way. Back in elementary school in Downey, California, he fought frequently with the other students—not because he couldn't control his temper, but to help keep the peace. "The principal would come and get me out of class to fight bad kids or kids who might have been picking on someone," Burleson explained. "We'd put on boxing gloves and after I'd beaten up the other kid a little bit, they'd stop it and break us up. Sometimes I even had to fight my friends."

Despite his less-than-sterling minor league statistics, Burleson worked his way upward with a relentless regimen of self-improvement. You could see the results in his batting average: in 1974, his rookie season, he hit .284 in 114 games, higher than he'd ever hit in the minors. Rick Burleson played, it was said, as if he was constantly expecting someone better to come along. "He comes to the ballpark mad and he goes home mad," said Johnny Pesky. "Some guys didn't like to lose," Bill Lee said, "but Rick got angry if the score was even tied." Burleson conceded the point. "I hate all opponents," he once said, and he hated the Yankees most of all.

"I don't think people really understand me," he explained in 1978. "The guys keep telling me to relax and enjoy what's happening. Hell, I enjoy it, but I enjoy it inwardly. I'm happy with the way things are going, but you'll never catch me celebrating until it's all over."

Burleson was the kind of player, and the kind of personality, whom Billy Martin respected, a red-ass, and Martin lamented the fact that Burleson wouldn't be able to play in the All-Star game. "I hate to see him out," Martin said. "I wish that, if he were going to get hurt, he'd do it the day after the All-Star game."

Rick Burleson was not the most gifted athlete on the Red Sox. He didn't have the most impressive statistics, and he wasn't one of the club's semiofficial leaders, like Yaz or Fisk. Burleson didn't even have the personality of a leader, really; he was too tightly wound. Yet the shortstop's intensity, the consistency of his determination to play as hard as he could every second of every game, was a battery that powered his team. He challenged his teammates to play with the same intensity he manifested. And then, of course, there was the fact that, as shortstop, he played a central position, second perhaps only to that of catcher in its importance.

The effects of Burleson's absence were not immediately apparent. Frank Duffy was thought more than capable of filling in for the week to ten days that Burleson was expected to miss. "I know my role," Duffy said, "and I accept it."

On July 13, in their first game after the All-Star break, Boston lost to the Texas Rangers, 12–7, and the next day the Rangers beat them again, 4–3. Still, there was no cause for alarm in Boston. In Minnesota, the Sox rebounded, taking four straight from the Twins. Unusual for the Red Sox, their pitching dominated the series; Boston pitchers gave up just eleven runs in those four games. Then the next day, the Sox trounced the Brewers, 8–2. It seemed nothing could slow Boston down.

On July 20, ninety games into the season, the Sox were 62–28, on track to win 112 games. Their defense had been seamless. Their hitting was, as expected, awesome. And their pitching had been better than Don Zimmer had dared to hope: Eckersley was 11–2, Lee, 10–3; Torrez, 12–5; and Tiant, 7–2. With seventy-two games to go in the season, Torrez had already equaled Louis Tiant's team-high 12 victories from 1977. It seemed unlikely not just that any competitor could catch Boston, but that they could even make it close. Milwaukee trailed the Sox by 9 games, Baltimore by 12½, and New York by 14.

The Red Sox and their fans knew what it was like to blow a big lead, to have victory snatched away at the last moment. But some were starting to believe that this year such an outcome could not happen—the Red Sox simply couldn't lose. In the *Boston Herald-American*, columnist Joe Fitzgerald wrote, "Honestly, did you ever think we'd get to the point where the Red Sox were too good, where our primary concern was not falling out of a pennant race, but falling asleep during one?"

Nobody in New York was likely to fall asleep following the Yankees. After the All-Star break, George Steinbrenner ordered Billy Martin to make some changes in the Yankee lineup, and Martin made them, in some instances without public objection, and in one instance, possibly with a secret pleasure. Steinbrenner, who'd never cared for the play of Roy White, installed recently acquired Gary Thomasson, formerly of the A's, in left field, meaning that the veteran White would be playing even less than he had been. (White would appear in just 103 regular season games in 1978, far fewer than the 150 he'd averaged for the previous decade.) Steinbrenner also insisted that Thurman Munson be moved to right field to rest his painful knees; Munson had never played the outfield in the pros. Mike Heath, a rookie just called up from the minors, would catch. That meant that Lou Piniella and Reggie Jackson, the previous right fielders, would now be dividing the designated hitter slot between them, depending on whether the Yankees were facing a left-handed or right-handed pitcher. The great Reggie Jackson was now a part-time player—probably the most expensive in baseball history.

At a clubhouse meeting, Steinbrenner informed the players of these changes and instructed them that they had no choice but to accept his decisions. "You're among the best-paid athletes in the world and I'm the man who signs your checks," he said. "If you don't want to do things my way, then I'll accommodate you by sending you somewhere else. This is my team. I pay the bills. I'll do what I want." Steinbrenner then read the team its new lineup.

The moves verged on the bizarre. Thomasson, a reserve throughout his career, was neither a better hitter nor a better fielder than White. Everyone knew that Munson could not catch forever, but to install him in the outfield in the middle of a season? ("I'm just happy to be here," Munson said.) He certainly wasn't a better outfielder than Piniella or Jackson. And what about asking the Yankee pitchers, who were struggling enough as it was, to throw to a catcher with no major league experience? But perhaps the strangest tactic was making one of the most feared sluggers in the game a part-time designated hitter. For Jackson, the move was even more damaging than it sounded, because Jackson was a streak hitter, prone to slumps. When Jackson was hitting poorly, the only thing to do was let him hit through it; when he came around, which he always did in time, he did so in a big way. But with far fewer at-bats than he was used to, Jackson was likely not just to hit less frequently, but to hit less well when he did get to the plate. Platooning him made no sense—unless one thought that Steinbrenner was simply trying to manipulate his players, to initiate change for its own sake.

Martin, who clearly had decided to accept whatever humiliation he had to in order to save his job, said little about the moves. Steinbrenner, always most likely to take charge just when he was announcing that the responsibility for the team lay with others, defended his actions. "Everybody says I should stay out, but I don't care," he said.

"If I don't get involved, we're not going to get better. We're going to get worse." The owner insisted that there was nothing wrong with his team that couldn't be fixed with greater mental toughness on the players' part. The players disagreed. They already played in the biggest market in the country, with the most aggressive media, a volatile, publicity-hungry owner and a volatile, hard-drinking manager. Toughness was not the issue.

"Last year," Lou Piniella said, "we had the most grueling year anybody could spend in baseball. All the problems we had, the toughness of the pennant race. Everybody got worn out; it takes the heart out of you. George with his theory of mental toughness—that's not true. He thinks it makes you mentally tough [to be publicly criticized], but it takes the heart out of you. There's no substitute for harmony and a good attitude. You're a professional ballplayer, but you're also a human being. You've got to have a happy atmosphere."

Piniella had put his finger on something that all the Yankee players were feeling, something that, up in Boston, Bill Lee would have agreed with as he lamented the dispatch of the Buffalo Heads to other teams: in order to play to their potential, the Yankees needed to enjoy what they were doing. They needed to have fun.

It was a simple concept, so honest and straightforward that it felt out of place amid the Yankee madness. Fun? That was for children. These athletes were being paid millions of dollars. (Well, more and more of them, at least.) They were famous and wealthy, and most people wouldn't have said their job was hard work by any traditional definition; it wasn't as if they were laying railroad track or working in a coal mine. Fun?

This tension between baseball as a business and baseball as a game was hardly a new problem for baseball players; the fundamental narrative of baseball history is a chronological line marking its transition from an amateur pastime to bigger and bigger business. The more "professional" baseball became, the harder it was to preserve the intangible element of pleasure—fun. And of course the more money was at stake, the more players found it hard to play as if baseball was still a game.

For Carl Yastrzemski, the erosion of fun had begun with the beginning of free agency. "Everything became more serious," he would say. "Imagine what it was like for us when you'd walk into the clubhouse and there were agents standing in the hallways, talking to the players. . . . Baseball went from a team orientation to an individual orientation. Nobody kidded around. It became . . . I guess the word is 'businesslike.' " And the ethos of business, of big-time bucks, permeated every aspect of a team's culture, corrupting the bonds that had traditionally united the players. Once salaries became public, "It went from twenty-five guys traveling together and seeing one another's families, to wives arguing over whose husband should be earning more money." On the other hand, no one was saying no to free-agency paychecks, either.

In New York, where everything was more intense than anywhere else in the league—except for fan ardor, where Boston at least equaled the Yankees—all of these trends were magnified. But for all the money and media attention that went along with playing baseball in the Bronx, it was still a game, essentially the same game that the Yankees had played when they were boys, hitting rocks in their backyards, playing catch after school, pretending that they were Mickey Mantle or Ted Williams or Sandy Koufax or Joe DiMaggio—who had himself said, on the occasion of his retirement in 1951, "When baseball is no longer fun, it's no longer a game, and so I've played my last game of ball." Fun was knowing, despite the pressure of money and competition, the expectations of fans and the media, the cultural climate in which fans felt comfortable wearing t-shirts saying "Boston Sucks" or "Yankees Suck" and throwing batteries and beers at the players, that once you trotted out on to that expanse of green, the parklike oasis in the middle of concrete and brick urban jungles, you could still lose yourself in the game, forget everything that happened outside the stadium. After all, wasn't that one definition of immortality—being able to return to your childhood day after day after day? And from a more practical perspective, wasn't it when you were having fun that you relaxed, forgot about the odds against you, the pressure you faced, and played your best baseball?

If George Steinbrenner understood the importance of fun, he gave no sign; he enjoyed himself when the Yankees won, but didn't seem to appreciate that the players had to have fun in order to win. "I don't think our owner liked to think we were having fun when we were playing," Graig Nettles recalled. "I don't think he could associate fun and baseball in the same breath. He wanted it to be work for us. I don't know if he understood that we *needed* to have fun—that once the game started, that was when the fun started, and we could go out and play."

"We have a good bunch of guys over here," Mickey Rivers said at the time, in his own inimitable way. "But [Martin and Steinbrenner] kill the spirit for the guys, and that don't leave too much. The pressure killed a lot of spirit. You could walk around the clubhouse, you see a guy with a bad opinion. Used to be a guy with a good opinion and laugh and tell a lot of jokes, and they don't do it no more."

The Yankee who was probably having the least fun that July was Reggie Jackson. The outfielder had been beaten down by the unpleasantness of his first season with the Yankees. He had rolled into New York loud and cocky and trash-talking, and he had been, if not humbled, at least bruised by the backlash. This season, he had tried to fit in. That wasn't always easy—not when, for example, thousands of fans threw candy bars bearing your name onto the field. But for much of the season, Jackson had gone out of his way to credit his teammates, to acknowledge the leadership roles of players such as Munson, Hunter, and Guidry, and to coexist in relative peace with Billy Martin.

Still, he could not wholly avoid controversy. On July 11, Jackson and his girlfriend went to the movies and wound up in a fight with an aggressive autograph seeker. The woman, who was black, asked Jackson for an autograph; Jackson said no, on the grounds that if he signed one for her, he'd have to sign one for everyone who asked. According to Jackson, the woman began hectoring him and, in particular, his girlfriend, who was white. "She started screaming at my girlfriend," Jackson said. He tried to stand between them and tried to restrain her. The woman toppled over backward and started screaming that Jackson had slapped her. As the *New York Post* put it, "pandemonium erupted" and the movie theater had to be emptied. The autograph seeker promptly filed charges against Jackson, who responded by counterfiling. "Sometimes," Jackson said later, "I wonder whether any of this is all worthwhile."

Jackson was having a good, if not great, season; on July 13, he was hitting .269, with 14 home runs and 50 runs batted in. Typical numbers for him, they would have been terrific for just about anyone else. Considering the constant uncertainty of his relationship with Martin and the stress it put on Jackson, those statistics were both more impressive than they looked and less than what they could have been had Jackson felt fully supported by his manager and teammates. The other Yankees didn't regard him with the hostility that they felt in 1977, but many still treated him coolly. While they were bemused by Jackson's apparent love affair with the media—he was still the player the reporters made a beeline to for quotes—some appreciated the fact that he took the spotlight off them. "It was easy to play when Billy and

Reggie and George were fighting for the headlines," Graig Nettles said. "The rest of us could sit back and watch and get a beer and not worry about it." Some of the newer players, such as Dent and Gossage, liked Jackson; they'd never responded to him as insiders resenting the intrusion of a self-promoting newcomer, and they could relate to the challenges of coming to New York as high-profile acquisitions, feeling pressure even greater than they anticipated.

In the past weeks, however, Jackson had been in a slump, hitting under .200 for July. His troubles at the plate came especially against left-handed pitchers; hence the decision to platoon him at designated hitter. Still, the news of his demotion embarrassed and frustrated Jackson, who started to sound as if he was psychologically throwing in the towel. "When you're me, nothing surprises you," he said. "I went to the movies last night and got sued." The man who'd powered the Yankees to their first world championship since 1962 was not a part-time hitter. Asked how he felt about the decision, Jackson made no secret of his feelings. "George owns the fucking team," Jackson told reporters. "He can do what he wants." Increasingly, what Jackson hoped Steinbrenner wanted was to trade him.

The Yankees did not respond well to Steinbrenner's personnel moves. Having come into the All-Star break losing three straight to Milwaukee, they came out of it losing two out of three to Chicago. The victory came on the 13th. Ron Guidry pitched, but again he looked tired and wasn't his usual dominating self; Guidry gave up six runs, including two home runs, in nine innings, before Jackson, who had doubled, scored the winning run in the bottom of the eleventh on a single by Graig Nettles. (Gossage got the win.) The next two days, the Royals beat Ed Figueroa and Jim Beattie. "Our backs are against the wall," Sparky Lyle said. "And after today they're farther against the wall. Soon we'll be in the wall." The press agreed, cranking up headlines such as, "Yanks cracking as season hits breaking point," and "Yankees Going, Going . . ."

Jackson's frustration grew steadily; he felt betrayed by Steinbrenner, the man who had wooed him to come to New York, the owner with whom Jackson thought he had a special bond, one that transcended and made tolerable his horrible relationship with Martin. He knew that Martin wasn't particularly bothered by Jackson's diminishing playing time—that if Martin had his way, Jackson would diminish himself right onto another team. The manager had not only gone along with Jackson's demotion without protest, he had added his own degradations, dropping Jackson to sixth in the lineup, sometimes using lefties Jay Johnstone and Jim Spencer instead of Jackson even when the Yankees were facing a right-handed pitcher. "I wonder," Jackson said, "if they are trying to break my spirit." It seemed a fair question.

And even though his fielding remained less than confidence-inspiring, Jackson hated the public suggestion that he was not a complete player. Even today, few hitters feel comfortable being thought of as purely a hired bat, and many players feel that they can't get in a rhythm at the plate if they're not out in the field as well. In 1978, the designated hitter rule was a novelty, having only been instituted by the American League in 1973. The sense that being a designated hitter meant inadequacy in other aspects of the game was even stronger then than now—especially for a proud man such as Jackson. "I'm not gonna DH for three years," the time left on his contract, he declared on July 16. "I won't ever be a DH, not until I feel I can't do the job in the outfield. I'm a baseball player, not a DH."

Jackson's frustrations came to a head on the afternoon of Monday, July 17. For weeks he had been requesting a meeting with Steinbrenner in which to vent his dissatisfaction and see if it could be resolved, likely either with a trade to another team or Martin's firing. Steinbrenner was inclined to do neither. The meeting did not go well; Steinbrenner not only told Jackson that he wasn't a good enough outfielder to start at the position, he lost his temper and added race to an already combustible mix. According to Jackson, as he and Steinbrenner argued over Jackson's desire to play more or be traded, Steinbrenner suddenly stood and yelled, "You better get your head on straight, *boy*!"

"Who the hell do you think you're talking to?" Jackson said, livid. No matter how famous he was, how much money he made, how many women of every skin color wanted him, he knew what that word meant when it came from the mouth of a white person. Every black man in America knew that.

"I'm talking to you," Steinbrenner answered.

"Don't you ever talk to me like that again as long as you live," Jackson said.

Jackson turned to Al Rosen, who was present, and asked Rosen how he would interpret the remark. Rosen struggled to answer diplomatically, but neither Jackson nor Steinbrenner would calm down. "Jackson, get the hell out of my office," Steinbrenner said. Jackson refused—so Steinbrenner stood up and stormed out of his own office. The meeting to clear the air was over.

That night, against Kansas City, Martin batted Jackson at cleanup for the first time in almost three weeks, starting him although the Yankees would face left-hander Paul Splittorff. Catfish Hunter was pitching for the first time since his shoulder manipulation on June 27. Hunter was rusty, but he threw well and without pain until the fifth inning, when he tired and was replaced by Sparky Lyle. Lyle shut out the Royals for two innings, then refused to pitch another. Announcing that he was not a long reliever, Lyle simply showered and left the stadium. Martin brought in Gossage, who gave up two home runs in the ninth that sent the game into extra innings tied at five.

In the bottom of the tenth, Jackson came up with no one out and Munson on first. Jackson was 0–3 with a walk, and he would be facing left-hander Al Hrabosky, a reliever known as the "Mad Hungarian" because of his overpowering fastball, his dramatic Fu Manchu mustache, and the fact that, before pitches, he would stand on the back of the mound, facing the outfield, to intimidate hitters. Martin hoped to surprise the Royals; he signaled to third base coach Dick Howser to instruct Jackson to bunt. No one would expect that from a home run hitter who wasn't exactly renowned for his bunting prowess.

Jackson pivoted to bunt on the first pitch, but Hrabosky threw him a fastball high and inside, almost impossible to bunt, and Jackson pulled his bat back. With the element of surprise gone—third baseman George Brett instantly moved closer to the plate—Martin and Howser signaled to Jackson to swing away. On the next pitch, though, Jackson again swung around to bunt, pushing the ball foul. The count was 1–1. Howser hustled down the third base line to confer with Jackson and remind him that Martin wanted him to hit away. No offense, Jackson told him, but I'm going to bunt. I hope you know what you're doing, Howser said.

On the next pitch, Jackson again bunted. Strike two. A third foul on a bunt would count as strike three. Yet once more Jackson leveled his bat, and once more the ball went foul. Munson was still sitting on first, Jackson was out, the Yankees would lose the game, 9–7, and Martin was furious beyond words. When the game was over, he retreated to his office, where he erupted. How dare one of his players defy him so blatantly? Martin threw his clock radio, breaking it. He hurled a beer bottle, shattering it. When he eventually agreed to see reporters, his eyes were red and puffy.

That night, Steinbrenner and Rosen suspended Jackson indefinitely without pay. Martin released a handwritten statement that said, "He was told verbally by the third base coach to swing. . . . Jackson was told to swing away but he said, 'I'll bunt instead.' "

Steinbrenner, who had telephoned the dugout after Jackson's at-bat demanding an explanation, backed Martin up. "What is paramount is a sense of command and discipline," he said. "If you don't have that, forget it. Forget the whole organization."

Jackson insisted that he had only been trying to help the team. He was in a slump; he felt that bunting was his best option. "If I get it down, I'm a hero. If not, I'm a butt . . . I can't win no matter what I do. . . . I come off as a big, greedy moneymaker." The image was unfair, Jackson said, and he'd had enough of it. "I've been saying nothing but 'Yes, sir,' ever since I came here. I'm going home to pack and go to California." And with that, Jackson fled his Fifth Avenue apartment, then went to Kennedy Airport and the West Coast.

For Martin, Jackson's retreat was a relief, and he tried to take advantage of the player's breach of conduct by laying down the rules of Jackson's return—rules so stringent that they would either break Jackson, or he would defy them and give Martin another chance to push for his exile, or Jackson would simply refuse to return. The latter was almost surely Martin's hope.

"If he comes back again, he does exactly what I say," Martin declared. "Period. . . . There isn't going to be anyone who defies the manager or management in any way. Nobody's bigger than this team. . . . I'm the manager." Just as Martin had bowed to Steinbrenner's dominion, now Jackson would have to accept Martin's. "He does what I say. I'm not getting paid $3 million; I obey my boss's orders. They tell me what to do and I do it." While a calmer response might have defused the situation, Martin could only ratchet up the drama. "I don't believe in apologizing," the manager said. "I won't talk anything out with him."

In Boston, the Red Sox and the media looked upon the goings-on in New York with a mixture of schadenfreude, bewilderment, and confidence. If the Yankees needed a miracle before, now surely they were up against it. In the *Globe,* columnist Steve Marantz wrote, "So now, with the Yankees suffering with a $3 million power hitter who wants to bunt, and the Orioles staggering behind a celebrated pitching staff with a 4.11 ERA, it appears only the Milwaukee Brewers remain between the Red Sox and 2½ months of tedium." On the day that column appeared, July 19, Mike Torrez beat the Brewers for his 12th win and

Ed Figueroa beat the Twins, 2–0, to raise his record to 9–7. The Red Sox were fourteen up on New York.

And then a strange and unexpected thing began to happen: the Red Sox started to lose, and the Yankees, in the aftermath of the storm, started to win.

First the Brewers pounded Bill Lee, knocking him out in three and a third innings, while the Yanks and Guidry beat Minnesota, 4–0—Guidry's 14th win against 1 loss. The pitcher had asked Martin for an extra day of rest, five instead of the usual four, and the added time off seemed to energize him.

Then, in Kansas City, the Royals took three straight from the Sox. Some said it was the Astroturf in Royals Stadium. While the Sox were used to swinging upward, for the fences, the Royals were accustomed to the crazy skips, slides, and bounces of their artificial surface, and tended to swing down at pitches, producing grounders that the Red Sox had trouble fielding; in the past three years, Boston was 3–12 when playing in Kansas City. (The Royals would replace the turf with real grass in 1995.) Perhaps it was the absence of Rick Burleson, the interrupted rhythm of a well-oiled machine; the Sox were now 5–7 since Burleson's injury. "We'll be all right as soon as we get out of here," Don Zimmer said. Another *Globe* columnist, Ray Fitzgerald, was unconcerned, writing that Red Sox fans were getting bored, since winning was so inevitable. "Several 'Hope they Go on a Ten-Game Losing Streak' societies have sprung up throughout Massachusetts," Fitzgerald wrote. He joked that the Sox were so firmly in control, Massachussetts governor Michael Dukakis was offering inoculations against boredom.

Things were not boring for long. The Sox lost that day, and split a doubleheader the next. The Yankees, meanwhile, had had an excellent week; between July 19 and July 23, they won five straight. Whoever was at fault in the bunt affair—and the team was divided about where responsibility lay—the violence of the episode had shocked the players into focusing on the game the way a defibrillator might stabilize a heartbeat. Most encouraging was a July 22 outing by Catfish Hunter against the White Sox; for five and two-third innings, he shut out the Sox. The win was Hunter's first since May 9, against Minnesota, and again he reported an absence of pain. It was too early to say for sure, but the Yankees could hope: had the Catfish of old returned?

By July 23, the Red Sox fourteen-game lead had shrunk to ten. On that same day, there came another eruption on the Yankees—one that, most of the players would agree, was essential to turning their season around.

According to baseball rules, the Yankees could not suspend a player indefinitely, and so the team announced that Reggie Jackson's absence would last for five days. Martin wanted at least seven; Al Rosen over-ruled him.

Jackson returned from his apartment in San Francisco on the after-noon of the 23rd, when the Yankees were playing the White Sox in Chicago. "It was difficult" coming back, he said before that afternoon's game, in which he would not play. "But I can't say I had any visions of not reporting." He'd had a lot to think about during his time off, Jack-son explained—"the magnitude of me, the magnitude of the instance, the magnitude of New York. It's uncomfortable, it's miserable." Asked whether Martin had spoken to him since his return, Jackson said no. Asked whether, if he were given the chance to redo his Kansas City at-bat, he would bunt again, Jackson answered, "I'd probably do the same thing, because I didn't realize what the consequences would be. I didn't regard it as an act of defiance. If I had known the consequences would have this magnitude, I would have rather swung and struck out and avoided the hassle."

Martin was unhappy about Jackson's return. The team's record during the hitter's absence appeared to have validated his complaints about Jackson, and the manager seemed irritated that Jackson had not simply stayed in California. After the Yankees beat the White Sox, 3–1, *New York Times* reporter Murray Chass ran into Martin in Chicago's O'Hare Airport and informed him of Jackson's comments. Martin responded, "I'm saying, 'Shut up, Reggie Jackson. We don't need none of your shit.' " (In place of the expletive, Chass would substitute "stuff" in the newspaper.) " 'We're winning without you. We don't need you coming in and making all these comments.'

"If Jackson doesn't shut his mouth," Martin continued, "he won't play, and I don't care what George says. He can replace me right now if he doesn't like it." His comments, Martin said, were on the record. Before the flight took off, Martin went to the airport bar and downed several drinks. Again spotting Chass, now accompanied by *New York Post* reporter Henry Hecht on the way to the flight, Martin asked if "they'd gotten all that in the paper." Chass, who had called in the story, replied, "Sure did, Billy."

"I didn't say anything before the game," Martin added. "I didn't disrupt the team. We won five straight. I waited until now.

"I'm a counterpuncher," Martin continued, a description that was only arguably true in the instance and certainly wasn't true generally; in his many fights, Martin almost always punched first. The manager mocked Jackson's assertion that he didn't realize the angry reaction his bunt attempts would spark. "It's like a guy getting out of jail and saying 'I'm innocent' after he killed somebody. He and every one of the other players knew he defied me." On the hitter's return to the bench that night, Martin said, Jackson had taken off his glasses, as if anticipating a fistfight. "He expected to get popped but good," Martin said. When Chass asked him if it had taken restraint not to hit Jackson, the manager replied, "The most it's ever taken in my life."

Martin wouldn't stop talking. As he and the reporters walked toward the airplane's gate, he insisted that Jackson was lying when he claimed that Martin hadn't yet spoken to him. "He's a born liar," Martin said. Speaking of Jackson and Steinbrenner, he added, "The two of them deserve each other. One's a born liar, the other's convicted."

Chass and Hecht wrote it all down.

When Chass called Steinbrenner at his home in Tampa, Florida, to ask for comment, the owner was understandably taken aback. Steinbrenner asked if Martin had been drinking, and Chass answered that he hadn't seen Martin drinking. (Alcohol, so obviously a factor in Martin's behavior that night and many others, would go virtually unmentioned during coverage of the incident, and indeed, in coverage of Martin generally.)

"I have no comment right now," Steinbrenner said. "I am stunned by it. He wins a few games and . . . I just don't know what to say."

The next afternoon, July 24, in the lobby of the Crown Center Hotel in Kansas City, Martin held one of the most surreal press conferences in the history of the institution—another Yankee contribution to the growing fusion of sport and celebrity cultures. In front of a pack of reporters and curious tourists passing by, Martin stood on a balcony in the hotel lobby and bade the Yankees farewell for the second time. He wore sunglasses to cover his eyes, but they couldn't hide the exhaustion in his face, the gauntness of his body, the shaking of his hands as he read from a hastily scribbled statement. Above his head there hung a sign that read "Antiques."

"There will be no questions and answers with anyone after the statement is made," Martin began. "That means now and forever, because I am a Yankee and Yankees do not talk or throw rocks.

"I don't want to hurt this team's chances for the pennant with this undue publicity. The team has a shot at the pennant and I hope they win it. I owe it to my health and to my mental well-being to resign. At this time I'm also sorry about these things that were written about George Steinbrenner. He does not deserve them, nor did I say them."

Martin did not explain why he would resign if he had not actually made the remarks attributed to him, but it is quite possible that he actually believed what he was saying: either he'd forgotten what he'd said while drunk, or he could not bring himself to admit that his own words had cost him the job he had wanted all his life. In any event, his resignation was a means of circumventing the inevitable: if Martin didn't leave voluntarily, Steinbrenner would surely have fired him.

"I've had my differences with George, but we've been able to resolve them," Martin continued.

"I would like to thank—" The words caught in his mouth and Martin began to cry. "The Yankee management . . . the press, the news media, my coaches, and most of all, the fans."

Before he could say "the fans," Martin's sobs grew louder, and it took him almost ten seconds before he was able to gasp the words.

With that, the press conference was over. "I can not recall another baseball farewell so lachrymose," Roger Kahn wrote in the *Times* a few days later. "Babe Ruth and Lou Gehrig went out of the arena more quietly to face their death."

Up in Boston, the *Globe*'s Peter Gammons made a similar point with a less delicate touch. "Martin had to be led away from the new conference in tears, which was good for a few laughs," he wrote.

Three years later, Yankee shortstop Brian Doyle, who would in a few years become a Baptist minister, was reunited with Martin when Martin was managing the Oakland A's from 1980 that 1982. He spoke with the manager about what had happened in 1978, and he thought that Martin opened up to him.

"We sat and had quite a few conversations, and at the time he was very sincere about trying to change some things," Doyle said.

"When you have a dependency on alcohol, you just don't think rationally. A lot of times, unfortunately, that's what was happening with Billy. Everybody understood that. Everybody knew that he was a great tactician on the field. But I don't think he liked himself a lot, and he was always trying to prove himself to everybody else instead of just resting in who God made him.

"At his best," Doyle said, "he was a lot of fun. He had a big heart, and when everything was cognizant—when everything was good in his eyes—he was fun to be around, and very likeable. And on the baseball field, he was brilliant."

But not everything was good in Martin's eyes, and that toxic mix of illness and insecurity had cost him his job with the New York Yankees. It was quickly announced that the team's new manager would be former Cleveland Indian pitcher Bob Lemon, who had recently been fired—amicably so—by the Chicago White Sox.

The next day, July 25, the Red Sox would leave eight men on base and lose to the Twins, 5–4. Ron Guidry shut out the Royals, 4–0, to win his 15th game with just a single loss.

In a week of turmoil and torment for the Yankees, Boston's lead over New York had somehow shrunk from 14 games to 9½.

THE FIFTH INNING

The late afternoon shadows were starting to crowd the field as left fielder Roy White led off the top of the fifth for the Yankees. It was one long shadow, really, a neat black border starting where the foul line converged with the stands in left field, then running toward home plate, nudging catcher Carlton Fisk as he lowered into his crouch, and then stretching out toward the right field stands.

The Yankees were struggling against Torrez. In four innings, they'd collected only two hits off their former teammate: Lou Piniella's chopped ground-ball single and Mickey Rivers's double past George Scott. Hitting left-handed, White had struck out against Torrez in his first at-bat, in the third inning, looking bad on a Torrez fastball. Torrez started him out with another one, but high this time. A slider followed, but that broke hard inside, too far inside, for a second ball. In quick succession there came another fastball high, and a third fastball that zipped by White's head, forcing him to fall backward. Ever polite, White slid his bat in the direction of the Yankee batboy, then trotted to first base. It was Torrez's second walk—the first was Rivers, in the first—and both had come on four pitches at the beginning of innings. Torrez, it seemed, lost accuracy after an interruption halted his rhythm. The Yankees had now put the leadoff man on in three of five innings; they had not yet been able to take advantage of the opportunity. Though thirty-four years old, White was still a base-stealing threat, and with second baseman Brian Doyle stepping into the batter's box, he edged off first.

Torrez's first pitch to Doyle was a waist-high fastball. His hands choked up high on the bat, Doyle, a left-handed hitter, took the pitch for strike one. On the next pitch, White took off for second. Doyle swung and struck a hard ground ball between first and second—a perfect double-play ball if White hadn't gotten an early start. Running to his left, Jerry Remy fielded the ball, spun around as if to go to second, decided against it, and made the play at first well before Doyle reached the bag. Doyle had done his job, pulling the ball so that White could safely advance.

Shortstop Bucky Dent, the ninth hitter, came to the plate. Dent had hit a bloop liner to Jim Rice in the third inning, a quickly dropping ball that Rice had had to sprint to catch. As he had with White and Doyle, Torrez started Dent with a fastball up; this was the bottom third of the order, and Torrez wanted to challenge them. Dent swung at the pitch, which came right down the middle of the plate—the kind of pitch that Reggie Jackson or Graig Nettles would have punished Torrez for—and popped it up behind second base. Raising his right hand over his eyes to block the sun, Rick Burleson made the catch. For the second straight at-bat, Torrez had beaten Dent. Even choking up as high on the bat as he did, the shortstop was still pushing the ball to the opposite field.

With two outs and Roy White still lurking off second, Mickey Rivers, who had walked and doubled, was the batter. Fisk ambled to the plate to chat with Torrez, while Scott, not forgetting that Rivers had smashed a line drive past him in the third inning, edged toward the line at first. Torrez gave Rivers a breaking ball just on the outside part of the plate, where it was hard to pull, and Rivers hit a high chopper to short. The ball almost hit White, who had to stop and contort his body to avoid it as he ran to third. As Rivers flew down the first base line, Burleson noticed White's awkward hesitation. He quickly threw the ball away from his body toward Jack Brohamer at third, who tagged White for the final out. White scowled and looked as if he was about to argue, then decided against it.

Torrez had started the inning with four straight balls, then had thrown four straight strikes. Swinging with their characteristic aggressiveness, the Yankees had produced three outs in those four strikes, and Torrez had escaped the inning throwing just eight pitches total. Except for his walk to White—a lapse of concentration? a moment to rediscover his groove after a break in his rhythm?—he had looked masterful.

Through five innings, Torrez had given up two hits and two walks. No Yankee had come close to scoring, and the Red Sox were coming to bat.

Ron Guidry was starting to feel it in the fifth, the lack of that fourth day of rest. As he started the inning, he could tell that his energy was a little lower than usual. He had to throw a little harder to achieve his normal velocity.

And so he started Fred Lynn, who had flied to Rivers in deep center in the second inning, with two sliders, the pitch breaking away from the left-handed hitter. The first was a ball; swinging awkwardly, Lynn somehow managed to pull the second one foul of the first base line. The third pitch was a fastball; Lynn tried to check his swing but failed, and poked the ball weakly to Guidry's left. If it got past the pitcher, it had all the makings of an infield single, but Guidry was an excellent fielder with fast reflexes, and he dove to his knees and stabbed the ball. Lynn was out by four steps.

Butch Hobson, who had grounded to Nettles in the third, stepped in, waving his long bat high over his head. Guidry came at him with heat. The first fastball was just below Hobson's knees, a ball. The second was up around the letters; Hobson took it for a strike. A third fastball cut the outside corner, and the right-handed-hitting Hobson fouled it into the stands behind first base. With the count at 1–2, Guidry threw his fourth straight fastball, this time putting it on the inside corner; Hobson nicked the pitch, and it struck Munson on the left shoulder, causing the catcher to fall back slightly, then shake himself off before throwing a new ball back to Guidry. Yet another fastball was fouled back into the stands. This one had been high, and Hobson had swung at a pitch likely to be a ball. That was a break for Guidry, who was working harder than he normally would have to, especially with two strikes.

Finally Guidry threw Hobson a slider, the pitch he loved to throw to right-handed hitters with two strikes. But it didn't break as sharply as Guidry's sliders usually did. Hobson drove it hard past third—a likely double, but the ball was just foul. So Guidry came back with a fastball, but this one was down the middle of the plate and lacked Guidry's usual zip. Hobson smashed it down the third base line so hard that Graig Nettles, back on his heels, let the ball bounce off the heel of his glove. Nettles usually made that play, but Hobson had hit the ball with such force, the third baseman hadn't had time to react. As the ball dribbled into the outfield, Hobson took a big turn around first, looking like he wanted to test Roy White's throwing arm, but settled for the conservative choice—the Sox, after all, were winning—and retreated to first. The Sox had their third hit of the game. Guidry had now thrown ten pitches in the inning, two more than Torrez had thrown the entire top half.

George Scott, who had doubled to center his first time up, lumbered to the plate. He set up well away from the plate, both because his bat speed was less than what it once was and because his stomach was more than it once was; Scott needed room to maneuver. His stance put him at a distinct disadvantage when it came to reaching outside pitches, however.

Guidry started him with a fastball right down the middle of the plate; Scott watched it all the way. A second fastball came outside and head-high, not even close to the strike zone; Munson had to stretch to grab it. It was the kind of pitch that a pitcher throws when he is tiring and his mechanics are starting to deteriorate. So Guidry brought another fastball in, a blazing pitch that he seemed to reach within himself to extricate. Scott swung, but barely made contact. His foul ball hit umpire Don Denkinger in the face mask. With the count 1–2, Guidry brought his fourth straight fastball; it had slightly less velocity than the one preceding it, and Scott, swinging wildly, was way out in front of it.

Fourteen pitches, two outs.

Jack Brohamer, who had bunted Scott to third in the third inning, half swung at Guidry's first pitch, a slider on the outside corner. It looked like Brohamer might have swung; in any case, the ball crossed the outside portion of the plate. Denkinger, however, called it a ball.

Munson then performed a subtle but important act, the kind of thing that made his pitchers appreciate him so much. After he caught the ball, he removed it from his glove, but held the glove exactly where it was—just above Brohamer's knee, well within the white of the plate, for a second, maybe two. Standing above him, Denkinger clearly looked down and saw the location. Munson then casually tossed the ball back to Guidry.

The next pitch was a fastball letter-high that missed the outside corner of the plate. Without hesitation, Denkinger signaled a strike. The count stood at 1–1, where it should have been, but it had taken a gentle nudge from Thurman Munson to get it there.

Another slider was well low and outside. Then a low fastball brought the count to 3–1, the closest Guidry had come to walking a batter.

After a casual throw to first to check Hobson, Guidry delivered a letter-high fastball, which Brohamer could only foul back into the stands. The count closer now, at 3–2, he put a perfect fastball low and slightly to the outside part of the plate. Brohamer looped a lazy fly ball about 280 feet to left, where Roy White, playing behind the extended shadow of a lighting tower, caught it for the third out. Guidry trotted off the field, making sure to honor superstition and hop over the third base line as he headed into his dugout.

Hobson had been stranded on first, but the Sox had made Guidry work hard; he had needed twenty pitches to get through the inning, almost triple what Torrez had required to put the Yankees down. Nonetheless, the comparisons between Guidry and Torrez were not all detrimental to the Yankee. While Guidry was laboring more than his usual, of the twenty pitches he threw, none were mistakes like the one he had served up to Yaz. He was working carefully, meticulously— pitching, not just throwing. Guidry knew that he wasn't going to throw a complete game, and in a sense, that knowledge liberated him. His job was simply to keep the Yankees close for as long as he could, and have confidence that the Yankee offense would eventually break through.

For his part, Torrez had obtained three outs on three consecutive pitches. But his initial four-pitch walk to Roy White suggested the pos- sibility of a mistake, whether from a dip in concentration or a break in his rhythm. The Yankees, as they repeatedly showed by swinging away on the first pitch, were aggressive hitters, and Torrez could not make many such mistakes or they would make him pay for it.

Still, at the end of five innings—more than halfway through the game—the Red Sox were hanging on to their 1–0 lead.

AUGUST

On July 23, the same day that Billy Martin resigned at a maudlin press conference in the lobby of a Minnesota hotel, the Yankees hired Bob Lemon, formally known as Robert Granville Lemon, to replace him. Lemon was fifty-seven years old but, with his white hair, glasses, and a Buddha-like stomach, looked amiably older. He was slow moving and slow speaking, and could not have been more different from Martin; he did not have an enemy in baseball, and it was said that the next person to say something bad about him would be the first.

Born September 22, 1920, Lemon was a friend of Yankee president Al Rosen from way back; the two had played together on the Cleveland Indians, most notably on the 1948 team that beat the Red Sox in the American League's first end-of-season playoff. He was a man who paid his dues without complaint. A native of San Bernardino, California, Lemon had begun his career in the minor leagues in 1938, then worked his way up to the Indians in 1941 as an infielder and outfielder. Unlike Martin, who had desperately tried to avoid wartime service, Lemon volunteered to serve and spent two years in the military, from 1943 to 1945. On his return, the Indians converted him to a pitcher, and he would go on to win 20 games seven times, including that 1948 season, when he also won two games in the World Series against the Boston Braves. In 1954, Lemon went 23–7 and the Indians would set a league record (since broken by the Yankees and the Seattle Mariners) with 111 victories.

When his pitching career was over, Lemon worked his way up the coaching ranks, finally landing a managing job in 1970 with the Royals, who had only come into existence the year before. Lemon guided the young team to a winning season in 1971, then lost the job in 1972 and returned to coaching. In 1976, he was the Yankees' pitching coach under Billy Martin. But when the season ended, White Sox

175

owner Bill Veeck hired Lemon to manage his team. Taking charge of a club with some strong hitters known as the "South Side Hitmen"— Jack Brohamer and Jim Spencer were both on that team—Lemon and the White Sox won 90 games in 1977 and finished third. (In one May game against the Indians, Spencer, who would also win a Gold Glove that season, drove in 8 runs.) Lemon had a talent for getting the best out of players who didn't know one another well and responded to a paternal but light touch; Veeck, who couldn't afford free agents, had adopted what became known as the "rent-a-player" concept, in which the Sox assembled a collection of players who were either past their prime or on the verge of hitting their prime—and would do so as free agents signed by other teams. (Other tightly budgeted sports teams would adopt the same approach as free agency took root.) But in 1978 the White Sox stumbled, and on June 29, when the team was 34–40, Veeck replaced Lemon with Larry Doby, who had been the second black player in baseball and now became the sport's second black manager.

Off the field, Lemon was a smoker who liked a few drinks of his own—whiskey and water—but alcohol affected him and Martin very differently. When Martin drank, he grew emotionally volatile, prone to mood swings ranging from anger and violence to a petulant self-pity. When Lemon drank, he became mellow and jovial. "I never took a game home with me," Lemon said on the occasion of his induction into the Hall of Fame in 1976. "I always left it in some bar." When one reporter sat with the new manager as Lemon smoked a cigarette and sipped a whiskey, Lemon jokingly cautioned him, "You better not say I look like a schoolteacher. The schoolteachers will raise hell if you put that in." But Lemon did look like a schoolteacher, the kind to whom generations of students would dedicate their yearbooks.

If Billy Martin sparked controversy everywhere he went, Bob Lemon had a talent for sidestepping, even quelling, it. Asked about the Yankees' ongoing dramas, Lemon said, "It's something I'm not going into because I haven't been here and I haven't been involved. Twenty minutes after I get here, I might have something to say, but I'm coming in with an open mind." He was by nature an optimistic man, as he showed when discussing the division race. "It could be interesting," he said on July 25. "I don't think Boston has won it yet." Optimistic, but not boastful.

The Yankee players were delighted to see Martin go—even the ones who liked him. His presence had become exhausting; he made it impossible to concentrate on the game, impossible to have fun. "Things were in turmoil when Billy was around," Graig Nettles said. "Once he got fired"—technically, Martin had resigned—"and we got Lemon in there, Lem was a real calming influence on the club. He basically let us go out and play."

Lemon's managerial style also differed from Martin's. He employed none of the psychological tactics that Martin had used: the badgering of umpires, the attempts to intimidate opposing players, the constant need to fight, whether the fighting be physical or psychological. Lemon didn't see the value in such conflict. When he joined the team, he held a meeting, and, as usual, spoke few words; Lemon was neither a cheerleader nor a manipulator. He believed in treating athletes like adults. "He came in and said, 'You guys were world champions last year. Just go out, relax, and play like you can, and everything will take care of itself,' " Bucky Dent said. "And everybody kind of went, *whew*, and just relaxed. The focus changed. It became more of, 'This is what we have to do, and this is what we're gonna do.'

"Bob was a funny guy in certain ways," Dent added. "He never said anything. He just let you play."

"Billy Martin basically had a good heart," Cliff Johnson said. "I feel it in my heart of hearts that he basically had a good heart. But he sometimes contributed to or created an environment that wasn't conducive to baseball." In contrast, Lemon did nothing to distract from the game at hand. "Lem just put the lineup on the wall, got up there and crossed his leg and watched the ballgame. He was a grandfatherly type—easygoing, could be a lot of fun, didn't draw any attention. He didn't put any undue pressure on, didn't pressurize you. If you did your job, he sat back, and once in a while he'd say, 'Way to go, Meat.' " ("Meat" was Lemon's all-purpose term of endearment for his players.)

Bob Lemon, Goose Gossage said, "was a breath of fresh air."

Certainly he was for Reggie Jackson. Among Lemon's first moves was to end the experiment of playing Munson in right field. He reinstalled Munson behind the plate, asked Lou Piniella to DH and play some outfield, and inquired of Jackson if he would like to start in right again. "Whatever you say," a delighted Jackson responded. "You're the boss. I'll shovel manure for you if you ask me like that." Lemon explained that it was his nature to be direct. "Beating around the bush takes work, and I'm lazy," he said.

Some reporters were glad to see Martin go. He made great copy, but even they tired of his erratic and often mean-spirited behavior. "He's a pathetic figure," wrote the *Post*'s Henry Hecht. "Self-destructive, childish, a man who will go to pieces if he can't get another job managing. . . . Billy is 50, but he still doesn't know how to handle himself.

In a later era, observers would surely have pointed out that Billy Martin was struggling with—and losing to—a disease, one that required treatment but was instead exacerbated by the hard-partying culture of baseball in which Martin had spent his entire adult life. Hecht would write that Martin had apparently consumed five drinks before making the airport outburst that preceded his resignation. But he would also claim that Martin was not drunk, because he had seen Martin drunk enough times to know that it took more than five drinks to get him inebriated. Later, Hecht wrote, when Martin once called him after midnight to chastise him for his columns and accused Hecht of being "anti-white"—then, Hecht said, Martin might have been drunk.

Things could easily have been different. Another owner might have compelled Martin to get treatment for his alcoholism (though Martin had worked for plenty of owners, and none had); another alcoholic might have taken that step himself, especially after losing the job that meant more to him than any other—more to him, probably, than anything else in the world. Ten or twenty years later, the symptoms of Martin's disease would have been easily diagnosed and openly addressed. But drinking was too much a part of Martin's identity for him ever to give it up, and he never would. Billy Martin loved the Yankees, but he loved the bottle more. Or, perhaps, he did not love it, but was not strong enough to beat it. Confronting his alcoholism may have been the only fight that Billy Martin should have picked, but didn't.

Two groups were less than happy to see Martin exit. The first was the Red Sox. When he heard the news of Martin's departure, Fred Lynn thought, " 'Oh, crap. That's the worst.'

"With Billy Martin," he explained, "they were playing us, and we were just beating the hell out of them. They were darn near coming to blows in the dugout. It was killer, when I read in the paper that he was fired."

As for Bob Lemon, Lynn said, "I don't know if he ever said two words. He just wrote down the lineup and let those guys go."

The second group of Martin supporters were Yankee fans, who, given the choice between Martin, Jackson, and Steinbrenner—if you believed the signs that popped up in Yankee Stadium, or man-on-the-street-interviews, or the letters to the editor—overwhelmingly supported Martin. "Billy's the One Who's Sane, Reggie's the One to Blame," said one sign when the Yankees returned home on July 26 and beat the Indians, 3–1. Another read, "Reggie, Are You Happy Now?" The police removed the obscene ones. And when Jackson came to the plate, some fans chanted, "Bunt! Bunt! Bunt!" in a sarcastic reference to the act that had prompted Jackson's five-game suspension.

The fans' loyalty to Martin was understandable. George Steinbrenner and Reggie Jackson were outsiders, new to New York. Before buying the Yankees, Steinbrenner had never lived in the city, and he never would; when Jackson was suspended, the first thing he did was fly to California. A part of New York since 1950, Martin was a connection to an era of unsurpassed glory, to Yankees with names like DiMaggio, Mantle, and Ford, and it was he whom the fans credited, not Steinbrenner, nor Jackson, for leading the Yankees to their first World Series victory in 15 years. Steinbrenner's Yankees, after all, had not gone to the World Series under Bill Virdon. And despite Jackson's awesome performance in that Series, for many fans it was still Thurman Munson and Billy Martin who stirred the Yankees' drink.

There was something even deeper, something primal, to the Yankee fans' love for Martin. They felt a spiritual connection to him. He was not rich and flashy, like Jackson and Steinbrenner; he did not eat at '21,' the pricey restaurant to which Steinbrenner had taken Jackson when he was courting the free agent, or rent an apartment on Fifth Avenue and drive Rolls-Royces, as Jackson did. Neither Steinbrenner nor Jackson could ever claim to be a man of the people. But Billy Martin could. He was passionate and emotional and obnoxious yet also vulnerable—had any New Yorker ever shed so many public tears?—and he worried about how the game was changing just as the fans did, worried that it was becoming a business in which the little guys, himself included, were less and less important, where money was all that counted. Steinbrenner epitomized those changes; so did Jackson. Martin was the man in the middle, confused and threatened by the forces transforming baseball, caught between the wealth and power of a business titan who knew little about baseball or New York and the glamour and ego—and, yes, skin color—of a new type of player, one Martin could not control and, for reasons sometimes understandable and sometimes lamentable, did not like. For the same reasons, Yankees fans gave their support to Billy Martin. In a changing game and a changing world, he was a throwback, an inspiration. He reminded the fans in the cheap seats that little guys could still be number one.

George Steinbrenner knew this; he knew that whatever he did for the Yankees, however much money he spent, however many championships he brought to the Bronx, the fans would never love him as they did Martin. Moreover, they would resent the owner for seeming to choose Jackson over Martin. And so he gave in.

On July 29, the Yankees beat the Minnesota Twins, 7–3, behind the pitching of rookie Ken Clay. Lemon gave Clay his first start since June 24, when the Red Sox had sent him packing and he had taken up indefinite residence in Martin's doghouse. Clay pitched capably and was helped by three no-hit innings from Goose Gossage, but the game was overshadowed by the bizarre spectacle that preceded it. It was Old-Timers' Day at the stadium, and as Yankee announcer Bob Sheppard announced the names of the returning Yankee alumni—a roster that included Phil Rizzuto, Yogi Berra, Whitey Ford, Roger Maris, Mickey Mantle, and Joe DiMaggio—he suddenly interjected, "Managing the Yankees in the 1980 season, and hopefully for many seasons after that, will be No. 1. . . ."

As Billy Martin ran onto the field, his name was drowned out, then and for the next seven minutes, by the roar of the crowd as it stood and cheered the return of its fallen hero. Just six days before, Martin had resigned from the Yankees in a way that cast into doubt not just his return, but his survival. Now, with the kind of drama that seemed to energize both Steinbrenner and Martin, he was back, raising his cap, soaking in the applause of 50,000 people. On a day intended to honor the Yankees' tradition of excellence, George Steinbrenner had shown that, much as he paid lip service to that tradition, he was more interested in showmanship, in theater—some would say farce—than in the quiet dignity that had long characterized the public face of the franchise. It was a bit of unfortunate symbolism that the man Martin passed as he ran up those dugout steps, Joe DiMaggio, embodied that dignity. Steinbrenner and Martin both claimed to represent Yankee traditions; both were starting new and unfortunate ones.

At a press conference following the game, Steinbrenner announced that in 1980 Martin would become the manager and Bob Lemon would move up to the front office, becoming the general manager. "All that happened in the past is meaningless," Steinbrenner asserted. "I didn't feel that what happened was right." Martin explained that in the days between his resignation and his rehiring, he had called Steinbrenner to apologize for the remark regarding Jackson's truth-telling and Steinbrenner's conviction. "I did say it," Martin admitted. "I don't know why I said it." That admission, of course, contradicted Martin's earlier insistence, at his resignation press conference, that he had not made the remark Murray Chass and Henry Hecht had attributed to him. As various press commentators would point out, Martin's turn-around meant that, either way, Martin himself was a liar.

Steinbrenner was the only person to whom Martin apologized, however. Not only was there no mea culpa forthcoming for Jackson, but Martin continued to insult him. Asked a few days later if he could manage Jackson, Martin replied, "I've always said I could manage Adolf Hitler, Benito Mussolini, and [Emperor] Hirohito. That doesn't mean I'd like them, but I'd manage them." A few days after that, he added, "I don't have any malice or dislike in my heart for Reggie Jackson. I've done everything I could to help the young man and now he has to help himself." (Jackson was 32 at the time.) With a year and a half to go before he was manager—give or take a week—Martin was already self-destructing.

Why had Steinbrenner handed Martin this reprieve? The self-deification of the act surely appealed to him, the fact that he could banish Martin one day, then restore him to glory days later. This was power! Martin's life may have depended upon Steinbrenner's forgiveness, and the owner unquestionably enjoyed the feeling of benevolent magnanimity that sparing Martin accorded him, the warm glow of having done something commanding and omnipotent, like the commutation of an exile or a death sentence. But Steinbrenner had also been taken aback by the vehemence of the fans' support for the manager, and much as he sought to entertain the crowd, he also feared it. Better to distract the fans of New York with more stagecraft than to have them turn their angry gaze upon the puppeteer. In any case, eighteen months in the life of Billy Martin was a long time. Anything could happen; Steinbrenner could always find a way to renege on his promise.

The players themselves were variously stunned, bemused, upset, and nonchalant. Some, such as Jackson, decided that one way or another they would simply be gone by the time Martin returned. (And indeed, in the days after the news of Martin's return, the Yankees were flooded with phone calls from teams around the league asking what they wanted for Jackson.) Most decided that anything could happen between August 1978 and spring training 1980, so what was the point of getting worked up about things? "Nineteen-eighty is a year and a half away," Lou Piniella said. "We can't worry about that." Most of his teammates shared the sentiment.

It helped that the Yankees were starting to win. They had taken five straight before Martin's resignation, and they continued their hot streak (although, in retrospect, few of the players thought that they could have done so had Martin stayed on). They were led by Guidry, of course, who beat the Royals, 4–0, on July 25, for his 15th win against 1 loss. On the 30th, he got a no-decision as the Yankees beat the Twins, 4–3. (Goose Gossage got the win.) On August 4, he lost only his second game when the Orioles' Doug DeCinces hit a two-run homer and the Yankees could score only one run off Mike Flanagan. The loss didn't slow Guidry much. In his next game, he threw nine innings and shut out the Brewers, 9–0. After that, he went nine again and shut out the A's, 6–0. Guidry would finish the month with a record of 19–2.

Another key element was the resurgence of Catfish Hunter. With his amiable personality and dry sense of humor, Hunter was one of the most popular men on the team, and his arm problems had weighed on the Yankees; it hurt to see a legend fall apart. In late July, Hunter pitched hideously against Cleveland, giving up six runs without recording an out. But in games after that, pitching pain-free, Hunter was simply, miraculously brilliant. The first sign of his comeback came on August 1, when he threw eight scoreless innings and beat the Rangers, 8–1 (Sparky Lyle gave up a run in the ninth). The Yankees had won 12 of 16 and put themselves 6½ games behind Boston. Five days later, he shut out the Orioles, 3–0, going nine innings and beating Jim Palmer. On August 11, he beat the O's again, 2–1. Then he beat the A's, the Angels, and the A's once more; Hunter would not lose a game in July. He was like the Catfish of old, and the Yankees could not have been happier to have him back.

In early August, the Red Sox came to the Bronx in trouble. Having not been shut out all season, they went scoreless three times in the last ten days of July. Though Rick Burleson had returned to the lineup, Jim Rice was slumping, George Scott's offense had vanished entirely, and Carl Yastrzemski was hurt. On July 26, in Texas, he'd started to swing at a breaking ball, then tried to stop, and instantly felt a sharp pain in his back. He struggled just to run to first on the weak ground ball he hit. Checked into the New England Rehabilitation Center, Yastrzemski was told that his lowest vertebra was jabbing into the surrounding muscle and nerve. The doctors informed Yaz that he'd be out for a couple of weeks.

"Near the end of my career, I started to have problems," Yastrzemski recalled. "I was getting a lot of cortisone shots, and that's no fun.

And [the back pain] would hit me without warning. I could be feeling great, and all of a sudden, bang, it would just go out."

At the rehab center, "they put me in traction, with the weights on," he said. "Stretch you out. And then they'd take me off that and put me in a pool—swim, kick your feet, stuff like that."

Yastrzemski was a restless patient. After four days in the hospital, the doctors told him that he would require another week of therapy. He would have none of it. When Red Sox doctor Arthur Pappas visited, Yastrzemski remembered, "I said, 'I'm ready. I'm ready to play.' He says, 'Well, we're gonna find out.' "

The two men were walking through the nearby University of Massachusetts–Boston campus as they spoke, and looked for some way to test Yastrzemski's back. "I don't know where the hell we went," Yastrzemski said, "but he found a shovel. Says, 'If you can swing this, you can play.' "

"Jesus Christ, a shovel's ten times heavier than a bat," Yastrzemski told Pappas. "And of course, it's got resistance, too"—the flattened steel at the tool's end.

"No, no, swing the shovel a few times," Pappas insisted.

Yaz picked up the shovel and swung it once, twice, three times. It hurt, but not so that he would let it show.

"You can play," Pappas said.

Yastrzemski would have to wear a steel corset to protect his spine, and checking his swing, or adjusting it in midstroke, would become especially difficult and worrisome. That pain—you never knew when it would hit. But he would not miss the games against the Yankees.

When the Sox came to New York on August 2, their lead over the Brewers was just 4½ games, over the Yankees, 6½. They had lost 11 of their last 14 games. But in a flukish two-game miniseries, they carved themselves some breathing room. On the 2nd, the two teams played fourteen innings before the 5–5 game was postponed due to base-ball's 1:00 A.M. curfew. The Sox's new left-hander, Andy Hassler, pur-chased from Kansas City on July 24, didn't last two innings before the Yankees drove him out, but Sox relievers clamped down. Goose Gos-sage had relieved Dick Tidrow in the sixth and pitched seven innings—not unheard of for Gossage, but remarkable for someone considered, in modern parlance, a "closer"—allowing just one run, before giving way to Sparky Lyle in the thirteenth.

When play resumed later that day, after the players had gone home and slept for a few hours, the Yankees lost on the kind of play that reminded everyone why, as a right fielder, Reggie Jackson made a heck of a designated hitter. With one out and Ken Clay on the mound, Dwight Evans fouled a 3–2 pitch down the right field line. Jackson chased the ball, but it landed in the seats. While Clay prepared to pitch, Jackson ambled back to his position, at one point stopping for no apparent reason. One of the other Yankees—perhaps backup catcher Cliff Johnson, who was starting that day—should have noticed that Jackson was taking his time, but none did. Clay delivered his pitch, and Evans hit a bloop to right field. If Jackson had been in position, the ball was easily caught. Instead, it fell for a single; in the dugout, the Red Sox were astonished but grateful that a player could be so unprepared. Butch Hobson then singled Evans to third, and Rick Burleson followed with a game-winning single. Jim Rice, who had hit just one home run in his previous thirty-three games, then drove in Hobson with an insurance run. In the second game, Mike Torrez pitched six shutout innings, Yankee rookie Jim Beattie got shelled, Fred Lynn and Bob "Beetle" Bailey homered for the Red Sox, and Boston won, 8–1, in a game cut short by rain. The lead over New York was back to 8½ games, and the Red Sox, it seemed, were out of their slump. "We're definitely turned around," Rick Burleson said. "It wasn't that we were doubting our abilities, but we were really wondering how long [this slump] was going to go on. Then we came out here today."

By August 14, the Sox had increased their lead, thanks in part to a bizarre game the Yankees played against the Orioles. Trailing 3–0 after six, New York took a 5–3 lead over Baltimore in the seventh inning—but when the umpires called the game because of rain, the score reverted to what it had been at the end of the last full inning. A five-run comeback was instantly erased, and when the Sox beat Milwaukee, 4–3, the Yankees were nine back, and Boston's lead seemed even more secure.

Nonetheless, the Yankees were feeling increasingly confident. Under Bob Lemon, they were having fun again, both on and off the field. One of the reasons they were able to enjoy this fun came in the form of an unexpected boon: a newspaper strike. The New York City dailies—the *Times*, the *Daily News*, and the *Post*—were being pressured by suburban papers such as *Long Island Newsday* and New Jersey's Bergen County *Record*, which operated without the burdensome union restrictions that characterized the printing business in the city. As an article in *The New Republic* put it, "Recent moves to automate the newspaper industry, through computer terminals right in the newsroom . . . have cut down on jobs . . ."

So when the management of those newspapers pushed to slash the number of union workers operating printing presses, William J. Kennedy, president of the New York Newspaper Printing Pressmen's Union, took his fifteen hundred members on strike for eighty-eight days. As of August 10, millions of New Yorkers who were used to reading one of those papers every day suddenly couldn't. The effects were painful for many constituencies. Department stores complained that they couldn't advertise their summer sales; Broadway lamented that it could not promote its new shows. The *Daily News,* creator of the most famous headline in New York history—"Ford to City: Drop Dead," about New York's 1976 fiscal crisis—would never fully recover. The paper had already been losing readers as middle-class New Yorkers fled to the suburbs in the 1960s and 1970s. Now, it lost about 350,000 readers from its prestrike circulation.

The strike was painful for many people who had to go without their news and/or their livelihood until November 5. But the Yankees loved it. Their clubhouse was usually flooded with dozens of reporters every day. Suddenly, most of the press was gone.

"The strike was one of the best things that happened that season," Graig Nettles recalled. "You could say stuff across the locker room, you could come in there and not worry about being misquoted or someone peeking over your shoulder."

"You weren't reading all the negative stuff that was being written," Bucky Dent said. "That made an impact."

With Martin gone, with the reporters gone, and with Lemon in place, the Yankees were free to relax and enjoy themselves, and they did. In particular, the Yankees bonded on their postgame bus rides, which were filled with relentless and hilarious teasing, particularly among the veterans. "You didn't want to screw up back then," Bucky Dent recalled, "because on the bus, they had a way of killing you."

If the bus was quiet, sometimes Catfish Hunter would start the proceedings. He'd call out to Lou Piniella, "Hey, Lou, how's your hair?" Piniella had a curious habit of smelling his hair—he didn't realize he was doing it, but he did it all the time, grabbing a lock of hair in his fingers and smelling it. So Piniella would shout something back about the frequency and distance of the home runs Hunter gave up, suggesting that Yankee outfielders ought to be equipped with fishing nets on those days Hunter pitched. And Hunter would point out that the Kansas City Royals had traded Piniella to the Yankees for Lindy McDaniel, then a thirty-eight-year-old, over-the-hill starting pitcher. Then maybe Mickey Rivers would join in, or Sparky Lyle, or Nettles or Munson.

"This ball club was unusually cool," Cliff Johnson said. "They didn't really wear it on their sleeves, but there were times when we'd lose a ball game, and it was like a party on the bus going back to the hotel or the airport"—those moments had infuriated Martin, who could never laugh after a loss—"and then we'd win and the bus would be subdued and quiet."

"If you lost a game, well, that bus ride or that plane ride, they were going to bury you," Rich Gossage said. "There was never any, 'We're just going to forget about this.' Nothing was sacred—nothing, not your family, not your mom and you and everyone else in it."

"We had some characters," Bucky Dent said. "That's what made that team special. We had guys with personalities. Sparky Lyle, Nettles, Piniella, Jackson, Munson. The one thing about it, though, is when they went between the lines, it was a different team. Between the lines, it was all for one thing, and that was to win."

"The Red Sox had been fourteen games ahead," Roy White said. "We really weren't focused on catching them. We just started playing our game after Lemon arrived. Then it was a twelve-game lead, then eleven, then ten. And we started thinking, 'Hey, we've got some games left with these guys. We can knock these guys off.' "

The Red Sox team culture was different; the intensity was there, but there was less humor and perhaps more individualism. The cliché about the Red Sox of the 1970s was that when the team arrived home at Logan Airport, twenty-five players hopped into twenty-five different taxis. And while that was probably too strong a characterization, it was true that the Sox didn't seem to enjoy themselves quite as much as the Yankees did. Yastrzemski was an icon, but he was quiet, not the rah-rah type. (He could be a prankster, though; Yaz was known for lighting fires in the bucket ashtrays scattered around the clubhouse in those days.) Jim Rice was also quiet, and could be moody. Fred Lynn was laid-back.

"They always talk about twenty-five cabs," Dennis Eckersley recalled. "It wasn't that bad. You can stick that chemistry up your ass, everyone's a professional and knows how to play, as along as you respect one another."

"The chemistry comes with the talent," Yastrzemski said. "Believe me, if you don't have the talent, you can have the greatest chemistry in all the world, and it's not going to work."

But Fred Lynn thought that the Yankees did play better than the sum of their parts. Somehow, he noted, someone in the Yankee lineup always found a way to contribute in a way that won games. It wasn't just Jackson or Nettles or Munson; it was Lou Piniella, laying down a suicide squeeze in the bottom of the ninth to win a game, or Willie Randolph driving in Mickey Rivers, or Roy White hitting an unexpected home run. "They were situational hitters," Lynn said, "pros' pros. It was like a blue-collar effect, where they're not real stars, but you put 'em all together and they play real well as a unity."

Eckersley thought the Yankees did have one advantage over the Red Sox. "The Yankees looked like they had more fun than us," he said. "They looked like they had a *lot* more fun. Zim was like the Gestapo—not that he was hard to play for, he was a great guy, but he was intense. And we had some fiery guys, but they were coming in all different directions. Some of our key players weren't a force from the emotional side. Freddy Lynn was not a force. A great player, but . . . there wasn't that one guy. Jim Rice, his personality wasn't the type to inspire a team. If anything it was Fisk, he ran the show, and he was like, Fisk and his pace, never in a hurry. And then you had Burleson, hothead, angry at the world, every day. . . . There was no one personality."

There had been personalities on the Red Sox, the Buffalo Head gang, but with the exception of Bill Lee, Don Zimmer had banished them to other teams. Lee may have been a little crazy, and without question his sense of humor could turn mean, at least when it was directed at Don Zimmer. But he helped break the tension the team was starting to feel at the end of July and early August. And he played the role that Reggie Jackson did in New York: he distracted reporters from guys who weren't as comfortable with media attention as he was. "If you haven't got a sense of humor, you're dead," said Graig Nettles. "And I think that's what hurt Boston. They were too uptight. They had a funny guy on their team—Bill Lee. But they didn't listen to him."

Not only did the Red Sox not listen to Lee, they benched him—or at least Don Zimmer did. Still recovering from the arm injury Graig Nettles had inflicted upon him in 1976, Lee had struggled since June, losing 9 times in 12 decisions. He lost some games he should, with more offensive support, have won, and he lost some games he should have lost. On August 19, he lost his seventh straight decision, and there were whispers that Zimmer planned to bring up a rookie, Bobby Sprowl, a fastballer who was 5–3 at Pawtucket. On August 22, when the Sox were in Seattle, Lee approached Zimmer to see if he would be flying back to Fenway a day early to rest for his start, as was customary for the first starter after a West Coast trip to do.

"Zimmer snapped on him," Mike Torrez, who overheard the conversation, recalled. "Zim says, 'No, you're not starting.' Period. He wouldn't give him a reason."

The truth, Torrez thought, was simply that Zimmer didn't like Lee. After all, the manager stuck with other players who were going through difficult streaks—as long as he liked them. The conspicuous example was third baseman Butch Hobson. Clell Lavern "Butch" Hobson, his full name, was one of the most likable Red Sox, a hardworking twenty-six-year-old with a positive attitude. He had joined the Sox in 1976, replacing Rico Petrocelli, one of the heroes of 1975, but with his good looks and unflagging work ethic—Peter Gammons called him "Paul Newman with a Reggie Jackson body"—Hobson soon won over Boston fans.

He grew up in Bessemer, Alabama. His father had played quarterback under the legendary Bear Bryant at the University of Alabama and was the most valuable player on a 1953 team that won the Orange Bowl. Butch would also play quarterback for Bryant.

But in his freshman year at Alabama, Hobson hurt his right elbow, his throwing elbow, playing on the school's artificial turf. The injury had never really healed, and throughout much of the 1977 season his elbow had hampered Hobson's play. Loose bone chips caused the joint to swell and fill with fluid, making it difficult for Hobson to straighten his arm. In the off-season, the Red Sox told Hobson that he wouldn't need surgery. But as the 1978 season progressed, the wear and tear on the elbow accumulated, and that prognosis revealed itself as significantly wrong. The elbow would fill with fluid and have to be drained with a needle almost daily. The procedure was unpleasant but imperative, because the fluid would cause the loose bone chips, some as big as a pencil eraser, to move, and occasionally they would get stuck in the joint.

"They would lock," Hobson recalled. "I knew pretty much when that feeling was coming, and I would try to get them out of the joint somehow. If I put a little pressure on the joint, then I could loosen it, and it would straighten out a little, instead of being locked in an 'L' shape, which is what it looks like today."

But Hobson couldn't always predict when his arm would lock up and refuse to bend. Sometimes it would happen in the middle of a game, sometimes in the middle of a play. The elbow problem also decreased the power of his swing, making it harder to drive the bat through the ball with the back elbow, and Hobson's home run production declined dramatically. His fielding became, over the month of August, unpredictable and costly. "There were times when I'd throw, and my elbow would lock and the ball would hit the pitcher's mound."

Hobson never complained, never asked to sit out a game, and Zimmer refused to bench him; the manager, who knew what it was like to play in pain, had a soft spot for players fighting through adversity. "For the last six weeks, the kid has played rotten, but he's played when others wouldn't play," Zimmer said in early August. "I want the good fans of New England to know what this young man is going through to play baseball for this team. He's playing in terrific pain. . . . I can't bench Butch Hobson. Not after what Butch Hobson has given the team this season."

Hobson was still capable of producing clutch, game-winning hits, and good things seemed to happen when he was playing. On August 10, for example, Hobson came up in the bottom of the thirteenth against Cleveland with the Sox losing, 5–4. He promptly hit a high pop-up in the direction of second baseman Duane Kuiper. But Kuiper lost the ball in the late afternoon Fenway sun, and when he dropped it, the ball bounced about thirty yards into the outfield. Hobson took second, then third, and when the throw to third came in wild, Butch Hobson had hit an inside-the-park home run on a pop-up, and the Sox went on to win, 6–5.

But in truth, Zimmer probably should have benched Hobson; he had a capable backup in Jack Brohamer, and Hobson's increasingly frequent errors were hurting the team. By late August, he had racked up an astonishing 30 errors; he would finish the year with 43 in 133 games at third base, the majority of them coming in the last two months of the season, for an embarrassing fielding percentage of .899. (Graig Nettles, who won a Gold Glove in 1978, had just 11 errors in 159 games at third, a .975 percentage.)

As the month progressed, the Red Sox did not play terrible baseball; in fact, they recovered from the slump into which they had fallen during Burleson's absence and compiled a record of 20–9 for August. But they could not shake the Yankees, who went 19–8. On September 1, the Red Sox had won 6 of their last 7 games, yet New York was closer to first than it had been on August 4—seven games back, instead of eight. And psychologically, the Yankees were hitting their stride.

"We started to get this feeling that, if we can make up one game a week till we get to September—we played them seven times in September—that we could catch them," Bucky Dent recalled. "It was just guys talking: 'If we could make up one game a week . . . we got a shot.' "

In August, the Yankees had not made up a game a week. But in the first week of September, they suddenly gained three on the Red Sox. Even as Boston announced plans for the sale of playoff and World Series tickets and the *Globe*'s Ernie Roberts wrote, "I can't work up a sweat over the Yankee threat," the Sox lost to the A's on the 1st and 2nd of September, beat Oakland on the 3rd, lost to the Orioles on the 4th and 5th—that game, in which Butch Hobson made his 35th error, was pitched by rookie Sprowl—until finally, on September 6, the ever-clutch Luis Tiant shut out the Orioles, 2–0.

In the previous two weeks, Ron Guidry had won his 20th, the first pitcher in the majors to do so, and the Yankees had won 12 of 14 games.

All of a sudden, the Red Sox lead was down to four, and the Yankees were coming to Boston.

CHAPTER 14

THE SIXTH INNING

When Thurman Munson came to the plate to start the top of the sixth, Mike Torrez had thrown just 54 pitches, about 11 per inning. At that low rate, he'd finish the game having thrown under 100 pitches, a number that would not bode well for the Yankees. To make the situation worse, the shadow had now crossed home plate; Munson would be the first batter to have to deal with the ball crossing a plane from sunshine to darkness. His performance against Torrez could hardly worsen. He had struck out twice, once in the first, with Rivers on second, and once in the third, also with Rivers on second. Munson hated to strike out, and he hated even more to strike out with a man in scoring position. In a game years before against Steve Stone, a White Sox pitcher who had been a teammate of his at Kent State, Munson struck out three times on breaking balls. "Throw me a fucking fastball," Munson said after the third one. The next at-bat, Stone did—and Munson grounded out. But at least he'd hit the damn thing.

Torrez started him with a slider inside, and Munson pulled it foul down the third base line. With Rivers on, he'd tried to push the ball into the opposite field, but now he felt free to try to drive it anywhere he could. There came another slider, another ball chopped down foul down the third base line. On both swings Munson had lunged awkwardly, as if he was having trouble seeing the ball.

Torrez threw Munson two high fastballs in a row, and Munson fouled both off, one into the right field stands and one behind the plate. After the second fastball, Munson wound up on the far side of the plate, and as he crossed back to the right-handed hitter's batter's box, he struck the plate with his bat handle in frustration. A few seconds later, he felt more frustration still. Torrez surprised him with a curveball; Munson tried to check his swing, but though he appeared not to have turned over his wrists, his bat crossed the plate. When Don

Denkinger didn't call a strike, Carlton Fisk leaped to his feet and pointed to first base umpire Jim Evans for a ruling. Evans made the strike signal, and Munson was down on strikes for the third time. He couldn't believe it. Standing in the batter's box, Munson stared coldly at Evans. All around him, Sox fans were cheering wildly. Munson turned and walked away, again pounding the ground with the handle of his bat, twice turning and staring down the first base line. That he would risk alienating an umpire was a measure of his frustration.

Lou Piniella came up next. He was 1–2, having grounded to third in the first and singled in the third. He would not remain at the plate for long. Torrez threw a fastball on the outside corner and Piniella drove it to deep center field. But Fred Lynn was off and running at the crack of the bat, and he hauled the ball in perhaps two steps from the wall—an especially difficult play given that, while Piniella stood in shadow, the sun in the outfield was still sharp and bright. Piniella had now seen four pitches in three at-bats.

He was followed by Reggie Jackson, perhaps the unluckiest Yankee of the day. Jackson's drive to left field in the top of the first would probably have drifted over the Green Monster if the wind, blowing from right to left—before it reversed itself inning later—hadn't pushed it into the glove of Carl Yastrzemski. Then in the third, Jackson had smashed a hard line drive to left field that might also have landed for a home run but for the fact that it was a low line drive, and the perfectly positioned Jim Rice had to move only steps to catch it.

George Scott strolled over to Torrez to remind him of these things, then strolled back to first, where he played tight against the line and behind the bag. Such close defense, intended to guard against extra-base hits down the line, was usually reserved for the later innings of a game. But with a one-run lead to preserve, Scott was taking no chances. In the background, the fans were chanting "Reg-gie sucks! Reg-gie sucks!"

Again, Torrez did not do well after an interruption. His first pitch, a fastball, bounced in the dirt before home plate and then skidded past Fisk. His second pitch was a curveball that didn't break much and wound up high and outside.

With the count 2–0, Torrez threw another curve, and this one dropped as if an invisible hand had reached out and shoved it down at the last second. Jackson swung so hard at the pitch that he almost toppled over. His right leg straightened and slid out toward first base, his left knee was just inches off the ground, and his head was pointing toward the right field foul pole, as if he were fully expecting to see the ball zoom past it any second now. Nestled safely in Carlton Fisk's glove, it did not.

Torrez followed the curve with a slider, and got the same result: a swing that looked like, had it connected, it would have driven the ball into western Massachusetts. *If* it had connected with the ball. Jackson had no intention of swinging to get on base with a single or a double; he was aiming to tie the score with one awe-inspiring swing. That desire to own the moment was why Reggie Jackson had hit so many dramatic home runs. It was also why Jackson would end his career with 2,597 strikeouts in 9,864 at-bats, still the most in baseball history by a substantial amount.

Torrez threw a curveball next, and when Jackson didn't swing and the ball nicked the inside corner of the plate, the pitcher thought he'd added one more strikeout to Jackson's long list; Torrez was halfway to first when he noticed that Denkinger hadn't signaled a strike. So with the count 3–2, a likely fastball count, he presented Jackson with a breaking ball that the slugger tapped weakly to Jerry Remy at second, who flipped the ball to George Scott for the third out.

Twelve more pitches, three more outs. Torrez certainly wasn't looking tired; if anything, he seemed to be getting stronger. The same could not be said of Guidry.

Shortstop Rick Burleson, 0–2 with a strikeout and a ground out, would lead off the bottom of the Red Sox sixth. He promptly swung at and missed consecutive fastballs. On a typical day, Guidry would have quickly put Burleson away; he wasn't the kind of pitcher who liked to noodle around, waste a couple pitches, then bring his out pitch. Guidry challenged hitters. Even if they knew what he was about to throw, Guidry believed, the knowledge wouldn't help them. But he was tiring; his out pitches were a little less automatic than usual. In the bottom of the fifth, he'd put up a 1–2 count on Butch Hobson, then seen Hobson foul a ball past third before singling into left. Then he'd required six pitches to get Jack Brohamer on a fly ball to left. Guidry was fighting hard, but his pitches lacked their usual power. He'd also thrown 66 pitches through five innings, 12 more than Torrez.

With the count 0–2, Burleson fouled back the next pitch, a slider. So Guidry put a fastball on the outside corner of the plate, and Burleson reached out and slapped it into left field. Roy White sprinted after the ball, but never had a chance; Burleson arrived at second base standing up.

Graig Nettles trotted to the mound to remind Guidry that the next batter, Jerry Remy, was an accomplished bunter. In the dugout, Bob Lemon called for Rich Gossage to start warming up. Gossage would not usually enter a game in the sixth inning, but he had done so more than once, and this was a special occasion.

Remy, hitless in two at-bats, stepped into the batter's box from the left side. At first, Chris Chambliss crept toward the plate; Remy was especially skilled at dragging bunts down the first base line. At third, Nettles positioned himself several steps in on the grass. Guidry was pitching from the stretch, leaning forward, his glove on his right knee, his left hand holding the ball tucked behind his back.

He did not want to give Remy an easy pitch to bunt, so Guidry threw two sliders, both of which broke away from Remy and missed the strike zone. With the count 2–0, he gave in and threw a fastball, still trying to make the bunt challenging by putting it at the letters and rising. But Remy bunted perfectly, angling the bat so that the ball rolled softly along the third base line. Guidry had no play, and Nettles, quickly scooping up the ball, could only go to first, where his throw barely beat the sprinting Remy to the bag.

With one out, Rick Burleson was perched on third base and Jim Rice, who had struck out in the first and flied out in the fourth, was coming to bat. The Fenway fans were roaring. The entire Yankee infield—Nettles, Dent, Doyle, and Chambliss—was crouching a couple of yards in on the infield grass, hoping to cut off any ground ball in time to make a play at the plate. It was a long shot; Rice didn't hit many ground balls, and the ones he did were usually better played from a safe distance.

Guidry's first pitch was a fastball that Rice fouled off; it hit Munson in the chest.

The crowd was chanting. *MVP! MVP! MVP!* Its roar was enormous, overwhelming, like a tornado whipping around the stadium.

In the Red Sox locker room, an ABC film crew started setting up cameras and a platform to interview the winners.

Creeping towards Guidry, the shadow had moved about fifteen feet closer to the pitching mound.

Another fastball; Guidry located it well, in on the hands, the place he considered Rice's weak spot. But the pitch lacked the velocity Guidry needed to blow it by Rice, who swung and connected late, but by sheer strength seemed to *push* a low line drive into center field. For a second, Mickey Rivers looked as if he was going to charge the ball, but the sun was in his eyes and he pulled up short. The ball bounced in front of Rivers and almost hit him in the chest; he managed to knock it down. Burleson scampered home. Rice stayed at first.

The Red Sox were now ahead, 2–0. That brought Carl Yastrzemski to the plate. Yaz was 1–2, having homered in the second inning and struck out in the fourth. Guidry was pitching carefully. The first pitch was a slider for a ball; the second was a low slider that Yastrzemski, fooled, swung at hard and missed by a good six inches. With the count 1–0, he'd been looking for a fastball. Three more sliders brought the count to 3–2, another fastball count. But again Guidry surprised Yastrzemski with a slider; he would not give in and throw Yaz the fastball. Yastrzemski swung awkwardly and hit a high chopper just to the right of Chris Chambliss. The first baseman fielded the ball cleanly, saw that he didn't have time to catch Rice at second, then made the play at first himself. Two out, and Carlton Fisk was coming to the plate.

Bob Lemon ambled to the mound, giving Goose Gossage more time to warm up. Munson trotted out and joined Lemon and Guidry. The three men chatted for a while, and it looked for a second as if Lemon was going to call for Gossage. But he turned and ambled back into the dugout, and when Guidry resumed pitching, the intention of his conference became clear: The Yankees would intentionally walk Carlton Fisk, so as to create a force at any base. The next batter, Fred Lynn, was left-handed, presumably a disadvantage against the lefty Guidry.

If it were possible, the noise level at Fenway grew even higher, an insistent, seamless roar. Rice was at second, Fisk at first, and with two outs Fred Lynn stepped into the batter's box.

In right field, Lou Piniella edged a few steps to his left. After Yastrzemski's home run, Piniella had talked with Thurman Munson, and the two veterans had agreed that Guidry's pitches were just a little slower than usual. It was unusual for anyone to homer off Guidry, and even more unusual to pull a home run. Piniella wasn't the most graceful outfielder—in a game against the Twins on July 30, he'd dropped an easy fly ball that allowed the tying run to score with two out—but he worked hard at being a smart outfielder.

Lynn took a slider, low and away; Guidry was struggling to nick the corner with his slider, as he usually could. Lynn drove the next pitch, a high fastball, into the left field foul territory, then pulled a second fast-ball foul behind first. The count was 1–2, another instance where Guidry would typically notch up a strikeout. But he missed inside, and then he missed outside, to run the count to 3–2.

As Rice and Fisk edged off their bases, preparing to run on the pitch, the roar, which seemed like it could get no louder, did.

Like Yastrzemski, Lynn got a slider on his 3–2 count. He swung and connected well. Hit high, hard, and far, the ball raced toward the right field corner. Piniella sprinted back, toward the wall, and sideways, toward the foul line. One, two, three, four, five, six, steps . . . With his body turned so that his right shoulder was facing home plate, Piniella stuck his glove out waist-high and turned upward. He was two steps away from the wall and he hadn't slowed. A few feet away, an obese Red Sox fan was screaming at Piniella, waving his arms up and down to distract the outfielder.

Rice, Fisk, and Lynn were flying across the base paths. *Two runs*, Lynn was thinking. *That's two runs*. Then Guidry would be gone, and the Sox up 4–0.

On the edge of the warning track, Piniella stuck his glove out . . . and somehow, the ball fell into it.

The roar stopped.

Piniella bounced off the wall near the heavyset fan, rested for a sec-ond, then turned to jog back to the Yankee dugout. The man shouted at Piniella again, leaning over the wall, his arms flapping up and down as if he were some giant bird, trying to take off.

Piniella stopped, turned, and said something to the fan—"Take that," he would recall later, in a way that sounded as if he were daring you to believe that his language was really so mild.

"Just getting their goat," Piniella would say.

Trotting back to his own dugout, Fred Lynn was, he would remem-ber, "freaked out." What were the odds? "I *never* pulled Guidry," he explained. "Barely hit a ball to the right side of second off him. The center fielder should be playing me left center, and as a right fielder in Fenway there's a lot of room in right center" to guard. There was no way Piniella should have been playing him to pull, no way Piniella should have come even close to making that catch.

Years later, Fred Lynn was working for ESPN and went to Seattle to cover a game involving the Mariners, whom Piniella was managing at the time. Lynn couldn't help but ask him about that play. "I said,

'What, was there a good-looking blonde that you needed to see? Why were you there?'

"And Lou gave me a smirk and said, 'I had a hunch.' "

At the end of six innings, the score was Red Sox 2, Yankees 0. Boston had added a run. But for New York, it could have been much worse.

CHAPTER 15

MASSACRE

As they readied for a four-game series against the Yankees at Fenway, starting September 6, the Red Sox were stumbling even as the Yankees were cruising. Boston had lost 5 of their previous 8 games against Toronto, Oakland, and Baltimore. The Yankees, however, were making the second half of their season look like the first half of the Red Sox's season. While the Sox were 25–24 since July 17, the Yankees were 35–14 during that time, 30–13 since Bob Lemon had taken over from Billy Martin. Individual Yankees were thriving under Lemon's firm but mellow stewardship; Reggie Jackson was hitting .319 since Martin's departure, while Graig Nettles was hitting .327 since mid-July. Both figures were about 50 points higher than was typical for Nettles and Jackson.

In the first half of the season, the Red Sox had been, by and large, healthy, while the Yankees had endured injuries to Mickey Rivers, Willie Randolph, Bucky Dent, Catfish Hunter, Don Gullett, and others. Now all of those players, with the exception of Gullett, were healed and productive. Boston, meanwhile, had lately been hampered by injuries to Bill Campbell, Rick Burleson, Butch Hobson, Carl Yastrzemski, George Scott, Dwight Evans, and Carlton Fisk, who was playing with sore ribs. From that perspective, that the Red Sox still maintained a four-game lead over the Yankees appeared almost impressive—even considering the fact that the lead had once been 14½ games.

On Thursday night, the first game of the series—the makeup for the game rained out back in July, when the Sox were the ones rolling and the Yankees didn't even have a starting pitcher—Mike Torrez started against Catfish Hunter. Torrez had been instrumental in the 1977 Yankee pennant drive, and he wanted to play the same role now for Boston—especially against his old team.

198

The Yankees destroyed him.

In the first inning, a throwing error by Butch Hobson put Mickey Rivers on second base; it was Hobson's fourth error in his last five chances. Singles by Munson and Jackson promptly gave New York a two-run lead. Hunter shut down the Sox in his half of the inning, and in the top of the second the Yankees went right back to work. Piniella, White, Dent, and Rivers singled, and faster than you could say "no outs in the second inning," Torrez was gone. Andy Hassler took the mound, and before long, he too was headed for the showers. The score at the end of two was 5–0; at the end of the third, 7–0; after four, 12–0. Thurman Munson had three hits before Butch Hobson even got to bat. In the sixth, reliever Dick Drago hit Munson in the head. "The balls were very slippery all night," Drago said after the game. "Maybe it was the weather." Munson was shaken up, but not seriously hurt.

All told, the Yankees had 21 hits that night, including three apiece by Munson, Roy White, and Willie Randolph, who also drove in five runs. The Sox nicked reliever Ken Clay for a couple of runs, but that hardly mattered when the final score was 15–3. The Yankees, with a record of 83–56, were now just three games behind 86–53 Boston. The Sox insisted that they weren't demoralized. Blowouts happen, and they are probably less painful and more easily forgotten than, say, a one-run, extra-inning loss. "Maybe we tired the SOBs out," Don Zimmer quipped, and that was the right approach to take; anxiety would be infectious. Before the game, the Yankees had asked to take extra batting practice on Friday, but, Zimmer joked, "they canceled that after five innings." Dwight Evans, who was struggling to return after a beaning by Seattle pitcher Mike Parrot, said, "There's always tomorrow—that's baseball."

For the Red Sox, tomorrow was no better.

On Friday, September 8, Boston started rookie Jim Wright against Yankee rookie Jim Beattie, the same pitcher who, on June 21, had gotten knocked out in the third inning by the Sox and dispatched to Tacoma before the sixth by George Steinbrenner. Now, having pitched a no-hitter at Tacoma, Beattie was back; he had a record of 3–7 with an ERA of 4.02, and against the Red Sox he was 0–2 with an 11.57 ERA, numbers mostly compiled before his current stint. Wright's numbers were considerably better. He was 8–2 with a 3.12 ERA; in four underwhelming innings against the Yankees, however, he had an ERA of 6.75.

That quickly went up. On Wright's first pitch, Mickey Rivers poked a single to right. On Wright's next pitch, Rivers stole second. When Fisk's throw got past Burleson, Rivers scrambled to third. On Wright's fourth pitch, Willie Randolph grounded to Rick Burleson . . . and the ball scooted under the glove of one of the league's best shortstops. Rivers raced home, and the rout was on. Wright would get four outs before Zimmer yanked him, a one-third improvement over Torrez's outing. Tom Burgmeier replaced him, and Reggie Jackson greeted Burgmeier with a three-run homer. And so it went. For the second night in a row, a Yankee, Mickey Rivers, would get his third hit before the Sox's number nine hitter, Butch Hobson, came to the plate. The final score was 13–2, and for Boston, the rest of the numbers were equally horrific. The Yankees had 17 hits. In one six-inning period, Jim Beattie retired 18 straight Red Sox. Meanwhile, Boston committed 7 errors, two by the normally perfect Dwight Evans, who dropped a fly ball and made an errant throw before having to leave the game, still seeing double after his beaning. Under less pressing circumstances, he wouldn't even have tried to play.

The Yankees were just two games behind Boston now, and the Red Sox were visibly shaken. "I can't believe we could have hitting, pitching, and defense all go like this at the same time," Carlton Fisk said. "I don't think they knew what hit 'em," Bucky Dent would recall. "We came in there and they had a four-game lead. All of a sudden, we won the first game, and it's down to three. We won the second game and it was like, 'Oh, boy . . . ' You could just sense the momentum starting to turn."

In the third game, Dennis Eckersley would face Ron Guidry. Eckersley was enjoying the finest season of his career to date; he was 16–6, and would win 20 games, including going 11–1 in Fenway. He would beat the Yankees four times that season. This was not one of them.

Eckersley started well, getting out of the first without giving up a run, something his predecessors had been unable to do. In the first, Guidry gave up a single to Rick Burleson and then an infield single to Jim Rice, but escaped the inning without permitting a run. Through three innings, the game was a pitcher's duel. That changed in the fourth. Munson, still feeling dizzy since Dick Drago hit him in the head two days before, singled to lead off. Reggie Jackson then hit an opposite field drive that looked sure to soar over the Green Monster, but a fitful, gusty wind slammed it down and Carl Yastrzemski made an acrobatic catch, colliding with the wall, then whirling to double off Munson, who was halfway to third, at first.

With two outs, Eckersley seemed to be out of trouble. But Chris Chambliss doubled into right field, and Eckersley then intentionally walked the hot-hitting Graig Nettles. Up next was Lou Piniella, who popped up toward center . . . and then the wind grabbed the ball and pushed it toward right. Fred Lynn chased it. So did George Scott from first and Rick Burleson from short. In right field, Jim Rice sprinted for the ball. Second baseman Frank Duffy, playing in place of the sore-wristed Jerry Remy, came closest; Eckersley later guessed that the pop-up had traveled about a hundred feet from where it first seemed likely to land. But Duffy lost the ball in the Saturday afternoon sun, and it dropped in front of him. The Yankees' short-lived logjam was broken. Chambliss scored, and there followed a series of plays that aren't supposed to happen to first-place teams: an intentional walk to Roy White led to Bucky Dent, who responded to the slight by slapping a two-strike single for two runs, and then came an error by Yastrzemski (Yastrzemski!), a wild pitch, and a passed ball, and suddenly the Yankees were up, 7–0.

Guidry, meanwhile, was his usual inexorable self, except maybe better. Walking only one, he did not give up a hit after the first, and the final score would remain 7–0. In the Boston papers the next day, there was much talk of Frank Duffy and the pop-up. Eckersley insisted that the fault was his, not Duffy's. "The thing that broke my back," he said, "wasn't the pop fly, it was Dent hitting an 0–2 pitch." But the shortstop had a way of coming up big; he would go 7–18 in the series, and his 7 runs batted in led the Yankees.

One hundred and forty-one games into the season, the Yankees were one game behind the Red Sox. For Boston, something could be salvaged if they won the series's fourth game; the Sox would still come away two up on the Yankees. Even though he was not scheduled to start, Luis Tiant wanted to pitch, as he always did in big games. Don Zimmer said no: he wanted Tiant to pitch against Baltimore's Jim Palmer on Monday. Bill Lee also wanted to start, but Zimmer would not use him; the manager was too irritated with Lee to turn to him now, in this crucial hour. Instead, Zimmer would go with the twenty-two-year-old rookie from the University of Alabama, Bobby Sprowl, who, five days earlier, had lost his first major league start, 4–1, to Baltimore.

Sprowl was probably best known around Boston for the fact that, some months earlier, he'd been shot. During spring training, he and his wife were asleep in their apartment when a neighbor thought he heard a prowler and fired his rifle; the bullet ricocheted and grazed Sprowl's arm. His minor league record had been less memorable. In Double-A ball, he'd gone 9–3, but after being promoted to Pawtucket, he was a less sterling 7–4 with a 4.15 ERA. Nonetheless, Zimmer thought the hard-throwing left-hander was ready to face the rampaging Yankees and pitcher Ed Figueroa, who at 15–9 was quietly working his way toward becoming baseball's first Puerto Rican 20-game winner.

Sprowl didn't pitch the kind of games that Torrez, Wright, or Eckersley had. He was worse; he didn't last an inning.

He walked Rivers and Randolph before getting Munson to hit into a double play. But Jackson singled, Piniella and Chambliss walked, and just like that, Don Zimmer was walking to the mound and looking toward the bullpen. The quick hook didn't matter: the Yankees won, 7–4, and for the Red Sox, the four-game series, soon to be dubbed the Boston Massacre, was finally, blessedly over.

Of all Zimmer's managing decisions that season, starting Bobby Sprowl was probably the most hotly debated—and the most unpopular, even among the Red Sox themselves. Most of the members of that team remember Zimmer with respect and admiration. Even so, few thought that starting Bobby Sprowl was wise. "I don't know if he even threw a strike," Fred Lynn remembered. "He was horseshit," Dennis Eckersley said. "I always felt that if Don Zimmer had let Bill Lee pitch. . . ." Mike Torrez said.

Sprowl would pitch again that season, but the experience of pitching against the Yankees, and the backlash he felt after getting yanked, appeared to have damaged him. In spring training in 1979, he developed control problems—mental in origin, it seemed—that left batters cowering at the plate, ready to dive before the pitch ever left Sprowl's hand. Balls zoomed behind their heads, thudded against the backstop. Sprowl never won a game for Boston, and in June 1979 he was traded to Houston, for whom he also never won a game. After 1981, Sprowl was out of baseball. In his four years in the majors, the pitcher, once considered a highly promising prospect, would throw a total of forty-six and a third innings and compile an ERA of 5.44, with a won-lost record of 0–3.

"To come into a pennant race like that as a rookie, and start—I think that was the stupidest move on the Red Sox's part," Torrez said. "That ruined him, bringing him up the way that Zimmer did in that pressure situation. After that, he was never the same."

Bobby Sprowl was not the only casualty of the Boston Massacre. So

was the Red Sox's division lead. After 142 games, the two teams were
tied, their records an identical 86–56. But the Yankees clearly had the
momentum. In the four games against Boston, they had outscored
the Sox, 42–9. The Yankees hit .396 for the series, racking up 67 hits
to the Sox's 21. Perhaps most damaging was the way they pecked the
Red Sox to death; 56 of the Yankee hits were singles. Every time the
Red Sox were in the field, the Yankees were cruising the base paths as
if they owned them. "I don't know if the Red Sox were spooked when
the series started," Dent said, "but they definitely were after we left."

In the aftermath, explanations for the Red Sox collapse were as
cheap and abundant as the irate phone calls that poured in to local talk
radio. The Sox were hurt. Boston lacked the bench depth to compensate for injured starters. Zimmer had overused his regulars—Hobson,
Fisk, and the pitchers in particular—until their bodies broke down. The
team lacked the cohesion to come together under pressure. Zimmer's
dislike of Bill Lee cost the team several wins that would have given
them a larger cushion against the Yankees. Pitching Bobby Sprowl was
stupid.

Whatever the reasons for the Red Sox's loss of their first-half
momentum, it was clear that the Yankees had gotten into their heads.
"As badly as we beat them early in the season, that's what they did to
us," Fred Lynn said. "It was really difficult: all we had to do was win
a couple" to maintain a four-game lead. "But we couldn't beat 'em,"
Lynn said. "The more we tried, the worse it got, and they knew it."

And then there was the simple fact that the Sox were playing a Yankee team that had been playing under pressure all season, had played
under pressure throughout the 1976 season, and was hardened by
those experiences. After what these players had been through with Billy
Martin, the simple pressure of a pennant race was practically a relief.
"Boston had no pressure all year," Bucky Dent said at the time. "This
club has been playing with pressure all year. And when you coast all the
time, it's tough to turn it on all of a sudden."

While being in second place, chasing the first place team, was
strangely liberating, the Red Sox had to cope with the pressure of worrying about a battle-tested Yankee team coming from behind. "We just
had this thing about us, we were not going to let Boston beat us when
it came crunch time," Cliff Johnson said. "You don't run your fastest
looking back, and there were times when they looked like they were
waiting on us."

The Yankees, Bucky Dent would argue, were more determined than the Red Sox were, and had a psychological advantage. "You know the history" of the rivalry, Dent said. "The Red Sox always trying to beat the Yankees, never being able to. You don't want to be the team that loses to them. You just don't want that tradition to stop."

But Mickey Rivers may have put it simplest and best. "We just outscared 'em," he said.

With twenty games left in the season, the two teams were tied, and they would meet again in five days for a three-game series at Yankee Stadium. But there were still games to play in between. Luis Tiant, the master of the big game, beat the Orioles on Monday the 11th, 5–4, while the Yankees were off. Mike Torrez gave up only five hits on Tuesday, but the O's won, 3–2, while the Yanks lost, 7–4, to Detroit, and dropped a half game back. The next day, Cleveland beat the Sox, 2–1, and the Yanks beat the Tigers, moving into first place by half a game—the first time since May 23 that the Sox had not occupied first. "It's where you are when the leaves turn brown, not when they turn green," that counts, Reggie Jackson said. New York was 87–57, the Sox, 87–58.

The next day, the Sox again lost to Cleveland, 4–3 this time; they'd been swept by the lowly Indians, and their record since the All-Star break fell to 30–33. As the team headed to Yankee Stadium, the Sox were angry and frustrated and a little bit confused. "Dammit, I just want to win," Jerry Remy said. "I want to win for Yastrzemski. He's the greatest player I'll ever play with, and he wants this thing so badly it must be killing him."

On Friday night at the stadium, with New York leading Boston by a game and a half, Ron Guidry beat the Sox again, 4–0, pitching his second consecutive two-hitter against Boston. Guidry was now 22–2, with 8 shutouts and an ERA of 1.71.

On Saturday, September 16, Mike Torrez took the mound desperately hoping for a win. The Sox played solid, tough baseball through eight innings. But the Yanks took the game in the bottom of the ninth when, with the game tied at two, Rivers tripled and Munson drove him home with a sacrifice fly to right field. The catcher was still suffering dizzy spells, but he managed to stroke the ball to the opposite field, doing what he had to do to push the winning run across the plate. The winning pitcher, Catfish Hunter, was now a more than respectable 10–5; Mike Torrez was 15–11, but he hadn't won since August 18. The Red Sox had lost 14 of their last 17 games. "It just seems like destiny has taken over," a despondent Rick Burleson said. "I don't see how we can win this thing." It was, he would later admit, the lowest day of his career.

With the Sox now 3½ games back, and the Yankees having beaten Boston six straight games, it fell to Dennis Eckersley to stop the bleeding. If Boston fell 4½ back, it was virtually impossible that they could catch New York in the season's final two weeks—not the way the Yankees were playing. New York had won 10 of its last 11 games.

Maybe it was because Eckersley was too young to worry much about the history of the Yankees and the Red Sox, or maybe it was just because he was a little, well, rambunctious. But the pitcher came through for his team; in six and two-thirds innings, he gave up just one run, while the Red Sox bats finally came to life. Boston pounded out 11 hits against Jim Beattie, Sparky Lyle, and Ken Clay, and beat New York, 7–3. After going 0–36, George Scott finally got a hit, an RBI double. Carl Yastrzemski—of course it would be Yastrzemski—led his team with a home run and a single, driving in two runs.

With fourteen games to play, the 90–58 Yankees led the 88–61 Red Sox by 2½ games. Boston had pulled back from the brink. Catching the Yankees would not be easy, but at least it wasn't out of reach. The Red Sox were still fighting, still alive.

The Pope Dies, the Sox Live

From August 30 through September 16, the Boston Red Sox had endured a miserable stint in which nothing went their way. Playing shoddy defense, pitching poorly, and vanishing at the plate, the Sox won just 3 games and lost a mortifying and demoralizing 14. In the process, they had gone from leading the New York Yankees in the standings by 7½ games to trailing the Yankees by 2½ games. The team, local commentators and furious fans charged, was choking under pressure. "Why do the Red Sox skitter and fall?" *Globe* columnist Leigh Montville asked. "The word is 'choke' and the word is appropriate. That is what they do. They choke. They have surrendered to the fear inside their minds."

At that point, the Sox promptly started to win again.

Dennis Eckersley probably saved the season by beating the Yankees 7–3 on the 17th, and then the Sox took two of three from the Tigers, staying 2½ back. "We've got to win," Carl Yastrzemski said after Luis Tiant beat Detroit, 8–6, on August 19. "We've got to keep winning, and I think everybody knows what he has to do. I went out tonight and took a full swing for the first time in weeks."

The next day, the Yankees began a three-game series against Toronto, and though his team had just won five of six from the Red Sox, George Steinbrenner announced, "If we don't sweep here, we don't deserve to win." The Yankees were promptly beaten, 8–1, as Ron Guidry pitched his worst game of the season, giving up five runs in one and two-third innings. Now 22–3, Guidry had pitched 21 innings without giving up a run until the first inning against Toronto, when he put two men on, then threw wildly to Graig Nettles at third and allowed two unearned runs to score. The rest of his much abbreviated night went about the same.

Also that day, Mike Torrez was thrashed by Detroit, and the Sox lost, 12–2. Yastrzemski, who was speaking out more as his team entered the final two weeks of the season, was unfazed. "All that means is that we've got to win ten in a row," he said. "We've still got a shot. This one is already forgotten. It's the next one that counts."

On September 22, the Sox lost to Toronto, 5–4, when Butch Hobson made his 43rd error of the season and Andy Hassler gave up a 4–3 lead in the bottom of the ninth. But in Cleveland, the Yankees' Ed Figueroa couldn't nail down his 20th win, losing 8–7, and the Sox remained two games back.

Boston's record was 91–63. The 1978 Red Sox would, that season and for many years to come, be saddled with the reputation that they had collapsed under pressure—"choked"—and certainly there had been stretches when Boston had played horribly and the pressure of first place seemed too much for the team to bear. But with eight games to go, the Red Sox were finally playing as they had in the first half of the season, hitting and pitching well and fielding brilliantly. When a single loss could mean elimination, the Sox would not lose.

Butch Hobson, meanwhile, had taken himself out of the lineup. "I was costing us some games," he would recall. "I just wasn't able to throw the ball to first. So I went to Zim and said, 'It's time for you to put someone in there who can throw the ball.' " Zimmer installed Jack Brohamer at third and switched Hobson, who had been hitting well, to designated hitter. That meant moving Jim Rice to right field and benching Dwight Evans, who had become ineffectual; since being beaned by Mike Parrot, Evans was just 9–54 at the plate. It was probably a decision that Zimmer should have made some time before.

On the 23rd of September, the Sox beat the Blue Jays, 3–1. Luis Tiant, of course, was the winning pitcher. Tiant flirted with disaster all game; 13 Blue Jays reached base. But Tiant would not give in. He threw 142 pitches, the Sox threw two runners out at home, Jim Rice hit his 43rd home run, and Jack Brohamer made the final out of the game on a check swing ground ball by John Mayberry—just the kind of slow roller that Hobson had been throwing into the stands. The Red Sox were themselves again.

In Cleveland, the Indians crushed the Yankees, 10–1, and Boston was one game back with seven games left.

The next day Mike Torrez took the mound against the Blue Jays, who were not the most formidable opponent; Toronto's record was 59–95. But Torrez had not won a game in a month. In seven starts since August 18, he was 0–6 with a 5.18 ERA. "He has not pitched well,"

Carlton Fisk said. "There have been a couple of good games, but mostly he has not pitched well." Fisk would walk to the mound and yell at Torrez, trying to get the pitcher mad at the batter, mad at Fisk, mad at someone—maybe if he got angry, he'd stop worrying and just start pitching. But it wasn't happening.

"I'm struggling," Torrez said, "but I'm not going to quit."

This game was a turning point. Torrez started shakily, giving up three runs in the first two innings. He settled down, though, and in the bottom of the eighth, the Red Sox were leading Toronto by a score of 4–3. But a tired Torrez put runners on first and third before being relieved by Bill Campbell, who gave up a game-tying single. Campbell gave way to Bob Stanley, who promptly allowed a double by catcher Rick Cerrone, and the Blue Jays were winning, 6–4.

Still the Red Sox would not lose. In the top of the ninth, Fred Lynn, George Scott, and pinch hitter Bob Bailey, batting for Brohamer, all walked. Rick Burleson doubled down the first base line, and the game was headed for extra innings. The Blue Jays had their chances. Twice, in the eleventh and in the thirteenth, Toronto loaded the bases and failed to score. In the fourteenth, Jim Rice, 0–5 to that point, singled, and so did Fred Lynn, and Butch Hobson hit a hard grounder that took a nasty hop off Toronto's artificial turf and hit third baseman Roy Howell in the throat. Rice scored, Dick Drago retired the Blue Jays, and after 296 minutes of baseball, finally Boston had won.

Even so, they did not gain ground. In Cleveland, Ron Guidry won his 23rd game for the Yankees, a two-hit shutout, 4–0, and New York retained its one-game lead. The Yankees had a record of 94–62; Boston was 93–63. Six games were left. Boston would play three against Detroit and three against Toronto, all at home. Playing in New York, the Yankees would take on Toronto and Cleveland. "There's less pressure on us," Dennis Eckersley said. "The Yankees look at the scoreboard more than we do. . . . We're just thinking about winning. They're thinking about not losing."

Maybe—but both teams were watching the scoreboard, and if the Yankees were watching it more, they showed no sign of being rattled by the pressure. On the 26th, Eckersley, quickly becoming Boston's most important pitcher, shut out the Tigers, 6–0, and Jim Rice hit his 44th home run. But the Yankees beat the Blue Jays, 4–1, as Ed Figueroa, victorious in 12 of his last 14 starts, won his 19th game of the season. New York had taken two straight, the Red Sox three.

They would make it four. On the 27th, Louis Tiant beat the Tigers,

5–2, as a resurgent George Scott singled twice and hit a home run. But in New York, Catfish Hunter beat the Blue Jays, 5–1, for his 12th win. Hunter had gone 9–1, with an ERA of 1.71, since the beginning of August—even better than Guidry. Jim Beattie was a weak link on the Yankee pitching staff, but Hunter, Guidry, and Figueroa were virtually unbeatable.

The next day, Thursday the 28th, Guidry won his 24th, going nine innings, striking out 9, and beating the Blue Jays, 3–1. Guidry was pitching on three days rest, a decision that Bob Lemon had made; if the Red Sox and the Yankees finished the season tied, there would be a playoff, and Lemon wanted Guidry to start it. "Starting with three days rest didn't really bother me until the last few innings, when I started overthrowing the ball," Guidry said. "Experiencing that for the first time, I learned that the thing to do is not to try and overthrow. The ball will get there anyway." Before the game, Thurman Munson received seven stitches in the index finger of his throwing hand after he accidentally pushed it through the window of a locker room sauna. Munson played anyway, and went 2–4 with a run scored.

In Boston, Mike Torrez finally pitched the kind of September game the Red Sox had expected when they signed the free agent; he shut out Detroit, Jim Rice hit his 45th home run, and the Sox won their fifth straight, 1–0. Though he walked seven, Torrez gave up just three hits and induced the Tigers to hit into four double plays. Rather than simply relying on his fastball and slider, a habit he had fallen into, Torrez mixed in changeups and breaking balls—a sign of a pitcher who had started 35 games and thrown almost 250 innings, and whose arm lacked some of its early season vigor.

Three games to go.

"You've got to figure that New York will lose at least one game," Fred Lynn said. "Of course, we've got to win all of ours."

On Friday the 29th, it was just like old times for the Red Sox. Against Toronto, they were up 8–0 after three innings, Bob Stanley cruised, and Boston won an 11–0 laugher. In New England, fans were transfixed; the *Globe* was covering the Sox on page one every day, and after Pope John Paul I died on the 28th, Charles Laquidara of radio station WBCN began his broadcast, "Pope dies, Sox still alive." No one questioned Laquidara's priorities.

But still the Sox could not gain. In New York against Cleveland, the Yankees scored three runs in the bottom of the eighth to beat the Indians, 3–1. Rich Gossage relieved Jim Beattie after seven and won the game. In the ninth, Gossage got the first two Indians out, then walked André Thornton before striking out designated hitter Wayne Cage. "I've been known to make it thrilling, too thrilling, sometimes," Gossage said.

There was one piece of bad news for New York, however. While running to first on the bouncing-ball single that started the rally, second baseman Willie Randolph pulled a hamstring. He would not play again until 1979.

Two games.

On Saturday the 30th, Eckersley won his 20th, beating Toronto, 5–1, as Fred Lynn, batting .455 in his last nine games, went 3–4. Eckersley set the tone early; he struck out the first two Blue Jays on six pitches. His season record: an impressive 20–8, with an ERA of 2.99.

But two hundred miles south, Ed Figueroa also won his 20th, beating the hapless Indians, 7–0. Thurman Munson went 3–4, Reggie Jackson hit his 26th home run, and Graig Nettles, Chris Chambliss, and Roy White—the middle of the batting order—each had two RBIs. An hour before the game, Figueroa had gone to his locker and prayed, which was something he customarily did before pitching. That day, he prayed a little bit longer than usual. After the last out in the ninth, a ground ball to Bucky Dent (0–3 on the day), he hugged Thurman Munson and started to cry. Finishing at 20–9, Figueroa had won eight straight and 13 of his last 15 games. "I win 20 games for the people of Puerto Rico and Bob Lemon," he said. Since July 19, Figueroa, Guidry, and Hunter had started 46 games, winning 34 and losing 6, for a winning percentage of .850.

The Yankees were 99–62, the Sox 98–63. In 1948, the Sox were down a game to Cleveland on the last day of the schedule, but they beat the Yankees and the Tigers beat the Indians to force a playoff. Thirty years later, the Sox were trying to be optimistic, but it was not easy. Cleveland was in sixth place with a 69–89 record. The Yankees were starting Catfish Hunter. "I believe we're going to win 99 games, but I don't have too much faith in Cleveland," Fred Lynn said. "If the season was a week longer, we'd catch the Yankees. But it looks like we're going to run out of time."

One game.

Luis Tiant won—of course. The apparently ageless pitcher made it look easy, giving up just two hits, for his third straight victory. In the fifth inning, the Sox scored two runs, and they knew the game was over; Tiant would not give up such an important lead. Third baseman

Jack Brohamer caught the final out, a pop-up in foul territory. The Red Sox had not choked.

As the innings passed, fans in the seats held transistor radios to their ears and the Red Sox watched the scoreboard. What they heard and saw astonished them. The Yankees were losing, decisively losing. Catfish Hunter, pitching on three days rest for the first time in two years, picked this day to pitch his worst game in two months. "As soon as I got out there, I knew I had no pop," he said afterward. In the top of the first, André Thornton hit a two-run homer that put the Indians ahead to stay. Hunter gave up four hits, one walk, and five runs, and was gone before the second inning was over. Dick Tidrow replaced him and gave up two runs. Rookie Larry McCall pitched two-thirds of an inning and gave up two runs. Meanwhile, Rick Waits, 12–15 at that point, was shutting down New York on five hits. "Waits pitched one of his better games of the year," Roy White recalled, "and Catfish wasn't sharp."

The Indians, with a record of 68–90, just a smidgen above last-place Toronto, had beaten the Yankees, 9–2.

The Yankees and the Red Sox had played 162 games, and each had won 99 and lost 63. New York was headed to Boston.

B.F.D.

In their dugout at the top of the 7th inning, the Yankees remained calm. They had come back from a fourteen-game deficit, they could come back from a 2–0 run deficit. And though Torrez was pitching well, they always believed they could get to him. They respected Torrez—well, some of them did—but they were not intimidated by him.

Were the Red Sox equally confident? They had taken their best shots against Guidry and hit him hard, but were ahead by only two runs. It should have been more. Why had Lou Piniella played Fred Lynn to pull, when Lynn never pulled Ron Guidry? Had Lynn's drive fallen for the double it looked to be, the pitcher would almost certainly have been yanked, it would have been a 4–0 game, Lynn standing on second, the crowd going nuts—the Sox would have been rolling. Instead, the game was still tight. Boston had seen leads, games, pennants slip away before. It was hard to feel confident with all that history, all those reminders, lurking just over their shoulders.

After changing his jersey for the second time that game, Mike Torrez took the mound in the top of the seventh having thrown a paltry 66 pitches. He felt strong; Torrez had thrown twice that many pitches in games before. And he was pumped up. Torrez was within three innings of beating the Yankees, the team that had cast him aside after two World Series victories. Torrez wanted to win this game as much as he'd ever wanted anything in his life.

He would face Graig Nettles first, starting the left-handed hitting third baseman off with a curveball; Torrez had thrown only two or three curves the entire game, and Nettles just watched as the pitch broke sharply down and in. The ball looked off the plate, but Don Denkinger called a strike, and for several seconds Nettles looked at him in disbelief.

Torrez followed with a fastball straight down the middle of the plate, just a little over waist-high, and Nettles swung at it as if he weren't going to see another fastball for the rest of his career. But the pitch was just a little above his power zone—Nettles liked his fastballs low—and he hit under the ball, driving an easy fly to Jim Rice in right.

Two pitches, one out. But the at-bat was deceptively easy. Nettles had been right; the first pitch wasn't a strike. And the fastball had been dangerous. Nettles had gotten around on it easily enough; he'd pulled the ball. It didn't take a lot of imagination to envision that ball soaring over the right field fence.

The scoreboard showed an out, one that required just two pitches, but Torrez had been luckier than the scoreboard could tell.

With the encroaching shadow now halfway to the mound, Chris Chambliss, who was also hitless, stepped into the batter's box. So Torrez started him off with a breaking ball, which Chambliss swung over. Perhaps trying to get away from the fastball—the pitch to Nettles seemed to have lost just a little velocity from Torrez's fastballs early in the game—Fisk called for a curveball. This one did not fool Chambliss, who reached down and lined the ball to the opposite field. It flew past Burleson and Brohamer into left field, where Yastrzemski scooped it up and threw it in to second.

The single did not seem important. Chambliss's was just the Yankees' third hit in the game, the first since Lou Piniella's ground-ball single in the fourth. It came with one out, and Chambliss, a large man, was not a threat to steal.

Switch-hitting left fielder Roy White, who had struck out and walked, stepped up to the plate from the left side. Odds were that if Billy Martin were still managing, White wouldn't have been playing, but that had changed under Bob Lemon and White was determined to make the most of the opportunity. He thought Torrez would throw him a slider; Torrez had a good slider, one that could really cut in on your hands, and he knew that Torrez liked to challenge left-handed hitters with it.

If he comes in with that slider, I'm going to really turn on it, White thought. *I'm going to be the hero.*

He guessed wrong. Torrez threw a high fastball, again not quite as fast as it would have been a few innings before. White waited on the pitch for a split second longer than Torrez would have liked him to be able to, and then he swung and punched it into center for a single.

Suddenly the tenor of the inning had changed. Chambliss on first was an irritant. White on first, Chambliss on second, was a threat. After three pitches, Torrez had compiled one out and a 1–0 count on the second batter. After five pitches, he had an out and men on first and second. In the Red Sox bullpen, Andy Hassler and Bob Stanley, left- and right-handed pitchers, jumped to their feet and began throwing. Carlton Fisk took off his mask and walked to the mound. Torrez impatiently rubbed the sweat from the hair along the edge of his cap.

Bob Lemon sent left-handed power hitter Jim Spencer up to bat for second baseman Brian Doyle. Spencer's season had not exactly gone as he had hoped since coming over from the White Sox, where he had played first base, in December 1977; he had batted only 150 times, hitting .228 with 7 home runs and 28 runs batted in, and like virtually every other Yankee, he had asked to be traded in the weeks before Billy Martin's departure. Spencer didn't like the frenetic, high-profile quality of playing for the Yankees, and he certainly didn't like the minimal amount of time he was spending on the field. He was a better hitter than his numbers would indicate, and he hit well under pressure; as a pinch hitter, he had a batting average of .304, with 7 hits in 23 at bats. He had also won several games with pinch hits. His solo home run in the top of the ninth had won an April game against the Orioles; on May 26, he smashed a seventh-inning, pinch-hit grand slam to beat the Blue Jays; on June 10, he stroked a pinch-hit single in the bottom of the tenth to help the Yankees beat the Mariners, 11–9. Against Red Sox pitching, he was 2–12, a .167 average. That statistic notwithstanding, Spencer was clearly a more fearsome hitter than Doyle. At six feet two and 195 pounds, he stood tall at the plate, waving his bat high above his shoulders. Mike Torrez certainly had no misconception about why Spencer was in the game—to drive a ball over the right field fence. Neither did Don Zimmer, who trotted out to the mound to talk things over with Torrez and Fisk. Zimmer was an ungainly sight—his belly and his rear extended an equal distance from his midpoint, giving him an oddly parabolic look—but he could he still get to the mound with agility that reminded one what a fine athlete he had once been. Zimmer asked Torrez how he felt. Good, Torrez said. Strong. Zimmer warned him to pitch carefully to Spencer, then turned and walked slowly back to the dugout.

In the on-deck circle, Bucky Dent was taking practice swings, knowing that, barring a double play, he would be up next. Bob Lemon could not pinch-hit for him. With Willie Randolph hurt, the Yankees' infield options were limited. Other than the rookie Damaso Garcia, whose defense was shaky, the Yankees had only one reserve infielder, Fred "Chicken" Stanley, and he would now have to take Doyle's place, because Jim Spencer certainly could not play second base. It occurred to Dent that, if Billy Martin were still managing the Yankees, Martin would almost surely have left Doyle in and pinch-hit for Dent, partly because Doyle was a left-handed hitter—in theory, an advantage against Torrez—and partly because he just seemed to like pinch-hitting for Dent. He would never bat in this situation if Martin were still the manager, Dent thought. Then again, Dent was convinced that, if Billy Martin were still managing the Yankees, they would never have come back to tie the Red Sox, and this game wouldn't be taking place.

As he'd shown previously during the game, Torrez had a habit of following breaks in his rhythm with pitches that missed their intended location. Torrez started Spencer off with a fastball right down the middle of the plate, and the left-hander swung like he couldn't believe his good fortune. He was just a little under the ball, though, and fouled it behind home plate.

Fisk jumped up and practically ran to the mound. He had wanted the fastball considerably lower and on the inside corner of the plate. A fastball straight down the middle could lead to three runs in a hurry.

Torrez followed Fisk's warning with a breaking ball, low and inside, a ball, but still more to the catcher's liking. It was, at least, unhittable—better a ball than a three-run home run. With the shadow now nibbling at the rim of the pitcher's mound, Torrez threw the same pitch, again for a ball. He too was nibbling.

But he could not afford to walk Spencer, and not wanting to miss with another breaking ball, Torrez came back with a second fastball down the middle. He put something extra on this one, though, just a little more zip; Spencer swung late and flied to the opposite field. Yastrzemski, playing Spencer precisely right, barely had to move to catch the ball.

There were two outs now, and though Torrez could not relax completely, he felt that the greatest threat had passed. All he had to do to escape the inning was to get past Dent, who was not the power threat that Spencer was; Dent had hit just four home runs all season. And unlike Spencer, Dent was a right-handed hitter, going against a right-

handed pitcher who was still—if just barely—throwing the ball from
sunlight into shadow. Two disadvantages before Dent had even taken
a swing. And Torrez wasn't the only one who knew that. At first base,
both Roy White and coach Gene Michael looked toward the Yankee
dugout, knowing that there wasn't anyone left to play shortstop but
still somehow thinking that Bob Lemon might send up a pinch-hitter.
White knew too that Dent had been complaining lately that he wasn't
swinging the bat well. So White had suggested that Dent try one of his
bats, one thirty-four inches long and weighing thirty-two ounces,
slightly shorter and lighter than his usual bat. White had ordered several of the bats, "but I never liked the feel of it," he would say, "so I
gave them to Mickey Rivers, who liked it," and before the game,
Rivers had given one to Dent. It was the second slight change Dent
made that day to try to tweak his play. He also removed the shin
guard that he'd been using since spring training, after he'd fouled a
pitch off his shin and developed a baseball-sized bruise. Dent had
been deeply frustrated with his efforts in recent weeks, with the sense
that while all of his teammates had pitched in to save their season, he
was letting people down with a mediocre September. He was willing to
try anything.

Dent stepped to the plate and went into his stance, a crouch that
looked defensive, as if he was more concerned with keeping the ball
away from Fisk than with driving it into the field. With his head just
barely above that of the squatting Fisk, Dent set his feet far apart and
bent his knees to shrink the strike zone. That, combined with the way
he choked up high on the bat, enhanced his ability to make contact
with the ball, but diminished his power.

Torrez delivered his first pitch, a fastball low—very different from
the high heat with which he had challenged Dent in the shortstop's first
two at-bats, a fly to Rice in the third and a pop-up to Burleson in the
fifth. Dent started to swing but then, awkwardly, yanked his bat back.
Ball one.

Out in left, Yastrzemski was playing Dent to pull. The wind was
blowing out now, from right to left. That typically happened at Fenway
between 4 and 6 P.M.; it always seemed to change from blowing in to
blowing out just around the time of batting practice for a night game.
Some days, right around five o'clock, the park would be just still,
totally free of wind. And then a minute later, you'd see the flags flapping.

At third base, Jack Brohamer was practically straddling the baseline;

better to let a ball go through the left side of the infield for a single, scoring only one run, than to permit a double down the line that could score two.

For the first time all day, the crowd had fallen almost completely silent. This was the only inning in which the Yankees had had two men on base. It was late in the game; the Yankees always seemed to pull something out of a hat late in the game . . . But there were two outs and the team's number nine hitter at the plate. If the Sox could get out of this jam, then there'd be just the eighth and ninth to go.

Torrez came with another fastball and Dent swung. But as he had done several times before that season when confronted with high, inside pitches, he fouled the ball almost straight down. It struck the instep of his left foot and bounced some fifteen feet high before being fielded by a batboy. For a second, Dent didn't react, and then he stumbled back out of the box a few yards toward the Yankee dugout. He rested his bat against the ground and leaned against it. He began gingerly rubbing his instep. The Yankees' trainer, Gene Monahan, quickly trotted onto the field to examine Dent.

At home plate, Carlton Fisk started a brief conversation with umpire Don Denkinger. Pointing to the shadows on the field, he said, "Have you thought about turning the lights on?" Denkinger replied that he hadn't because no one had complained. "But if my team was ahead, I don't think I'd be very interested in turning the lights on."

"Oh," Fisk said. "Forget it."

Mike Torrez stood on the mound, occasionally looking into the Red Sox dugout, pacing a little, tossing the ball into his glove, then plucking it out and doing it again. He didn't think about throwing Fisk a couple of warm-up pitches during the interruption. He would say later that it lasted about four minutes, maybe five.

Off to the side, Gene Monahan was spraying Dent's ankle with ethyl chloride, a chemical compound once used in leaded gasoline, more recently used as an inhalant drug during sex. In aerosol form, it chills the skin, numbing pain.

Dent stood up, shaking off the pain in his ankle, and Monahan patted him on the left calf as if to say, "You're ready."

In the on-deck circle, Mickey Rivers was watching the whole thing intently, and he noticed something no one else did. During batting practice, backup catcher Cliff Johnson had been using one of Rivers' bats, and he'd put a hairline crack in it just around the edge of the tape. "I grabbed another bat, and left that one on the side," Rivers said. "Later on, Bucky got up and picked up the broken one." And as Dent leaned against his bat, Rivers saw that the shortstop was still using the cracked one. "I said, 'Homey, homey, that's the wrong bat.' "

So Rivers handed batboy Tony Sarandrea another of White's bats and told him to take it to Dent. "Give this to Bucky," Rivers said. "Tell him there are lots of hits in it." Sarandrea got to the plate just before Dent did, and the switch was made.

One minute and twenty-five seconds after Dent had fouled the ball off his foot—it only seemed longer—he stepped back into the batter's box and took a couple of practice swings. The crowd, which had kept quiet during the interlude, sensed weakness—Dent was hurt!—and began to cheer again.

The count was one ball, one strike. Torrez thought about throwing Dent a slider, but Fisk called for a fastball. The idea was to jam Dent, put the pitch exactly where he was likely to foul it off again, and set him up for a slider outside—the out pitch.

But Torrez didn't jam Dent. His fastball sailed right over the plate, and not all that fast—another misplaced pitch following a break in Torrez's rhythm.

Dent swung, a smooth, fluid stroke, and he hit the ball in the air toward left field.

Torrez thought the ball sounded funny coming off the bat—there wasn't that telltale *crack* of a well-hit ball. This sounded more like *whump*. He turned and saw Yastrzemski pounding his glove.

Good, Torrez thought. *He didn't get it.*

Jerry Remy saw Yaz pound his glove, and relaxed just a bit. So did Carlton Fisk, who breathed a sigh of relief.

"Hit high in the air to left field . . ." ABC announcer Keith Jackson said.

Inside the Red Sox dugout, right fielder Dwight Evans was worried. He knew how the wind could carry balls. *Hit the wall,* he thought. *Hit the wall.*

In center field, Fred Lynn positioned himself to back up Yaz. He was sure it wasn't going out. But when it hit the wall, it would hit high, and those could come straight down and bounce high—a fence scraper, they called balls like that. Not many outfielders could catch the ball on such a carom, but Yaz could. The chances of him missing the ball altogether were almost nonexistent. But just in case, it was Lynn's job to back him up.

In the Yankee dugout, Ron Guidry didn't think it was going out,

either. Dent hadn't hit a home run in two months. This one looked like
it would be caught at the wall.

Rounding first, Dent couldn't see where the ball was going to land,
because of the shadow on the wall. He was running full-out.

So was Roy White, who was sprinting and watching Yastrzemski at
the same time. *It's off the wall*, White thought as he rounded second. If
Yaz missed the carom, White might be able to score all the way from
first.

Yastrzemski was running toward the left field foul line, crossing into
the shadow on the field, about six feet from the warning track. He'd
seen a hundred balls just like this one over the course of the season. He
didn't think it was going out. Yaz prepared to play the ball off the Green
Monster and make a throw, either to try to hold Dent to a single or to
throw him out at second. Maybe even catch White trying to go from
first to third. Yaz had made that play countless times before as well.

"Going into the corner, Yastrzemski . . ." Keith Jackson said.

Next to the mound, Torrez happened to look at the flag. *Oh, no.*
The flag was pointing out. *Dammit, the wind changed.*

At home plate, Fisk saw Yastrzemski look toward the top of the
wall.

And then Dennis Eckersley, watching from the dugout, saw something bad. "Yaz just sort of drooped."

"His shoulder went down and his head slumped," Dwight Evans
said.

Inches above the top edge of the wall, the ball vanished.

Yastrzemski bent both knees and fell forward for a fraction of a second, as if he'd been punched in the gut.

"It's over the wall!" Keith Jackson shouted. "It's a home run for
Bucky Dent!"

"A fucking piece of shit home run," Dennis Eckersley said.

"I was just shocked," Yastrzemski would say. "Really, I was. I
could see him hitting a double or something like that. A base hit. I
would have expected that more.

"But a home run . . ."

Nearing third, Roy White didn't hear any sound of ball against
wall, but he saw Yaz's head drop. The ballpark, he noticed, had suddenly gone completely silent, as if someone had flipped a switch. He
looked up and saw the third base umpire, Steve Palermo, making cir-
cles with an upraised right hand.

About halfway toward second base, Dent saw second base umpire

Al Clark circling his arm. He clapped his hands together once, pumped his right fist, and his sprint became a home run gambol.

Outside Fenway Park, in a nearby dorm room, a college student yanked his television's plug from its socket and threw the television out his window, several stories high. Similar reactions were occurring from Maine to Connecticut and across the country.

"The last guy on the ball club you'd expect to hit a home run just hit one into the screen," Yankee announcer Bill White said.

Chris Chambliss crossed home plate and waited. Roy White touched the plate and did the same. As he turned from third to home, Dent heard nothing. Thirty-three thousand people in the stadium, and he ran ninety feet of silence. It took only seconds to get to the plate, but they were seconds filled with the best, most amazing feeling Bucky Dent had ever known. Everyone dreamed of doing something special. Everyone dreamed of being a hero just once. Every athlete lived for a moment like this. Sure, all the thousands of hours of practice helped you get to the big leagues, maybe land a big contract. But deep down, this was why young boys played baseball: to grow up and become a man and hit a home run with two on and two out and put your team in the lead in the season's most important game. Bucky Dent had never done anything like this before and he never would again, but that didn't matter, that was irrelevant. Most players never got this lucky. Most never got to feel this feeling of sheer, utter, complete joy even once.

And to feel it when you'd come from where Bucky Dent had come . . . when you'd spent most of your life searching for your father, running away from your biological mother . . . sleeping on a mattress on the floor of a tiny apartment when you were barely getting paid in the minor leagues . . . wading through the Florida surf day after day, trying to heal the leg that kept giving out on you . . . knowing that when it did heal, you'd go back to your team and the manager would keep sending others to the plate in important situations, to hit in your place, because he didn't think you were good enough, because he just didn't like you very much . . .

As he crossed the plate, Dent was congratulated by White and Chambliss, then turned to the Yankee dugout to see his teammates spilling onto the field. They hugged him, patted him on the back, slapped his hands.

In the press booth of WPIX, the New York television station that broadcast the Yankees, announcer Phil Rizzuto turned to his colleague and said, "Don't ask me to say anything, I've been holding my breath,

Bill White. . . . I'm in a state of shock, so I'm not going to be much help up here. I'm like a hen on a hot rock, I don't know whether to jump or sit or lay an egg."

The Red Sox tried to regroup. They were only one run down with three Sox at-bat to go. "The home run didn't beat us," Jerry Remy said. "We had had a 2–0 lead, but 3–2 . . . big deal."

Torrez had a hollow feeling in his stomach. But still . . . it was just 3–2. He still felt good.

Shit, that's nothing, Torrez thought—made himself think. *That's nothing.*

Mickey Rivers, who'd already walked and doubled, came up. Torrez threw him eight pitches; Rivers fouled off two before Torrez walked him on a 3–2 count.

Shit. Shit, Torrez thought. He was convinced that his last pitch, a fastball well inside, had been a strike. *Now I'm really going to bear down, take it to another level, be aggressive, go after Munson.*

He had struck out the catcher three times already, and he was sure he could do it again.

But Don Zimmer was walking to the mound, and when he was about halfway there, he waved his right hand, calling for reliever Bob Stanley.

Torrez couldn't believe it. He'd struck Munson out three times! Zimmer couldn't take him out now.

Torrez waited for a moment to leave the mound, as if considering a protest. He kicked dirt back and forth, and he looked out to the Green Monster, as if to say, *How could you?* Finally, he started to stride toward the dugout, holding his glove in his right hand. The crowd applauded Torrez's effort; through six and two-thirds innings, he had pitched brilliantly. But he didn't look up, didn't acknowledge the courtesy. Had there ever been anything that he wanted any more than to beat the Yankees? He had already been a hero once, in Game Six of the 1977 World Series. He would not be a hero again.

Torrez strode down the dugout steps and fired his cap and glove at the bench, accompanied by an epithet. He sat down and folded his arms across his waist, and no one came near him.

"I really felt I could beat them," he said many years later. "I knew we'd score some runs."

Relief pitcher Bob Stanley had had a sterling season. In 52 appearances including three starts, he had compiled a 15–2 record with 10 saves and a 2.55 ERA. In August and September, his record was 10–1.

Stanley was a right-handed pitcher with a strong sinker ball, a pitch thrown with heavy topspin so that it drops down as it reaches the plate, often causing batters to swing high and hit ground balls.

Before the at-bat started, Stanley threw to first to try to keep Rivers honest. Rivers scrambled back. Stanley threw over a second time. Rivers hustled back to the bag again.

On the first pitch, a slider, Rivers took off for second. Playing the part of the dutiful number two, Munson swung, but missed the pitch. Fisk threw a one-hopper that took a perfect bounce, but Rivers was safe with his second stolen base of the game.

Fisk walked to the mound again, said a few encouraging words to Stanley, then slowly strolled back, taking his time to set up.

Stanley gave Munson a slider, up and slightly in, and Munson turned on it, lining the ball to center. A sprinting Lynn fielded the ball as it bounced toward the wall, but then bobbled it—though it wouldn't have made any difference if he'd fielded the ball cleanly. No one was going to keep Mickey Rivers from scoring on that play. Munson trotted easily into second, so delighted to have broken his string of strikeouts that he hopped on the bag and clapped his hands.

Lou Piniella, 1–3 with a single, came up. Piniella was having an overeager day; he had seen four pitches in three at-bats. On Stanley's first pitch, Piniella hit an opposite-field line drive that Jim Rice, raising his glove to block the sun, caught without much difficulty. Five pitches in four at-bats for Piniella, and the Red Sox finally had three outs.

Still, the game had entered a new phase, one even more tense and pressure-laden than were the first six innings. The Yankees had scored four runs to take a 4–2 lead. The Red Sox had three innings in which to come back. Plenty of time to score two runs. Still, the Fenway fans were nervous, the shadows were growing longer, and Goose Gossage was warming up.

But Guidry took the mound for the bottom of the seventh, and the Yankees' only substitution was Fred Stanley, taking over at second for Brian Doyle.

Butch Hobson, 1–2 with a single to left in the fifth inning, stepped in against Guidry, who would hold nothing back. What would be the purpose now of saving his strength? He threw Hobson a low fastball, which the third baseman swung on and missed. A fastball straight down the middle was fouled back into the screen—another big swing from Hobson. Guidry was pitching even more quickly than usual.

With an 0–2 count, Guidry put a slider on the outside corner that just missed. Hobson was set up, though. Expecting Guidry to come back inside, he looked at a fastball that didn't miss the outside corner, and became Guidry's fifth strikeout.

George Scott came to the plate, while Bob Bailey, the right-handed reserve about whom Don Zimmer had enthused earlier in the season, stepped out of the dugout to pinch-hit for the left-handed-hitting third baseman, Jack Brohamer.

Guidry gave Scott a high fastball on the outside corner, and Scott was happy to see it; he poked a ground ball past Fred Stanley into right field. Bob Lemon quickly stood up, strolled onto the field, and waved his right hand toward the Yankee bullpen. When Lemon reached the mound, Guidry was not happy. "My job ain't finished," he said to Lemon. "Leave me." Munson, who had joined them, said, "He's still throwing the ball well." Lemon shook his head no. "I got Goose," he said to Guidry. "He's warmed up, he's ready to come in. You did a hell of a job."

Guidry left the game having pitched six and a third innings, striking out five, giving up six hits, one walk—intentional—and two runs. His numbers were almost identical to Mike Torrez's, who had pitched six and two thirds, striking out four, giving up five hits, and walking two. Each man had made one mistake. Torrez's however, had come with two men on base.

Goose Gossage trotted in from the bullpen and began to warm up. His record was curiously mixed: 26 saves, an ERA of 1.91, and 10 wins—but also 11 losses. Most of those losses had come early in the season, when Gossage was adjusting to the pressure of being a free agent in New York, superseding the popular Sparky Lyle, and coping with the irrational antipathy of Billy Martin. There was no question in Gossage's mind that if Martin were still managing the Yankees, they'd be home resting on this day. At the same time, he was a proud man who probably felt the pain of losing even more than he did the joy of winning. If he'd pitched better early in the season, Gossage felt, the Yankees would never have needed a playoff. "I lost us a lot of games," he said. "It would never have been the greatest comeback in history if I hadn't dug us that deep hole."

The Red Sox were not happy to see Gossage enter the game. "You don't want to face Goose in the shadows," Fred Lynn explained. Not with that fastball in the high 90s, sometimes hitting 100, zipping and darting, cutting in, breaking down. Not with that cap brim pulled down so you couldn't see his eyes. Not with those big arms, those pow-erful legs, driving toward the plate. What made Guidry so impressive was his speed and his control, the efficiency of his game. What made Gossage so intimidating was that he had slightly more speed than Guidry and just as much control—but as he threw his body all over the mound, he *looked* like he was out of control. Which, with a 98-mile-an-hour fastball headed their way, posed certain psychological issues for batters. It was hard to feel secure in the batter's box with the Goose on the mound.

But—and you would never have known it to look at him—Gossage was nervous. He'd never pitched in a game that big. True, no one on either team had, but at least some of the Yankees had playoff and World Series experience. Not Gossage. Even in the bullpen, things had been a little crazy. As he was warming up, guys in the stands were screaming at him, calling him names you'd be more likely to hear in a prison than in a baseball park. Gossage turned around at one point and one of the shouters spat at him, spraying his face with saliva. The secu-rity guys were football players from Boston College, big, strong men, and they hauled the guy away and came back and said, "We took care of him, Goose."

So Gossage was a little rattled. As he finished his warm-up pitches, his legs were shaking. He wasn't sure he'd be able just to throw a real pitch.

And then he caught a break. Don Zimmer realized that he had made a mistake, sending Bob Bailey onto the field before Scott had actu-ally hit. The move might have made sense if Guidry remained in the game—a right-handed hitter versus a left-handed pitcher. Now, with the right-handed Gossage coming in, the advantage reverted back to the Yankees. Zimmer asked Don Denkinger if Bailey's substitution was offi-cial. Was it too late to change his mind? It was, Denkinger told him.

When Gossage saw Bailey approaching the plate, he breathed a lit-tle sigh of relief, and thought, *Thank you.*

Once upon a time, Bob "Beetle" Bailey had been a very promising power hitter. Once upon a long time before. Originally from Long Beach, California, he'd been signed by the Pittsburgh Pirates for a six-figure bonus in 1961, reportedly the largest bonus in the history of the sport to that point. But Bailey had never lived up to expectations, and he'd bounced around the National League from Pittsburgh to Los Angeles to Montreal to Cincinnati, who had shipped him to Boston for a minor leaguer and a few bucks during the 1977 season. In

1970 he hit 28 home runs, but that was a rare high point; in 17 seasons he'd totaled just 189 home runs and a batting average of .257. And though he'd come into the pros one year after Carl Yastrzemski, he had not been quite so diligent as Yaz about maintaining his physique. Bailey was officially 188 pounds, but to look at him, you'd think the number was plagiarized from his high school yearbook.

Even from their spot high above the field, the Yankee announcers couldn't help but notice how Bailey's stomach pressed enthusiastically against his uniform. "Looks a little out of shape, doesn't he?" Phil Rizzuto asked of Bill White. "Well, Beetle's been around a while . . ." White said, chuckling. "Got a lot of money [from the Pirates], put it all in California real estate. That's why he's got that big, um . . ."

"Big what?" Rizzuto asked.

"Big bank account," White said, and both men laughed.

Bailey's statistics were not as large as either his bank account or his stomach. In 93 at-bats that season, he had hit just .194, with 4 home runs and 9 runs batted in. It seemed unfair to send him to the plate with so much at stake. "A right-handed hitter coming to the plate against Gossage . . ." Carl Yastrzemski would say later. "That's a hard job."

And, of course, the shadows weren't going to make it any easier.

Zimmer then made what was probably his second mistake of the inning. He could have sent left-handed hitter Gary Hancock to the plate in place of Bailey. Hancock was only a rookie, and he'd only hit .225. But .225 was still 30 points higher than Bailey's batting average. And Hancock was left-handed. But Zimmer chose to stay with the veteran.

Gossage started Bailey with, no surprise, a fastball, but it was way outside. The next fastball was down the middle and rising, and Bailey swung—slowly, so slowly, it seemed, compared to Gossage's pitch— only managing to foul it back. Then Bailey watched as a fastball nipped the outside corner, and the count was one ball and two strikes. You couldn't take a close pitch on that count, and Bailey didn't. Instead, he watched as Gossage threw a fastball right down the middle for strike three—not a close pitch. The crowd booed, and a defeated Bailey shuffled back to the dugout. He would never have another at-bat in the major leagues.

There were two outs now, and George Scott remained on first base. Scott was not exactly a fast baserunner, and it would probably require a triple to bring him home. Rick Burleson, another right-hander, was the batter. In his career, he was 5–29, or .172, against Gossage, and this at-bat started ominously. Gossage caught the inside corner with a fastball for strike one, then froze Burleson with a fastball on the outside corner for strike two.

So far Gossage had thrown six pitches, five of which were for strikes, only one of which had been swung on. But now something happened that suggested that Gossage was a little tight—that maybe things weren't going to come easily for him on this day. With the count 0–2, Munson set up way on the outside corner, hoping that Burleson would chase a bad pitch; the catcher's entire body was out of the plate area.

But Gossage's pitch didn't go outside. Slipping and sliding like a dog on ice, it skidded toward the inside part of the plate, and Munson waved his glove but couldn't catch it. The ball bounced toward the backstop, and Burleson, without even looking backward, waved his hand for Scott to advance. The big man took second base easily. It wouldn't take a triple to score him anymore.

On the next pitch, though, Burleson bounced a ground ball to Dent, who made a quick throw to nail the speedy Burleson at first by half a step. Gossage's wild pitch might have suggested something, but it hadn't cost the Yankees anything.

With two innings to go, Boston was still down, 4–2.

THE EIGHTH INNING

Reggie Jackson began the top of the eighth having had an unusually quiet day for him. It was not for lack of trying. Jackson was 0–3, but he had narrowly missed a home run to left field in the first inning and narrowly missed a home run to right in the fourth. Nonetheless, Jackson's contribution to the game felt strangely minimal, a function of him not playing in the field and not having come to the plate during the Yankees' seventh-inning rally.

Bob Stanley, who had replaced Mike Torrez in the seventh and promptly given up Thurman Munson's run-scoring double, started Jackson off cautiously. His first pitch was a fastball that missed outside, where Jackson couldn't pull it. So was his second. Aggressive on a 2–0 count, Jackson fouled the next pitch into the left field stands. The 2–1 count was still in his favor. Down 4–2, Stanley had to pitch more defensively than if the Red Sox were still winning.

And so, almost inevitably, he made a mistake. Needing to throw a strike so as not to fall behind 3–1, he came with a breaking ball straight down the middle of the plate—and Jackson just destroyed it. His bat whipped across the plate like a snake flicking its tongue and the ball shot to deep center field. Jackson stood in the batter's box a moment and watched in admiration. Fred Lynn ran back to the warning track, and then he stopped and watched also, though not in admiration. The ball disappeared about six rows into the stands in the deepest part of Fenway.

The crowd went silent for the second time, so eerily quiet it would not have felt surprising if tumbleweeds had started blowing across the outfield. Jackson chugged around the bases. It had seemed impossible that he would not make his presence felt in a game of such import, and, predictably, characteristically, he had. It was a classic Jackson contribution—dramatic, powerful, drawing attention to himself—but there was also something almost lonely about it in a way that seemed to parallel Jackson's entire season, if not his Yankee career. His was the definition of a solo home run. Jackson shook hands with Graig Nettles, who was waiting to bat next—each man now had 27 homers for the season—and on his way back to the dugout, he detoured to shake hands with George Steinbrenner, who was seated in a front-row box between the Yankee dugout and home plate. No other Yankee would have made that gesture. Even if you liked the owner, you didn't shake his hand in the middle of a game.

Still, the run was what counted and New York was glad to have it. At Fenway, you could not have a large enough lead—the Red Sox could score quickly and in abundance—but with the score now 5–2, the Yankees had a little breathing room.

Graig Nettles had also had a quiet game at the plate, going 0–3, popping up twice and flying to right. To face the left-handed hitter, Don Zimmer yanked Stanley and brought in reliever Andy Hassler, the lefty with a lively fastball whom the Sox had bought from the Royals in late July. He had done so with only moderate success, compiling a record of 3 wins and 5 losses with an ERA of 3.95. Against the Yankees, his record was underwhelming; in ten and two-thirds innings, he had given up seven earned runs, walking six and striking out ten.

Nettles fouled off Hassler's first pitch, then check-swing-fouled the next, quickly falling behind on the count. Hassler next gave him a curveball that skimmed the inside part of the plate, and Nettles toppled backward to the ground in self-defense. The pitch was close, but not that close, and his overreaction—and the previous check swing—suggested that Nettles too was affected by the shadow that now extended almost all the way to the pitching rubber. Having set up Nettles with a high inside pitch, Hassler now followed with a fastball low and away, hoping the third baseman would chase it. Nettles didn't, but he did go fishing for the next pitch, a shoulder-high fastball. Now he was 0–4.

Chris Chambliss, who was actually hitting better against left-handers than against right-handers, .292 versus .254, socked Hassler's first pitch hard into the hole between first and second. On the outfield grass, Jerry Remy dove and snared the ball in the very tip of his glove. Quickly hopping to his feet, he threw to first, and though it was impossible to tell which arrived first, hitter or ball, umpire Jim Evans called Chambliss out. The Yankee first baseman, perhaps the mildest-mannered player on the team, couldn't believe it. He turned and stormed up to Evans, nudging the umpire with his chest, shouting his protest. First base coach Gene Michael hastily inserted himself between the two men. Umpires would tolerate a lot in big games, but their patience would not long accept being bumped by a player.

There were two outs, and when Roy White hit an easy grounder to Remy on Hassler's first pitch, there were three. The reliever had done his job, shutting down New York on seven pitches. But the Yankees had picked up another run.

The Red Sox had two at-bats left.

Jerry Remy, who was 0–2 with a bunt, would lead off against Rich Gossage. Gossage had looked strong in the bottom of the seventh, and as Remy stepped into the box, the reliever continued to do so, nipping the outside corner with a fastball for a strike. Gossage threw little else besides fastballs, but his fastballs were rarely similar; they moved, they darted, they skidded, yet somehow Gossage managed to put them consistently almost exactly where he wanted them. When Remy defensively fouled off the next two pitches, Gossage seemed to be rolling.

Then Munson decided to try to confuse Remy; he called for a breaking ball, which Gossage would throw every so often. Gossage went along with the call, and he put the ball in an almost impossible place for Remy—way inside, surely not a strike, and about ankle-high. Somehow the left-handed Remy turned on the pitch and drove the ball hard down the first base line, past Chris Chambliss, who had not been playing the line (not many batters pulled Gossage), and into right field. Piniella fielded the ball cleanly and made a strong throw to Dent covering second, but Remy was too fast; he chugged into second standing up.

The leadoff batter was in scoring position, and Jim Rice was up.

Gossage started him with a low fastball for ball one. Rice had an advantage, but he forfeited it on the second pitch, a high fastball—out of the strike zone—that he swung on and drove in the air to right field. Lou Piniella had to make a long run to get to it, and as he ran, he seemed to be fighting to see through the glare of the sinking sun. Fred Stanley, the veteran infielder substituting for Brian Doyle, ran back into the outfield, his right arm pointing out the ball as it flew straight through the sky, making sure that Piniella would not lose track of it. Piniella made the catch, and though Remy bluffed taking off for third, the ball was really not hit far enough to take that chance—not when your team was losing by three runs, and Remy would score on a single anyway. The last thing Remy wanted to do then was run his way into a second out.

Besides, Carl Yastrzemski was coming to the plate.

Yaz was 1–3, with that second-inning home run, but Guidry had beaten him since, giving him sliders and breaking stuff on fastball counts, making Yastrzemski guess wrong. Yastrzemski had a different approach to hitting Gossage than he did for Guidry, though.

Yaz didn't think about pulling Gossage, because his fastball just exploded on batters. Up and down, it had much more movement than Guidry's fastball had. Guidry's was straight like uncooked spaghetti. Gossage's moved like a fishing fly being tugged and jerked by an expert angler. Facing Gossage, he had to be disciplined. He wasn't going to hit the ball out of the park. He had to be thinking, *Just get the head of the bat on the ball, let him supply the power. Always up the middle on him. Up the middle, up the middle, up the middle.*

Yaz watched a fastball inside for a ball. Gossage had now started behind on two straight batters, which was unlike him. Like Guidry, Gossage had remarkable control for a power pitcher and strongly believed in the importance of the first-pitch strike. Before this game, Gossage had struck out 120 batters and walked just 58 over the course of 131 innings that season.

Yastrzemski took another fastball inside—another ball. Not that a fastball from Gossage would be a huge surprise—*Who the fuck are you going to trick?* Munson had once said to Gossage, waving his hand. *Bring on the heat*—but with the count 2–0, Yaz could almost surely count on one. He got a fastball he didn't like, a nasty strike on the outside corner. A tough pitch to hit; a smart pitch to let go.

Keeping guard in the outfield, Lou Piniella was shading his eyes with his glove, struggling now just to see the pitches as they neared home plate.

Gossage missed again with an inside fastball. At 3–1, the count was distinctly to Yastrzemski's advantage. He looked for a fastball, and he got one—right over the plate this time.

Up the middle, up the middle, up the middle.

Yas stroked the ball cleanly up over second base for a hit. Off at the crack of the bat, Remy scored easily. Standing at home plate, Carlton Fisk raised his arms to indicate that Remy need not slide.

The fans were roaring again; the tumbleweeds had been banished; winter would not come without a fight. Carl Yastrzemski, the man who always rose to the occasion, was 2–4 with 2 runs batted in, and the Sox were back in it. Boston fans had seen this scenario before. Thirty-one times that season—almost one-third of their victories—the Red Sox had scored the winning run in the eighth inning or later. This was not a team that gave up.

With Carlton Fisk stepping up to the plate, the score was 5–3, and Yastrzemski was on first with one out.

For the third straight time, Gossage started a batter off with a ball. He wasn't comfortable. He felt like he was trying to throw the ball 200 miles an hour, like he was trying to squeeze the ball to death, and even though he knew it, he kept doing it anyway. As a result, the ball wasn't moving the way it normally did for him; it was going up straight to the plate, and the Red Sox were seeing it.

Fisk smacked the next pitch foul, yanking it toward the lights overlooking left field. The shadows coming from that direction had now crossed the field and crept past first base.

A called second strike, low around the knees. Nothing but fastballs now.

Fisk fouled off the next pitch, then another. He was fighting Gossage, swinging defensively, waiting for a mistake.

A second mistake, really. Munson had set up outside before that last pitch. But just as Gossage had in the seventh, when Rick Burleson was batting and Munson set up outside and Gossage threw it inside all the way to the backstop, Gossage couldn't put the ball where he wanted it. Fisk had only fouled it off—but he'd taken a good cut.

Fisk fouled another back, his third straight. An inning before, he'd asked about turning on the lights, but decided it was a bad move when the Sox were winning. They weren't winning anymore, but Fisk was so locked in, he'd completely forgotten he'd asked.

Glove on his left knee, ball tucked in his right hand, curled behind his back like a weapon, Gossage leaned forward to take Munson's sign. He came just low and outside, a hard pitch to let pass, but Fisk checked his swing and Denkinger called a ball. The count was 2–2.

From low and outside Gossage went to over the plate and high, and the count went to 3–2. Fisk had fought his way back to a hitter's advantage.

In the Yankee bullpen, former Red Sox reliever Sparky Lyle and right-hander Ken Clay started to warm up. Neither was an attractive option for Bob Lemon. Clay was a rookie who'd had an erratic season. Lyle had pitched just twice in the last seventeen days.

Fisk smoked a foul ball past third.

Then he hit another, even harder foul ball past third. For Gossage, that was worrisome. Right-handed hitters did not usually pull him. And he had now thrown ten pitches to Fisk.

On the eleventh, Fisk finally got a pitch he could do something with, a fastball waist-high, by far the most hittable pitch of the at-bat. Fisk lined it smartly to center field, where Mickey Rivers fielded the ball. There were Red Sox on first and third with one out, 5–3 the score, and Fred Lynn, who had been robbed of an extra-base hit by Lou Piniella just one inning prior, advanced to the plate. He was now 0–3. Were it not for Piniella, he would have been 1–3 with 2 runs batted in.

He fouled the first pitch back. The second pitch from Gossage was a high fastball, tailing toward the outside part of the plate, and Lynn timed it perfectly, slapping it into left field for a single. Yastrzemski scored. It was 5–4 now, and the noise had returned to Fenway. Lynn was on first, Fisk on second with one out.

Bob Lemon ambled to the mound, where Munson joined him and Gossage. But with two right-handed hitters coming up—Butch Hobson and George Scott—Lemon wasn't about to yank Gossage. After just a few moments, he turned and strolled back to his dugout with all the mellow tranquility he'd shown on the way out.

Gossage delivered to Hobson low—yet another first-pitch ball. But finally, he got a break; Hobson swung at an outside fastball and poked it, in much the same manner as Jim Rice had earlier in the inning, out to right field. Piniella caught the ball on the heel of his glove and almost dropped it. Had he not been struggling to see the ball as it hurtled from the infield shadow, the play would have been routine, even boring. Not now. But at least Gossage finally had two outs.

George Scott, 2–3 with a double and a single, stepped up to bat. The crowd was calling his nickname. *Boo-mer! Boo-mer!*

Gossage's first pitch was, yes, a ball. And then Scott got his mistake: a fastball waist-high, right across the plate, exactly where the Boomer liked to crush it. Put a fastball there against the George Scott of old, and he would make you pay.

Scott fouled the ball off.

After that, he went down easy. Gossage gave him two fastballs too high to hit, really, out of his power zone. Scott swung away. The first one, he swung so hard and missed by so much that he almost fell over, saving himself only by propping himself up with his bat.

The second pitch, Scott just missed. Strike three.

In 1979, George Scott would play for three different teams: the

Red Sox, the Royals, and yes, the Yankees. He would hit .254 in 346 at-bats, and he would then make his exit from baseball, a very fine player, just never the superstar he was supposed to be.

But that was a year away. Here at Fenway, both teams had reason to take satisfaction. The Red Sox had shaved the Yankees lead from 5–2 to 5–4. They had shown that the Yankees' best reliever was fallible, and pulled within a single run.

But with one inning to go, the Yankees were holding on.

Sunday Night

"Now we'll see who's the best," Louis Tiant had said after beating the Toronto Blue Jays, 5–0, on October 1. Tiant considered the victory—which, coupled with a Yankee loss to Cleveland, resulted in a season's-end tie—the most important win of his career. "This is the best of all," he said. "The playoffs in 1975, the World Series—they were important games. But we were already there. This is a game we had to win or we wouldn't even get a chance to get there. . . . Probably the toughest game I've ever had to pitch."

The Red Sox felt confident about playing the Yankees the next day. "Bring your bags to the ballpark, we're going to Kansas City," Mike Torrez said, even though his record against New York in 1978 was less than awesome. In four starts against them, he was 1–3, had given up 28 hits in nineteen and a third innings, and had an ERA of 7.45. "I've been given a chance to redeem myself," Torrez said. "If I win this, this is what people will remember."

The Red Sox had been on a remarkable roll. Since September 17, they had won 13 of 15 games. In their last six games, the Red Sox had allowed only three runs. The team pushed back that damning label, "chokers," that so frustrated and infuriated the players. "We had heard so much the 'collapse,' 'we choked,' this and that," Rick Burleson said. "We took a lot of pride in coming back and being able to play the way we did at the end, and I don't think we got a lot of credit for that, because you're really not collapsing when you're winning 13 out of the last 15 games to get the tie." The last time an American League race had come down to the final day of the season was in 1967, when the Sox, the Impossible Dream team, beat the Minnesota Twins, 5–3. Among the 35,770 people in the Fenway stands that day was fifteen-year-old Jerry Remy, sitting in the right field seats, watching as Carl Yastrzemski willed the Red Sox to victory, going 4–4, with 2 runs batted in and a run scored.

Don Zimmer was not big on pep talks, but he sat his team down after that October 1 game against Toronto and had a few words with them. It had been a tough season for Zimmer. Though he'd managed a team that had won 99 games—four more wins than any other team in baseball, except the one three hours down Interstate 95—fans and pundits had ripped him all season. They'd called for his head after the Red Sox started with one win and three losses. Now, Zimmer knew, if the Sox didn't beat the Yankees, the abuse would get uglier still.

He was proud of them, Zimmer told his players, proud that they had hung in there and fought their way back after injuries, after losing streaks, after being written off. He did not mention the ghastly four-game blowout by the Yankees in early September, the Boston Massacre, but he did not need to. Everything was supposed to have come easy to the Red Sox. It hadn't, and the team had been forced to prove that it had not just talent, but heart.

Down in the Bronx, the Yankees were disappointed but not demoralized. The Indians had beaten them by playing as if they had nothing to lose, which they didn't. "Last game of the season," Cliff Johnson said. "They were going home." The Yankees had been through too much to get bent out of shape about having to play one more game. "We remembered that just a month earlier we had beaten Boston four straight," Piniella said. "We went up to Boston confident." And the Yankees were proud of their season as well—coming back from chaos, controversy, and a 14½ game deficit. That mattered to all of the players, but perhaps it mattered most to the quiet ones, who just wanted to play the game like pros, to do what they loved, to win, to have fun. "Now people can respect us for the way we play, instead of thinking we're some kind of soap opera," Bucky Dent said. He'd had enough melodrama in the rest of his life. Baseball was supposed to be different; baseball was the joy that healed the pain you felt from life's hard realities.

Anyway, it felt right, playing this decisive game. These were the two best teams in baseball, constituting the best rivalry in baseball. It was only one game, but it felt like the World Series, and both teams belonged there.

In Yankee Stadium, Bob Lemon called his players together and did something that he had not done since taking over from Billy Martin: he reamed someone out. In the top of the ninth, Mickey Rivers had loped after a base hit by Cleveland's Gary Alexander, playing the ball so casually that Alexander wound up on second. Now, Lemon shut the door to the clubhouse. He began by thanking the Yankees for the way they had played in the season's second half. When he took the job, he had told them that they were world champions, that he just wanted to let them do what no one did better, and they had risen to the challenge. Lemon was proud of them.

And then he laid into Rivers. You loafed on that play, Lemon said. Rivers mumbled that he was tired from running down balls all day. Lemon answered that that wasn't good enough. The Yankees weren't going to Boston just to show up, but to win. "Do you want to play or not?" he said to Rivers. "You sleep on it, you tell me one way or the other tomorrow."

That night, Red Sox went to their homes and apartments, while the Yankees took a bus to La Guardia Airport, flew to Boston, and dispersed for dinner. Afterward, a bunch of players wound up drinking beers at Daisy Buchanan's on Newbury Street, just a few blocks from the ancient ballpark. Thurman Munson, Lou Piniella, Sparky Lyle, Reggie Jackson, Bucky Dent, Goose Gossage—it felt like the whole team was there. The Yankees were like that, a tough, rambunctious crew. They liked to have fun. It kept them sane.

Back in the hotel later, Goose Gossage tried to sleep.

Not too far away, Carl Yastrzemski lay in bed and wondered if this was going to be his last opportunity to get to and win a World Series. Eighteen years in major league ball had taught him that these chances, these teams, did not come often. They took years to coalesce, but they could fall apart between the end of one season and the beginning of another, especially now, in the era of free agency. A team's excellence was like a perfect swing; so many things had to go right to make it happen, but to wreck it, to shatter its rhythm, required only one mistake. Yaz thought that this was the best team he'd ever played on, and that this game against the Yankees was the moment he'd been preparing for ever since he was a boy, getting strong, throwing sacks of potatoes in a Southampton field, swinging through the chill of a winter night at a leather ball hanging from a string in his garage.

THE NINTH INNING

As shortstop Fred Stanley stepped to the plate to begin the Yankee ninth, Fenway Park was taut with collective tension, an individual anxiety multiplied some 33,000 times, fueled by the heavy knowledge that the Red Sox had to keep the Yankees from further scoring—and then had to score at least one run themselves to tie the game at five and send it into extra innings. After 162 games and eight innings, only six outs remained, and if the Sox did not come from behind, the shadows that had been stretching across the field would just keep right on going all the way into winter. A season of promise would come to a bitter end, and that bittersweet axiom, "Wait till next year," would kick in—though it was hard to believe that you could start any spring with greater optimism than Sox fans had enjoyed six months before, and so "wait till next year" couldn't be said with much vigor, because how could the team get better than it was supposed to have been in 1978, the season of greatest expectations?

But if Boston could somehow claw back, just as it had done in forcing this playoff in the first place only one day before (it seemed like more now), then the weight of disappointed hopes could be lifted, and that season of hope could continue for just a little longer.

But first, the Yankees had to be retired.

Fred Stanley did his part.

Back in June, the shortstop had hit a grand slam home run off Mike Torrez to beat the Red Sox. It had accounted for much of his offensive production during the season, during which he had batted .220, with 1 home run and 9 RBIs. Now, he swung at the first pitch from Andy Hassler and hit a bouncing ball to Jerry Remy for an easy out.

The fans rumbled as Bucky Dent approached the batter's box, but there was no onslaught of full-throated boos. Perhaps the Boston crowd was too tense to show that much emotion, or perhaps it was hunkering down, saving its energy for the Red Sox half of the inning.

Dent took a sinker low for a ball, but Hassler came right back with a fastball down the middle that Dent watched for a strike. Dent swung at the next pitch and hit it hard, considerably harder than he'd hit his home run. It soared foul onto the roof overlooking left field, where a group of fans standing on the roof watching the game scrambled to retrieve it. For the first time all day, the fans gave off a sound that could be described as anger, a frustration that Dent, who by all logic should never have homered in the first place, could even dare to try again.

But Hassler followed with an inside fastball that Dent fouled to the ground near his instep, and then the pitcher delivered a perfect curveball that looked headed well off the plate, but, as Dent stood frozen, dove back to nip the edge of the strike zone. Dent knew he was out before the umpire bothered to confirm it.

Two away.

Batting for Mickey Rivers, Paul Blair, the former Oriole, came to the plate. Blair was a right-handed hitter who hadn't had much chance to hit; his season average was only .169, with 2 home runs and 13 RBIs in 124 at-bats. But as a pinch hitter he had struck 4 hits in 15 at-bats, and he was a far better center fielder than Rivers was, with a much stronger arm; he had won eight Gold Gloves with the Orioles.

In theory, Blair should have been an easy out; Hassler looked strong, and Blair was rusty. Instead, the hitter worked the count to 2–1, then ripped a single past Frank Duffy at third. Regular third baseman Butch Hobson might have had the ball, but it bounced under Duffy's outstretched glove. Don Zimmer quickly hopped out of the dugout and, just as he was crossing the first base line, waved his hand for right-handed pitcher Dick Drago to come in to face Thurman Munson. Zimmer was taking no chances. The Sox could not afford to be down by more than one run, as the odds of scoring two runs in each of consecutive innings against Goose Gossage were minuscule.

Originally signed by Detroit in 1964, Drago was a thirty-three-year-old right-handed pitcher who had played for the Sox in 1974 and 1975, after which he was traded to the Angels, who then traded him to the Orioles. After that, Drago became a free agent, and the Sox had signed him in December 1977 as part of their effort to boost their pitching staff. Drago had generally done what the Sox had hoped he would do. He'd thrown 77 innings in 36 appearances, with a 3.04 record, 4 wins and 4 losses, and 7 saves. Eight days before, against

Toronto, at the start of the run that had brought the Sox into their tie with the Yankees, he'd thrown four and two-thirds crucial shutout innings. Against the Yankees, however, his record was mixed. In five appearances, he had a 0–1 record and an ERA of 4.30. And though Drago claimed that control was his pitching strength, he had also hit Thurman Munson below the helmet the last time the teams had played.

Munson went through his rituals—checking the batting gloves, tapping the edges of the plate, settling his batting helmet with each hand—and stared at Drago. He was 1–4, with three strikeouts, but also had lined the double that had driven in Mickey Rivers for the Yankees' fourth run.

Drago threw to first to hold Paul Blair to the bag. Then he did it again. Blair scrambled back to first base. Before throwing the ball back the second time, George Scott picked up a handful of dirt from the base path and firmly rubbed it on the ball. Umpire Jim Evans did not seem to notice.

Drago threw Munson two fastballs, both of which were outside. Other than the occasional isolated cheer and scattered applause, there was almost total silence in Fenway Park.

Drago came with a breaking ball on his third pitch, and Munson knocked a bouncing ball between third and short. Once again the grounder scooted under the glove of Frank Duffy, but Burleson fielded it on the edge of the outfield grass and made a quick, hard throw to second. It was close, but second base umpire Al Clark called Blair out—as if he, too, were impatient to get to the Red Sox half of the inning.

Three outs, and the Red Sox had Frank Duffy, Rick Burleson, and Jerry Remy coming to the plate—and after them, Jim Rice and Carl Yastrzemski.

As the bottom of the ninth began, the entire field was covered by shadows except for a slice of center and most of right field, which were still bright with sun; they looked like they existed in a different time zone than the rest of the field. Right field was particularly bright, as if the sun had picked that corner of Fenway to wage a last stand. Standing in right field, Lou Piniella looked curiously spotlighted. If someone hit a high fly ball, the sun was manageable; the arc of the ball would take it over the rays of the sinking sun. But line drives were another matter. Their flight path aligned with the rays of the sun, and to pick them up, Piniella would have to look directly into the October sunlight.

Standing fairly far back toward the wall, Piniella hoped no one would hit the ball his way—he wasn't sure how he would catch it if someone did. "In about the fifth or sixth inning, that sun got in your face and just stayed there," Piniella would explain. "That day it was just a big, big ball." Three innings before, he had returned to the dugout and said to Bob Lemon, "If that ball is hit to me on a line, we're going to have some problems."

The Yankees made two defensive changes. In center field, Paul Blair had taken Mickey Rivers's place, and in left field, Gary Thomasson was entering the game as a defensive replacement for Roy White, an embarrassment to White, since it was obviously a commentary on his arm strength. But with just half an inning to go, Bob Lemon did not feel the value of sentimentality.

Don Zimmer also made a change: in lieu of the light-hitting Frank Duffy, he sent right fielder, and right-handed-hitter, Dwight Evans to the plate. Zimmer wanted a home run to tie the game, and though Duffy had hit a respectable .260 in 104 at-bats, he had not hit a single home run. Evans, however, did hit with power. He had 24 home runs and 63 RBIs in 496 at-bats, despite a subpar (for Evans) .248 batting average.

Evans, though, was really in no condition to be batting. On August 29, he had been hit in the head by a pitch from Seattle's Mike Parrot, and the effects were serious and persistent. "It hit me right behind the left ear," Evans would say, "and it stopped me from playing." His equilibrium thrown off, Evans frequently lost his balance. "I couldn't even step off a curb without spinning," he said. At night, Evans would lie in bed and the room would spin as if he were on a bad drunk. "I'd wake up throwing up," he recalled. Evans loved to play—only Carl Yastrzemski would play in more Red Sox games than Evans did during his career—but even though he looked fine to outsiders, his condition was so debilitating that he grew demoralized, and, on the field, nervous. "As long as my head didn't move, I was okay," he said. "It was just horrible. I went out to right field and I would see three or four balls coming at me. People would just not understand. They would say, 'Catch the one in the middle.'"

In one week in September, Evans dropped four balls, about twice as many as he would typically drop in an entire season—and these were easy catches. During the second game of the Massacre, he left the field after dropping a fly ball and complaining of dizziness. Evans was not just a great outfielder but also a proud one. His defense mattered greatly to him, and his condition unnerved him. His hitting was suffering as well. After his beaning, he would go 9–54 the rest of the season. It was scary. You couldn't play on the Red Sox and not remember what had happened in 1967 to Tony Conigliaro, hit beneath the left eye by a pitch from the Angels' Jack Hamilton, never really to recover.

Standing in the dugout now, watching Evans walk to the plate, Carl Yastrzemski thought about what it would have been like in '67 if the Sox had had Conigliaro, what might have happened in 1975 if Jim Rice hadn't broken his wrist and missed the World Series. Would things have been different? And how would this game have been different if Dwight Evans had been able to play? Twice now Yastrzemski had gone to the World Series only to lose in seven games. How many more chances would he get?

Evans's performance had deteriorated so much that Don Zimmer had finally benched him a week before. For Zimmer to bench a veteran who was clearly trying so hard, things had to be bad. That was why sending him to the plate now was an understandable move, but one with a low probability of success. If Zimmer had not hit for Jack Brohamer with Bob Bailey, he would not have had to use Frank Duffy in the field, and it would have been the left-handed-hitting Brohamer now coming to the plate—a better matchup against Gossage than a right-handed hitter who hadn't played in a week because his vision was suffering.

But Gossage was not his usual self, either. Starting his third inning of relief, the pitcher had had struggled to find the plate, especially with first pitches. The pattern held true now. Gossage started Evans with a fastball low for a ball. His next pitch, however, was a fastball right down the middle—by Gossage standards, more than hittable. Evans tried. He swung hard, but his location was off; he hit slightly under the ball and lofted a gentle fly to left field. Thomasson had plenty of time to settle under the ball and make the easy catch.

The Red Sox were two outs away from winter.

Rick Burleson, 1–4 with a sixth-inning double, stepped up to the plate. And suddenly Gossage's control vanished.

The first pitch was low. So was the second.

Gossage stood on the mound and took a deep breath. His cheeks swelled as if he were about to play the trumpet, and then he shot the air out of his lungs.

The third pitch was a fastball outside. The crowd, which had fallen silent after Evans's fly ball, started to cheer again.

With the count 3–0, Burleson parked his bat on his shoulder and watched the next pitch, a fastball that darted across the inside corner. At last, a strike. But Gossage's fifth pitch wasn't even close; Munson had to stretch to grab the outside fastball. Burleson flipped his bat toward the dugout and ran to first base. With one out, the tying run was on first, and Jerry Remy, who had doubled against Gossage in his previous at-bat, was coming to the plate. Fenway roared back to life. The fans were on their feet now, the noise overwhelming, and that would not change until the game was over.

Remy fouled the first pitch into the left field stands. He swung at and missed the second fastball entirely. But even with the count 0–2, he felt good. Gossage didn't seem to have as much on the ball as during Remy's prior at-bat against him.

He's running on fumes out there, Remy thought.

Not fumes, Gossage would have told him. Adrenaline. Nerves. Too much of both. He still felt like he was overthrowing, trying to throw the ball too hard, and when he did that, his pitches straightened out and actually slowed down.

Remy didn't like the next pitch, an outside fastball, and swung defensively, poking the ball the opposite way into the stands. With the count 0–2, Gossage inexplicably gave Remy a fastball smack in the heart of the plate. Remy whacked the ball, and not to the opposite field this time; he pulled it, a line drive toward Lou Piniella in sun-soaked right field. As the ball came off the bat, Piniella saw it clearly. But then, as it arced over Fred Stanley's head and into right field, it disappeared in the sun. Piniella had no idea where Remy's line drive was going to land, and where it might go after that.

The right fielder started to back up slowly, just a bit. Three steps, total. He didn't want the ball to go by him—Burleson could score from first if it did—but neither did he want to give Burleson any sign that he had lost the ball.

Burleson ran toward second, then slowed. The outfielder's deke was working.

Sprinting toward first, Remy had no doubt. *It's going to drop,* he thought. He could tell the second he hit it.

The ball bounced in front of Piniella and to his left, and Burleson took off around second.

And then, something amazing: as the ball actually bounced *past* Piniella, he twisted his body and lunged for it, stretching out his glove arm like a wide receiver leaping for a pass just at the edge of his fingertips. And, with his body pointed toward the corner of right field, Piniella found the ball wedged in the tip of his glove. He landed, planted his feet, and pivoted to throw to third. About thirty feet past second base, Burleson saw Piniella's play, and he quickly planted his own feet and scrambled back to second. Piniella's throw was a rope, straight and hard to Graig Nettles a yard or so in front of the third base bag. If Burleson hadn't returned to second, he would almost surely have been tagged by Nettles for the out. But if he hadn't slowed between first and second . . .

It didn't seem to matter, though. Jerry Remy was on first, Rick Burleson was on second, and the Red Sox had Jim Rice and Carl Yastrzemski coming to bat. Five minutes before, after Dwight Evans at-bat, Fenway had been near-silent. "And now," Red Sox announcer Ned Martin said, "the thunder of Fenway Park descends." The Red Sox, and their fans, had come to life.

Jim Rice was 1–4, having struck out, grounded to short, singled home a run, and flied to right. He was, in short, overdue. Just as it seemed implausible that Reggie Jackson would not make his presence felt, how could a man having one of the greatest offensive seasons in baseball history play a game so important and compile only a single in five trips to the plate?

Gossage threw Rice a rising fastball, and the slugger fouled it back directly behind the plate—a good cut, but Gossage had put the fastball just where Guidry had tried to pitch to Rice, just around his wrists.

The next pitch came to the outside part of the plate, and Rice swung and connected. The ball soared toward the right field fence, an obstacle Rice had cleared many times in the past. But he would not do it this time. Just in front of the warning track, Lou Piniella stood waiting for the ball to descend. It was no line drive; it curved above the sun's rays, and Piniella had it in his sights from the time the ball left Rice's bat to the time it settled in his glove. When it had done so, Burleson left the second base bag and scurried to third. Piniella's throw to second blocked Remy from advancing.

If Piniella had not acted as if he would catch Remy's line drive—if Burleson had not stopped running between first and second—then Burleson would have been standing on third when Rice hit his deep fly ball, and he would have tagged and scored the tying run easily.

And then, Mike Torrez would say years later, "No one would have talked about Dent's hit."

But Piniella had looked as if he was fully capable of catching Remy's single, and Burleson had paused between first and second, and maybe, just maybe, it didn't even matter, because although there were two outs, there were runners on first and third and Carl Yastrzemski was the next batter and the thunder of Fenway, if it were even possible, boomed louder still.

How many times had Yaz come through for the Red Sox when it counted? Perhaps no one on either team knew the answer as well as Graig Nettles, who had been with the Twins in 1967, when Yastrzemski, in that amazing Triple Crown season, had taken it upon himself to carry the Red Sox into the World Series. It was the last weekend of the season and all the Twins had to do was win one game of the two against the Red Sox. Yastrzemski went seven for eight, Boston won twice, and the Twins were gone.

Oh, no, Nettles thought. *He's going to do it again.*

Standing on first, Jerry Remy thought so, too. *We're going to win. First and third, and we've got Mr. Red Sox up there . . .*

Yaz was not infallible, of course. In 1975, he had made the last out in Game Seven of the World Series, lofting a gentle fly ball to Cesar Geronimo in center field in the bottom of the ninth. But was there anyone in baseball the Yankees would want to see up there less? Watching the game in the clubhouse, where he had gone to ice his arm—after all, if the Yankees won, they'd start playing the Royals the next day—Ron Guidry didn't think so. He was worried. Yaz may have been older now, but he was still a good fastball hitter. He'd already homered and singled today, driven in two runs. The man was always dangerous.

On the mound, Lemon, Gossage, and Munson were conferring, ostensibly discussing how to pitch to Yastrzemski, really just giving Gossage a moment to relax and catch his breath.

Remy stood on first. Swatting the mud off his pants, Rick Burleson waited on third. Not far from Burleson, Graig Nettles was setting up close to the infield grass, because you never knew, there was always the chance that Yastrzemski would bunt. If he played too far back, Nettles thought, Yastrzemski would be a fool not to bunt. All Yaz had to do was square around and push the ball down the third base line, and if Nettles wasn't expecting it—what a mad, risky, brilliant play it would be. Nettles wasn't going to let that happen.

As he walked toward the batter's box, holding his bat in his right hand, Carl Yastrzemski was nervous.

He looked focused and resolute. But the noise was incredible, every person in Fenway Park was standing on his or her feet, screaming and clapping, and Yastrzemski could feel his stomach jumping up and down. It was not a feeling he knew well. Generally he was too prepared, too methodical, and too experienced to be nervous. And he was this time, too—prepared, that is. The night before, he had visualized exactly this situation. Now, he wanted to be the batter at the plate. He wanted it just the way Bucky Dent had wanted to hit a home run and be a hero; this was the situation little boys dreamed of. Two out, two on, the Red Sox down by one run, 5–4. The chance to be a hero, now, tomorrow, for the rest of your life, for longer than that. Tens of thousands of people cheering for you, *believing* in you. This was when baseball was a game. Not only a game—the greatest game.

And so perhaps it was not a surprise that Yastrzemski was nervous. Seventeen years he'd been in the majors, and had there ever been a more important at-bat?

Then he got to the plate and Fenway somehow, impossibly, got even louder, an enormous roar of support and faith and goodwill all directed at Yastrzemski, and he started doing what he always did at the plate, checking his helmet and shirt, slightly hitching up his pants, getting comfortable in the batter's box, thinking to himself.

Lay off the high pitch, lay off the high pitch. Get something down and in to pull. Anything down. Doesn't have to be a line drive. Doesn't have to be a home run. No one hits home runs off Gossage. A ground ball will do. Chambliss is holding Remy at first. A ground ball between first and second. That's all you need. That's all you need.

Yastrzemski picked up a handful of dirt in his right hand and sprinkled some on his bat handle. He gripped his bat and got into his stance. And as he did, the sound of the crowd just disappeared. Gone. As if someone had hit a mute button. It was just him and Gossage. The way it should be; the way he'd dreamed of it.

Don't let him beat you. Don't let him beat you. Get the head of the bat out, don't let that ball beat you.

Gossage delivered a fastball inside, and Yastrzemski watched it, and when the umpire called it a ball, Yastrzemski grew more confident.

Man, he's gotta throw me a strike.

With the count 1–0, Yastrzemski knew that he could afford to take a pitch. But if Gossage gave him something low and inside, something he could drive through the hole where the first baseman would ordinarily be . . . he was going to swing at that pitch.

Standing on the mound, staring toward home plate, Rich Gossage was also nervous, and he was talking to himself. Not so you could see it, of course. Just in his head, a hell of a conversation between himself and himself, standing there on the mound.

This is what you went to bed last night thinking about. Well, here it is. Why are you so nervous? What's the worst thing that can happen to me?

At first, his mind didn't give him a chance to answer that one. The conversation continued.

This is what you play the game for! The love of it and the fun of it. Again: *What's the worst thing that can happen to me?*

This time, his mind answered the question. *What's the worst thing that can happen? If we lose, tomorrow I'll be home, elk hunting in Colorado.*

And when he thought that, Gossage felt calm. It was the first time he'd felt calm all day.

He threw an inside fastball toward the plate, just where Yastrzemski loved to swing, just where he could hit the ball like the Yaz of old. Yastrzemski saw it coming, knew exactly what it was—he'd seen this pitch a thousand times before—and he started to swing.

And then the ball changed direction. As if someone had suddenly tugged it, Gossage's pitch seemed to speed up those last few feet before the plate, and it darted even farther down and in, away from Yastrzemski's sweet spot. For a fraction of a second, Yastrzemski looked surprised. He tried to adjust his swing, but it was too late. He got under the ball, undercut it, and he popped the ball up toward third base.

He knew right away. *Get in the stands, get in the stands. Go foul. Give me another chance.*

Graig Nettles hated pop-ups. He was one of the best-fielding third basemen in the history of the game, but he just didn't like pop-ups. "It's a hard play because you never practice 'em," not after spring training was over, he would say. "Everyone assumes that you can catch a pop-up, but sometimes they get up there and you lose sight of the ball. I tried to make 'em look easy, but believe me, I wasn't comfortable with pop-ups. If it had been a towering pop-up, I probably would have called for Bucky." Dent had played in the swirling winds of Chicago; he was good with pop-ups.

But Nettles couldn't have called for Dent, because just as the shortstop saw Nettles position himself under the ball, he felt something fall down his shirt. The chain on his Saint Christopher's medal had broken and the medal slid down inside his shirt. Dent thought that a bug had flown inside his shirt, and was momentarily distracted. He would later find the medal inside his uniform, but for now, he was taken out of the play.

Standing just inside the third base line, about a yard behind the third base bag, Nettles raised his glove to his left shoulder and caught the ball and squeezed his glove about as tight as he ever had.

The thunder that had descended upon Fenway was gone, and for long moments all that remained was a stunned silence, a disbelief that it could end this way. Carl Yastrzemski had popped up. The Yankees had won, 5–4. They were celebrating on the field, running joyfully into their dugout. Within hours they would leave for Kansas City. The Red Sox would take the bags they had packed for the trip west and go home for the next five months.

The Yankees swarmed and hugged and leaped on top of one another. For a moment, George Steinbrenner, who had clambered from his first-row seat onto the field, tried to join in the hugs, but the players rushed by him and into their locker room. Boston police officers on imposing horses filled the perimeter of the field, but there was no need for that. The fans were too stunned to move.

Still, they pulled themselves together in time for a gesture of gratitude. They knew then—in a way that some Boston fans would forget in later years, as the memory of the loss took root—how hard their team had fought. Down to the last out, the Red Sox had never given up. After 163 games, which was the better team? The Yankees had a better record, 100–63, to the Red Sox's 99–64. But that one-game difference was really just a one-run difference, and that one-run difference was really just a one-swing difference, and when you thought about it that way, how could you possibly say that one team was better than the other?

And so the fans in Fenway Park stood and cheered their team as the Boston Red Sox walked off the field for the last time in the 1978 season.

Carlton Fisk and Jerry Remy lingered near the walkway to the clubhouse. They did not want to leave, were not ready to leave. Carlton Fisk, who had been on deck, still had his batter's helmet on.

Alone in the Red Sox trainer's room, Carl Yastrzemski buried his head between his knees and sobbed. The home run, the RBI single in the eighth—none of that mattered. He had popped up.

I let everybody down, was all he could think. *My teammates. The fans in the park. All of New England.*

I let everybody down.

Carl Yastrzemski would play for the Red Sox through the 1983 season, an incredible 23 years with one team, something hard to imagine in the age of free agency. In 1979, he would strike his 3,000th hit. In 1989, he would be inducted into the Hall of Fame on the first vote.

But he would never reach again reach the playoffs, never play in another World Series, and never win a championship. He had been right. This had been the most important game of his career.

In the Yankee locker room, when all the shouting was over, all the champagne bottles popped and poured, Thurman Munson found Goose Gossage in the trainer's room, where he had gone to ice his arm.

"Where'd you get that fastball?" Munson asked him. That last one, to Yastrzemski. "Hell, that pitch had another foot on it than anything else you'd thrown all day."

Gossage said that that was the first pitch on which he'd relaxed.

Munson looked at Gossage in that mischievous way he had.

"Took you long enough," he said.

EPILOGUE

It was probably impossible that the 1978 postseason could live up to the drama of the Yankees' victory over Boston. Players on both sides felt that Boston and New York were baseball's best teams, with the records to prove it, and nothing that followed could equal the intensity of their one-game matchup. Not even the specter of Billy Martin could create drama. When the Yankees headed to Kansas City to play the Royals, whom they'd barely beaten in the American League championships the past two years, Royals pitcher Larry Gura pointed out that "if [Billy] Martin was still here, we'd probably be playing the Sox." But Martin wasn't with New York, and the Yankees were a confident and relaxed team without him.

Jim Beattie won Game One for the Yankees easily, 7–1, as his teammates pounded 16 hits. In the second game, Ed Figueroa pitched uncharacteristically poorly and the Royals won, 10–4. In Game Three, Rich Gossage finished for Catfish Hunter, who was showing signs of fatigue after his up-and-down season, and got a 6–5 win. That brought up Guidry, and the result was predictable: a 2–1 victory and the third straight American League championship for the Yankees.

Against the Dodgers, they quickly fell behind two games to none, losing 11–5 and then 4–3 when, with Bucky Dent on second and Paul Blair on first, a hard-throwing rookie named Bob Welch struck out Reggie Jackson in an exciting nine-pitch, six-minute at-bat. (Jackson had earlier hit his sixth home run over four consecutive World Series games, breaking a record set by Lou Gehrig.) Yet the Yankees weren't rattled. Back in New York for Game Three, Ron Guidry was pitching, but he was not sharp. Guidry would later admit that he "left his fastball in the bullpen," and the Dodgers hit him hard. At third base, though, Graig Nettles made a series of astonishing plays—leaping, diving, scrambling, and throwing—that likely prevented seven runs from scoring. Despite giving up seven walks, Guidry won, 5–1. The Yankees evened the series in Game Four, when Lou Piniella singled in the suddenly ubiquitous Roy White in the bottom of the tenth and the Yankees won, 4–3. Game Five's greatest drama came in the third inning, when Dodger shortstop Bill Russell doubled with shortstop Davey Lopes on first base. With Lopes sprinting toward home, Graig Nettles ran deep into the outfield grass to take Roy White's throw. His relay to Munson arrived at home plate a fraction of a second after Lopes did. The Dodger was safe, and Munson was hurt. As Lopes bounced up and dusted himself off, Munson tried to stand, then toppled over onto his side in obvious agony, one new wound added to the pain of a long season, of eight long seasons catching for the Yankees. Munson pushed himself onto his knees but still couldn't stand. Propping himself up with his mitt, he dragged himself along the ground like a dog that's been hit by a car, as if he knew that if he stopped moving, starting again would hurt even more. A few feet down the first base line, Munson pushed himself off the ground with his arms and straightened his body. His face tight with concentration, he waved away the trainer who was running from the dugout, then hopped up and down a little as if to shake out the pain.

Whether he succeeded in that effort or not, Munson seemed to draw strength from the collision. That day he went 3–5 with 1 run scored and 5 runs batted in, accounting for half the runs in the Yankees' 12–2 victory. All told, the Yankees collected 18 hits in a manner reminiscent of their relentless performance during the Boston Massacre: 16 of those hits were singles. Jim Beattie pitched the first complete game of his career for the win.

Back in Los Angeles, Catfish Hunter gave up a leadoff home run to Lopes. The Yankees scored three in the second off Don Sutton, but in the third the Dodgers threatened again. Brian Doyle would remember that Munson called time out and trotted to the mound. "I ran out, thinking that they were going to change something," Doyle said. "And Thurman comes up and says, 'Catfish, you don't have anything.' And Catfish says, 'Don't you know I know that? Now, get back there.' "

The Yankees would win, 7–2, and take the Series four games to two, becoming the first team ever to win the World Series in four straight games after being down two to none. The unlikely duo of Brian Doyle and Bucky Dent was New York's greatest surprise. After sitting out the first two games, Doyle racked up 6 hits, batting .438, and scoring 4 runs. Dent, the Series MVP, would go 10–24, a .417 average, with 7 runs batted in and 3 scored. The Yankees were champions for the second year in a row.

No one could know it or would have even believed it at the time, but eighteen years would pass, ushering in an entirely different era in the team's history, before the Yankees would win their next World Series. When the 1979 season began, it was clear that this year could not match 1978 for memories; both the Red Sox and the Yankees had changed since the previous October, and their internal tensions kept them from squaring off against each other as they had in 1978. In November, the Yankees traded Sparky Lyle, so unhappy after losing his status as the team's stopper, to Texas. But in a move that devastated the Red Sox, George Steinbrenner signed Luis Tiant to a two-year contract for $840,000. Red Sox president Haywood Sullivan thought Tiant too old, but the pitcher meant more to the Sox than could be so easily quantified: his wit and toughness helped hold the team together. "When they let Tiant go to New York," Carl Yastrzemski would say, "they tore out our heart and soul."

Nor was that the only departure for the Sox. The last of the Buffalo Heads, Bill Lee, was dispatched to Montreal in December for a utility infielder named Stan Papi, who, after some years in the minors, had compiled 46 hits in two major-league seasons. Papi would hit .188 in 51 games for Boston before the Red Sox sent him to Philadelphia in 1980, which two weeks later forwarded him to Detroit, where the efficacy of his hitting did not change before his retirement in 1981. But the best part of Lee's career was over as well; he would never really recover from the injury suffered in the fight with Graig Nettles. In a little over three seasons with Montreal, Lee won 25 games and lost 22.

George Scott would also depart the 1979 Red Sox. After the big first baseman went 0–25 early in the season, Zimmer benched him. "Play me or trade me," Scott said. The team honored his request by shipping him to Kansas City. The Royals cut Scott in August, after which the Yankees signed him for September, then released him. The next spring, Scott rented a car and drove around the training camps of the Red Sox, the Tigers, and the White Sox. "Money? I don't care about money," he said. "Let me play." No one did.

Over the next years, the Sox would continue to shed the personnel who had dominated the team during the late 1970s. After Boston finished fifth in 1980, Zimmer was fired, and he would wind down his career, among other places, in New York, as a trusted adviser to Yankee manager Joe Torre. Rather than renegotiate new contracts with

Rick Burleson and Butch Hobson, Haywood Sullivan traded them to the Angels in late 1980. Fred Lynn and, most painfully, Carlton Fisk would leave the Red Sox on a technicality; when their contracts for 1981 arrived after a league deadline, both players filed grievances. The Sox hastily traded Lynn to the Angels, but Fisk would become a free agent and sign with the White Sox. Though he would actually play more years for Chicago than he had with Boston, the second half of Fisk's career had an anticlimactic quality. The rivalry with the Yankees had helped define him. Without it, Fisk was just a very fine catcher on a not particularly good team.

Carl Yastrzemski, forty-four by then, would retire at the end of the 1983 season. He had compiled incredible statistics since starting with the Red Sox in 1961—3,419 hits, 452 home runs, 1,844 runs batted in—but Yastrzemski would never know what it felt like to win a championship, for he never again came as close as he had that October day in 1978. Still, Yastrzemski never regretted being the man to come to the plate against Rich Gossage with two on and two out in the bottom of the ninth.

"That was some season," he would recall almost thirty years later. "I wish it would have ended differently, but it was a great season. And what made it a great season was that we won all those games at the end to force the playoff game. And who ever thought that we would come back and score those runs off Gossage? I'm glad we did, because it gave me the chance to come up in the ninth inning and tie the game or win it. I loved that throughout my whole career, absolutely loved that. I wished that every time I came to the plate it was in that situation.

"I wanted to be there, I'll tell you that," Yastrzemski said.

Before the last game of the 1983 season, on October 2, Yastrzemski slowly jogged around the perimeter of the stands at Fenway, shaking and slapping hands with as many fans as he could touch. "New England, I love you," Yaz said, and after all those years, and everything Yastrzemski and Sox fans had been through together, the feeling was unquestionably mutual.

The Yankees' 1979 season started ignominiously. In April, a locker room scuffle between Goose Gossage and Cliff Johnson resulted in torn ligaments in Gossage's right thumb. The Yankees traded Johnson to the Indians, and Gossage would miss 83 games. That was one reason why the team started off a mediocre 34–31, and in June, George Steinbrenner reluctantly fired Lemon and brought Billy Martin back sooner than planned. That didn't work, either; Martin, who had gotten into an off-season brawl with a sportswriter in Reno, Nevada, hadn't changed a bit, and the Yankees weren't all that happy to have him back.

But the team's greatest loss in the 1979 season had nothing to do with its place in the standings. It was the death of Thurman Munson in a plane crash on August 2.

Munson had purchased a Cessna Citation, a twin-engine, seven-seat jet with the registration N15NY, earlier that year. He had been a pilot for fewer than eighteen months, not a lot of experience for flying a jet. Munson had 516 hours of flying time, but before August, only 33 in the Citation.

His body hurting more than ever, Munson was having a subpar season, hitting .288 with just 3 home runs and 39 runs batted in. His career as a catcher was winding down, and in 1980 Munson would probably have been shifted to first base and designated hitter roles. With the end of his career in sight, Munson felt the day-to-day absence of his family even more deeply. On Wednesday, August 1, he flew home to Canton to be with his wife, Diana, and their children after a game against the White Sox. The Yankees' next game was not until Friday. On Thursday, Munson decided to practice takeoffs and landings at the Akron-Canton Regional Airport. At around 4 P.M., Munson came in some five hundred feet to low for the runway approach, and his plane lost speed and more altitude. With the jet some three hundred feet off the ground, Munson, desperate to regain control, floored the throttle. It was too late. Trees sheared off the plane's wings. Tearing through a barren field, the Cessna plowed through a ditch, then skidded through some saplings, and finally hit a large tree stump and slid to a halt on Greensburg Road, about nine hundred feet from the runway.

Munson's two passengers, flight instructor David Hall and friend Jerry Anderson, managed to scramble out. Munson could not. His neck was broken, his legs pinned under the dashboard. Anderson and Hall tried to pull him to safety, but Munson's door was crumpled and jammed. The plane was burning. As flames started to engulf the cockpit, the two men had to back away.

Thurman Munson was thirty-two and the Yankees would not be the same without him, not that season, not for many seasons to come.

In 1980, sports columnist Corky Simpson tracked down Munson's sixty-four-year-old father, Darrell Munson, who was working as a part-time parking lot attendant. He hadn't seen his son since 1974.

Thurman's death, Darrell said, "didn't hit me so hard. If you're really close to someone, it's different. I just wasn't in his world. People used to say I criticized him too much. Maybe that's what I did wrong. But he resented me. He got carried away with his own self-importance. He hated me."

He himself could have been a great ball player, Darrell Munson said. "I had natural talent. . . . I wish I could have made it to the big leagues because I think I could have outdone Thurman. I would have been better than him."

The heartbroken Yankees finished fourth in 1979, below the third-place Red Sox. At season's end, Catfish Hunter, 2–9 in 1979, retired. In the off-season, Martin got into another fight, this time with, of all people, a marshmallow salesman. Steinbrenner fired him again. The process—rehiring, then refiring—would occur thrice more during the 1980s, even as Steinbrenner's endless personnel machinations and fondness for giving exorbitant contracts to over-the-hill free agents pushed the Yankees into a trough of mediocrity while pushing away the players who had formed the core of the 1978 team. Chris Chambliss was traded after 1979, Reggie Jackson signed with the Angels in 1982, and Bucky Dent was traded to the Rangers in that same year. In 1984, the Yankees sent Graig Nettles to the San Diego Padres. Rich Gossage left New York that same year to pitch for the San Diego Padres. After all those years, "it just didn't seem like the fun was there, and I felt myself changing," he said. "I felt like I was getting a bad attitude . . . a bad attitude about not wanting to come to the park. Even when you won, it wasn't fun." Gossage had started his career in 1972; twenty-two seasons later, in 1994, he would finish it with the Seattle Mariners. "Make them tear the uniform off you," a former manager had once told Gossage, and he felt the same way.

Ron Guidry would never have another season as miraculous as 1978 had been, but he had several more than good ones after that. In his understated way, he would retire in 1988 with 170 wins and 91 losses and head home to Louisiana, returning to the Yankees eighteen years later for a stint as their pitching coach.

The last remaining Yankee from 1978 to leave was Willie Randolph, who signed with the Dodgers as a free agent in December 1988. Randolph would end his career with the New York Mets in 1992; thirteen years later, he would rejoin the Mets as their manager.

On Christmas Day, 1989, Billy Martin died in a car crash while either driving or being driven home—the truth is unclear—from a bar. His finances and personal life in a shambles, Martin had never been able to stop drinking, and his life had become increasingly sordid. In death, he aspired to greater nobility. Martin would be buried at the Gate of Heaven Cemetery in Hawthorne, New York, about 150 feet away from the grave of Babe Ruth. His tombstone read: "I may not have been the greatest Yankee to put on the uniform, but I was the proudest."

In late 1997, Catfish Hunter was diagnosed with amyotropic lateral sclerosis, better known as Lou Gehrig's disease. The illness progressed quickly, and when he visited his teammates the next spring training, his deterioration was plainly visible. "I'm doing all right," he said. "It's just my hands and arms don't work right." He died on September 9, 1999, at age fifty-three.

Mike Torrez would pitch for four more years with the Red Sox, but his productivity would steadily decline after 1978; his record from 1979 to 1982 was just 44–41. The Boston fans never forgave him that home run; he was booed every time he pitched at Fenway until he left Boston in 1983 to wrap up his career with the Mets. For years, Torrez was angry about that, frustrated with the fact that he'd pitched a good game but for one mistake, that it wasn't even Dent's home run that had beaten the Sox, that a home run hit by a shortstop who almost never hit home runs had kept him from taking revenge on the team that rejected him. When, in the sixth game of the 1986 World Series, Red Sox first baseman Bill Buckner let a ball scoot between his legs that allowed the Mets to win the game, Torrez couldn't help but feel relieved: at long last there was another Red Sox goat. Always business-minded, he would capitalize on his part in baseball history, once re-creating the at-bat with Dent and signing baseball memorabilia commemorating the home run.

But to this day, Mike Torrez is a competitive man, frustrated that he is only remembered for one thing and not his many years of pitching, not the 100 games he won between 1974 and 1979, the two World Series games he won for the Yankees in 1977. When he talks about Bucky Dent's home run his voice is tinged with a mixture of wistful acceptance, regret, frustration, and disappointment. "I'm not going to complain," he says. "I've made some money off it—sometimes bad does turn into good. It's enabled me to make a few bucks."

Still, he has always wondered about that home run, the strange *thunk* sound he thought he heard when the ball came off Bucky Dent's replacement bat. Some years after that game, Torrez says, he was talking with former Yankee Mickey Rivers, and "Mickey told me that Dent used his corked bat." He nods at the memory. "I don't know if Mickey was kidding, but he did tell me that. He said, 'Mike, why is Bucky getting all this notoriety?' I said, 'I don't know.' "

According to Torrez, Rivers replied, "Well, you know, I gave him my damned corked bat to use. I saw that bat was cracked. I said, 'Hell, use this one.' So he used that one."

"Mickey was sincere, I think," Torrez says.

Roy White, the bat's rightful owner, denies that story. "Absolutely not," White says. It is, he says, wishful thinking on Torrez's part. (Bucky Dent declined to respond to Torrez's assertion, and Mickey Rivers did not reurn phone calls asking about the quote.)

For Dent, that home run has come to define his baseball career. In New York, he is remembered for little else (but that is plenty). In New England, he is generally known as "Bucky Fuckin' Dent," the words a disbelieving Don Zimmer uttered while driving home after the game. Until the Red Sox's dramatic American League Championship Series comeback victory against the Yankees in 2004—a series that capped the resurgence of the Red Sox–Yankees rivalry—Dent represented the embodiment of Boston's futility against New York, the way that, year after year, the Sox's hopes were so cruelly dashed in the most unexpected ways. Even though it was not Dent's home run that scored the winning run against Boston—that honor belonged to Reggie Jackson—his was the blow that changed the momentum of the game. When Bucky Dent's fly ball off a 1–1 fastball slid over the edge of the Green Monster, Carl Yastrzemski slumping underneath it, Boston fans knew instantly that, in allowing themselves to believe that their team might finally win, they had been duped again by the gods of baseball, and it was easier simply to accept the inevitability of crushing defeat. Nothing that happened in the next quarter century would change their minds.

"There isn't a day that goes by that people don't talk about it," Dent says now, and there is still wonder in his voice at the idea that, through some bizarre stroke of fate or luck or divine intervention, he has played a part in the great history of baseball. One swing of the bat is the sole act for which Bucky Dent will be remembered, and he has come not only to accept that, but to be thankful for it, to understand that to be remembered for something, no matter how exceptional or fleeting, is a gift.

"People will come up to me," Dent explains. "They'll say, 'I was a Red Sox fan back then, thirteen years old, you ruined my life.' Or it'll be a Yankee fan: 'That was the greatest day, I can tell you what I was doing, where I was at. . . . ' "

They tell him stories, too many stories to remember. The guy who skipped school to watch the game, the guy who heard the news from a bus driver's announcement, the kid with the transistor radio hidden in his desk drawer . . .

"I like to hear the stories," Dent says. "That's the thing that stays with me more than anything, is the impact that that one-game playoff between those two teams had, that it still affects people so that they come up to me and talk about it. That is pretty special.

"Those two teams and that day, that doesn't happen very often," Dent says. "The Yankees, the Red Sox, all the things that went into that game, all the great players who were on the field, Guidry pitching, crystal-clear day. It seemed like everything stopped. Everything shut down for this one game."

Once every couple of years, Dent will sit down and watch the game again. "I still sweat when I watch it," he says. "I do."

He runs a baseball school in Delray Beach, Florida, now—"Bucky Dent's Baseball School." He's proud of the work the school does with young kids and their fathers. They come down, dads and sons and daughters, too, to get better at baseball, to hit and pitch and field under the Florida sun. But they also come, whether they know it or not, to get better at being dads and sons and daughters. That means a lot to Dent, who knows something about the relationship between a father and his child and how a game can help bridge the space between them. No matter how baseball has changed in the intervening years— nine-figure salaries, three-figure ticket prices, powerbroker agents, steroids, asterisks—that hasn't changed. When you get on those fields with a bat, ball, and glove, it remains a game.

There are seven baseball fields at Dent's school, but he is particularly proud of one. Its left field wall is a reconstruction of Fenway's Green Monster, correct in every dimension except that it is 35 feet high rather than 37—a quirk of construction. The scoreboard stops at the seventh inning. Every year, with gloves in hand, new children take the field, the scoreboard behind them forever frozen in that moment, reminding them that they too are part of the greatest game.

NOTES

INTRODUCTION

My description of Goose Gossage's and Carl Yastrzemski's pre-game feelings is drawn from interviews with both men. The story of Yastrzemski's childhood comes from my interview with him, as well as Yastrzemski's two autobiographies, *Yaz* (Carl Yastrzemski and Gerald Eskenazi, Warner Books, 1990), and *Yaz* (Carl Yastrzemski and Al Hirshberg, Viking Press, 1968).

CHAPTER ONE

This chapter and others are informed by the sportswriters of the New York and Boston newspapers, specifically the *New York Times,* the New York *Daily News,* the *New York Post,* and in Boston, the *Boston Globe* and the *Boston Herald-American.* Foremost among those writers were the two men who most frequently covered the Red Sox and Yankees, Peter Gammons and Murray Chass. Other sportswriters whose work was informative include Dave Anderson, Roger Angell, Steve Cady, Larry Craig, Joseph Durso, Gerald Eskenazi, Ray Fitzgerald, Joe Giuliotti. Henry Hecht, Roger Kahn, Parton Keese, Leonard Koppett, Tony Kornheiser, Larry Merchant, Leigh Montville, John Powers, Bob Ryan, Red Smith, and Larry Whiteside.

The portraits of George Steinbrenner and Billy Martin are drawn from Roger Kahn's *October Men* (Harcourt, 2003), Jonathan Mahler's *Ladies and Gentlemen: The Bronx is Burning* (Farrar, Strauss and Giroux, 2005), Marty Appel's *Now Pitching for the Yankees* (Sport Classic Books, 2001), *Damn Yankee—The Billy Martin Story* (Maury Allen, Times Books, 1980), *The Last Yankee—The Turbulent Life of Billy Martin* (David Falkner, Simon & Schuster, 1992), and Peter Golenbock's *Wild, High and Tight: The Life and Death of Billy Martin* (St. Martin's Press, 1994).

Archival material from the National Baseball Hall of Fame-A. Bartlett Giamatti Research Center was also valuable.

Three articles on Martin's early years were particularly instructive: "Billy the Tiger" (Les Woodcock, *Sports Illustrated*, March 31, 1958), "The Damndest Yankee of Them All" (Paul O'Neill, *Sports Illustrated*, April 23, 1956), and "He's Never Out of Trouble" (Al Stump, *Saturday Evening Post*, August 18, 1956).

Useful sources on Reggie Jackson included *Mr. October—The Reggie Jackson*

Story (Reggie Jackson and Maury Allen, Signet, 1982), *Reggie: The Autobiography* (Reggie Jackson and Mike Lupica, Villard Books, 1984), and *Reggie: A Season with a Superstar* (Reggie Jackson and Bill Libby, Playboy Press, 1975). Archival material from the National Baseball Hall of Fame was also helpful.

CHAPTER TWO

Descriptions of the game were taken from the ABC broadcast, the WPIX (New York) broadcast, and the WBET (Boston) broadcast. Jonathan Schwartz's *A Day of Light and Shadows* (The Lyons Press, 2003) is a poetic and well-told account of the game.

A helpful source for information about Fenway Park was *Red Sox Century* (Glenn Stout and Richard A. Johnson, Houghton Mifflin, New York and Boston, 2005).

For Mike Torrez's biography, I drew upon articles from the National Baseball Hall of Fame and a lengthy interview with Torrez, as well as the remembrances of his teammates and opponents. Two websites were enormously helpful with information about Torrez and virtually all the players mentioned in this book: Baseball-reference.com and Baseball-almanac.com. For information on free agency, I drew upon Brad Snyder's *A Well-Paid Slave—Curt Flood's Fight for Free Agency in Professional Sports* (Viking, 2006), *Baseball—A History of America's Favorite Game* (George Vecsey, Modern Library, 2006), and *Catfish—My Life in Baseball* (Jim "Catfish" Hunter and Armen Keteyian, Berkley, 1989).

Material on Lou Piniella comes from interviews with Piniella, his teammates and opponents, as well as material from his file at the A. Bartlett Giamatti Research Center.

CHAPTER THREE

For background information on the Red Sox, I drew upon Peter Gammons' *Beyond the Sixth Game* (The Stephen Greene Press, 1986) and *Red Sox Century* (Glenn Stout and Richard A. Johnson, Houghton Mifflin, 2005). Carl Yastrzemski generously shared some of his memories of Tom Yawkey with me. Don Zimmer's biography is drawn from archival material from the National Baseball Hall of Fame and from his autobiography, *Zim—A Baseball Life* (Don Zimmer and Bill Madden, Contemporary Books, 2001). Butch Hobson and other players also shared their memories of Zimmer. Material on Bill Lee and the Buffalo Head Gang is drawn from Lee's autobiography *The Wrong Stuff* (Bill "Spaceman" Lee and Richard Lally, Three Rivers Press, 2006) and the 2006 documentary, "A Baseball Odyssey," directed by Brett Rapkin and Josh Dixon.

CHAPTER FOUR

Material on Ron Guidry comes from interviews with Guidry and other players, as well as Guidry's autobiography, *Guidry* (Ron Guidry and Peter Golenbock, Prentice-Hall, 1980).

CHAPTER FIVE

Material on the beginning of the Red Sox season is drawn from the *Boston Globe* and player interviews. Jim Rice's autobiography is drawn from player interviews and archival material from the A. Bartlett Giamatti Research Center at the National Baseball Hall of Fame. Gossage material is drawn from interviews with Gossage and other players, as well as archival material from the Hall of Fame. The incident involving Billy Martin and Bill Sample was related to me by Gossage.

CHAPTER SIX

Material on Graig Nettles comes from interviews with Nettles and other players, as well as archival material at the National Baseball Hall of Fame. Material on Roy White comes from interviews with White and other players, as well as archival material. My biography of Carl Yastrzemski comes from his two aforementioned autobiographies, archival material from the Hall of Fame, and interviews with Yastrzemski, his teammates, and others.

CHAPTER SEVEN

Johnny Pesky, Carl Yastrzemski, Bucky Dent, Brian Doyle, Cliff Johnson, Gene Michael, Dennis Eckersley, Graig Nettles, Mike Torrez and others spoke to me about the historical rivalry between the two teams, as well as the relationship between Thurman Munson and Carlton Fisk. Additional material on Fisk and Munson came from archival records at the National Baseball Hall of Fame. Munson's autobiography, *Thurman Munson* (Thurman Munson and Marty Appel, Ace Press, 1980), provided helpful background. Roger Kahn's *October Men* and Peter Gammons' *Beyond the Sixth Game* were also informative.

CHAPTER EIGHT

Portraits of the players in this chapter are based upon interviews with them and others, as well as archival material from the Baseball Hall of Fame and contemporaneous newspaper accounts. The story of Dent's childhood has been explored in magazine articles, particularly "Bucky Dent's 15-Year Search for His Father" (Richard O'Connor, *Sport*, January 1979). Roger Kahn also discusses it in *October Men*. My portrait of George Scott comes from interviews with his teammates and archival material.

CHAPTER NINE

The story of Billy Martin and the little boy comes from the *New York Times* of June 5, 1978. My account of the weeks of the season preceding the All-Star Game is drawn from the aforementioned newspaper reportage.

CHAPTER TEN

My account of the fourth inning is drawn from the game itself, of course, and from interviews with players.

CHAPTER ELEVEN

My portrait of Rick Burleson comes from interviews with Burleson and other players, a description of Burleson in Bill Le and Richard Lally's book, *The Wrong Stuff*, as well as archival material from the National Baseball Hall of Fame and newspaper accounts. The description of Reggie Jackson's meeting with George Steinbrenner comes from *Reggie—The Autobiography*, by Reggie Jackson and Mike Lupica, and is also detailed in Roger Kahn's *October Men*. That book was also helpful in detailing the events that led to Billy Martin's resignation, as were the aforementioned biographies about Martin and, of course, contemporary reporting by Murray Chass, Henry Hecht, and others.

CHAPTER TWELVE

My account of the fourth inning is drawn from the game and from interviews with players.

CHAPTER THIRTEEN

My portrait of Bob Lemon is based upon interviews with players, archival material, accounts of Lemon in Roger Kahn's *October Men* and Sparky Lyle's *The Bronx Zoo: The Astonishing Inside Story of the 1978 World Champion New York Yankees* (Sparky Lyle and Peter Golenbock, Triumph Books, 2005). My description of Carl Yastrzemski's return from injury is based upon an interview with Yastrzemski and Peter Gammons' *Beyond the Seventh Game*. My portrait of Butch Hobson is based upon interviews with Hobson and other players, as well as contemporaneous newspaper accounts and archival material from the National Baseball Hall of Fame.

CHAPTER FOURTEEN

My account of the sixth inning is drawn from broadcasts of the game and interviews with its participants.

CHAPTER FIFTEEN

My account of the four-game Red Sox–Yankees series known as the Boston Massacre is based upon newspaper accounts and interviews with the participants.

CHAPTER SIXTEEN

My account of the game's seventh inning is based upon interviews with its partici-pants, in particular Bucky Dent and Mike Torrez.

CHAPTER SEVENTEEN

My account of the last weeks of the season is based upon newspaper accounts and interviews with the players.

CHAPTER EIGHTEEN

My account of the game's eighth inning is based on broadcasts of the game and inter-views with its participants.

CHAPTER NINETEEN

My account of the season's last day is drawn from newspaper accounts and inter-views with the players.

CHAPTER TWENTY

My account of the game's ninth inning is based upon broadcasts of the game and interviews with its participants, particularly Goose Gossage and Carl Yastrzemski.

EPILOGUE

My account of the Yankees' post-season is drawn from newspaper and magazine reports. My account of Thurman Munson's death is drawn from archival material at the National Baseball Hall of Fame. Information about the death of Billy Martin comes from Peter Golenbock's *Wild, High and Tight: The Life and Death of Billy Martin.*

Acknowledgments

I was at soccer practice one golden October afternoon when someone, another boy, came running to the edge of the hill above the Connecticut field where my schoolmates and I were kicking around. "Bucky Dent just hit a home run!" he shouted. "The Yankees are winning! The Yankees are winning!" Our game stopped instantly. Some kids jumped up and cheered, others glowered and booed. I was thirteen years old and would never forget the drama of that moment, the excitement we all felt. The enduring memory of that afternoon is a big reason why I wrote this book, but of course it took the invaluable help of many people to make *The Greatest Game* happen.

At the William Morris Agency, Suzanne Gluck helped me shape and sell the idea of a book about a legendary baseball game, two remarkable teams, and a classic season. Working with Suzanne has made writing *The Greatest Game* not only possible, but unquestionably saner and calmer than it otherwise would have been. The result is a better book.

I have also benefited from the great help of numerous others at William Morris, including Jay Mandel, Andy McNicol, Georgia Cool, and Sarah Ceglarski.

My editor at Free Press, Martin Beiser, believed in this project from the beginning and throughout the process—even, I think, when I gave him reason to wonder if he'd made a terrible mistake. Patient when necessary and impatient when necessary, Marty hung in there through more missed deadlines than either of us cares to remember. Throughout, his editorial guidance was insightful, inspiring, and essential.

Publisher Martha Levin has been a great supporter of this book, for which I am deeply grateful.

I also want to thank Kirsa Rein at the Free Press, as well as Jessica Chin and Tom Pitoniak, and everyone who helped bring this book to fruition in ways I'm not even aware of.

All organizations should be as much of a pleasure to work with as the Boston Red Sox have been. Everyone at the Red Sox has been helpful, patient, and welcoming. I probably need to thank more folks than I know for that help, but I want specifically to mention Dr. Charles A. Steinberg, Dick Bresciani, Debbie Matson, and Jim Rourke, who opened doors, scorebooks, Rolodexes, and files for me, helping me write about a season that, it's safe to say, not all Sox fans remember fondly. Their faith in their players' and fans' willingness to reconsider such a season speaks immensely well of all parties.

In a time of transition for the Yankees' organization, a number of people with the Yankees took time from their busy schedules to help with this book. They include Debbie Tymon, Rick Cerrone, and Rob Bernstein. Former Yankee public relations director Marty Appel was also an enormous help.

In addition to the two teams, a number of people helped me contact former Yankees and Red Sox and provided their own insights into the 1978 season. They include Dave Baudoin of the Speaker's Corner; Dick Gordon; Kevin Kernan; Andrew Levy, of Wish You Were Here Productions; Cabot Marks; Alan Nero; Frank Perry, of ReggieJackson.com; Kenneth Thimmel, of AllAmericanCollectibles.com; and Noel Wax.

For the second book in a row, Tina Peak and Greg Pearce provided essential research assistance, as did everyone at the National Baseball Hall of Fame and Museum, and especially librarian Claudette Burke. The World Umpires Association helped me reach the umpires who worked the game, and Rick Ambrozic helped me locate the various video records of it. Nick Trotta and Dan Von Behren at MLB.com also provided invaluable help with archival research.

The Greatest Game couldn't have been written without the tangible and intangible help of family, friends, and colleagues. My siblings and siblings-in-law, parents, and stepparents have all been patient and encouraging. Sarah Haberman has been a patient and tireless source of support during the writing and publication of all my books. She is a great ally, a savvy reader, and a shot in the arm, and I have been incredibly fortunate to have such a loyal advocate. I also want to thank David Asman, Andrew Auchincloss, John Berman, Mindy Berman, Rebecca Boyd, David Bradley, Evan Cornog, Peter Critchell, Townsend Davis, Laurie Dhue, David Duffy, Bradley Dwight, Joni Evans, Katie Finneran, Neal Gabler, Judith Geis, Georgia Gruzen, Wendy Hinton, David Hirshey, Bom Kim, Meredith Kopit, Daniel Loss, Katharine MacIntyre, Ricardo Madrigal, Timothy McCarthy,

Lauren McCollester, Patrick Mitchell, Amy Mendel, Abbey Nayor, Bruce Nichols, Ann O'Connell, Maria Padro, Tony Perez, Rita Rodin, Maria Cristina Roratto, Stephen Rodrick, David Salz, Bruce Sandys, Eric Sandys, Nicole Smith, Daniel Solomon, Califia Suntree, Rob Tannenbaum, Marcelline Thomson, Nick Trautwein, Zoe Trodd, and Tim Walker for their support, encouragement, and patience. My apologies to anyone I've neglected to mention. If for some reason I have forgotten to include you here, know that I have appreciated you along the way.

Above all, I want to thank the players from both teams for taking the time to talk with me and for providing so many wonderful memories in the first place. We all grow up, of course. But you help us to remember what it feels like to be a child playing a game, and really, is there anything better than that?

Richard Bradley
New York City
November 2007

INDEX

About the Author

The executive editor of *02138* magazine, Richard Bradley is the author of the number one *New York Times* bestseller *American Son: A Portrait of John F. Kennedy, Jr.* and *Harvard Rules: The Struggle for the Soul of the World's Most Powerful University*. His writing has appeared in the *New York Times, Vanity Fair, Rolling Stone,* and the *New Republic,* and he was the executive editor of *George* magazine. He is a graduate of Yale College, and received his M.A. in American history from Harvard. Bradley lives in New York City.